The Connecticut River Boating Guide:
Source to Sea

Help Us Keep This Guide Up to Date

Every effort has been made by the authors and editors to make this guide as accurate and useful as possible. However, many things can change after a guide is published—trails are rerouted, regulations change, techniques evolve, facilities come under new management, and so on.

We would love to hear from you concerning your experiences with this guide and how you feel it could be improved and kept up to date. While we may not be able to respond to all comments and suggestions, we'll take them to heart, and we'll also make certain to share them with the authors. Please send your comments and suggestions to the following address:

The Globe Pequot Press
Reader Response/Editorial Department
P.O. Box 480
Guilford, CT 06437

Or you may e-mail us at:

editorial@GlobePequot.com

Thanks for your input, and happy travels!

The Connecticut River Boating Guide: Source to Sea

THIRD EDITION

The Connecticut River Watershed Council
John Sinton
Elizabeth Farnsworth
Wendy Sinton

FALCONGUIDE®

GUILFORD, CONNECTICUT
HELENA, MONTANA
AN IMPRINT OF THE GLOBE PEQUOT PRESS

Falcon and FalconGuide are registered trademarks
of Morris Book Publishing, LLC.

Text and table design by Nancy Freeborn
Maps created by Multi Mapping LTD with contribu-
tions from M. A. Dubé © Morris Book Publishing,
LLC
Photo credit: Photo on p. vi, motorboats on
Barton Cove, by John S. Burk.

Library of Congress Cataloging-in-Publication Data

Connecticut River Watershed Council.
  The Connecticut River boating guide : source to
sea / by Connecticut River Watershed Council,
John Sinton, Elizabeth Farnsworth, Wendy Sinton.
— 3rd ed.
     p. cm. — (A Falcon guide)
  Includes bibliographical references and index.
  ISBN-13: 978-0-7627-4097-0
  ISBN-10: 0-7627-4097-3
  1. Boats and boating—Connecticut River.
2. Connecticut River Region—Description and
travel. I. Sinton, John, 1939– II. Farnsworth,
Elizabeth, 1962– III. Sinton, Wendy. IV. Title.
  GV776.C83S56 2007
  797.109746—dc22   2006026212

Manufactured in the United States of America
Third Edition/First Printing

To buy books in quantity for corporate use
or incentives, call **(800) 962–0973**
or e-mail **premiums@GlobePequot.com.**

To all who use and love the river that connects us.
May its future be clean and full of life.

Contents

Acknowledgments

This book could not have been written without the inspiration, guidance, and editing of many people who love this river. The vision of Connecticut River Watershed Council's (CRWC) Chelsea Reiff Gwyther and Ed Gray spurred us to undertake this project in the first place. For careful reviews of our reach descriptions, we are extremely grateful to the CRWC river stewards: David Deen, Andrea Donlon, and Megan Hearne. Adair Mulligan, Beth Goettel, Terry Blunt, and Judy Preston gave us careful feedback. For sharing their knowledge of the river, we thank Ann Colson, Ken Hastings, Beth Lapin, Suellen Nesler, Mike Payton, Judy Preston, Lisa Savard, Bill Schomburg, Bill Schweikert, Robert Staley, and Al Werner. Thanks to Ed Klekowski and Boyd Kynard for sharing their scientific insights and to Jon Caris of Smith College who loaned us a GPS unit and data layers and guided us through the steps of making river maps.

To all the anglers, scientists, and boaters we met while out on the river, our thanks. Thank you to the many members of CRWC and local watershed associations who wrote us about what they wanted to see in this guide and corrected information in the old edition.

Al Braden improved this guide immeasurably by giving us permission to use a large number of his photographs. We thank all the other photographers who contributed photos to this book: John Burk, Ruth Bergengren, Joaquin Cotten, David Deen, Chris Joyell, and Tom Miner. Thanks to Jerry Weinstein for photo help. The staff at CRWC, Christine Luis-Schultz, Pat LaMountain, and Alan Morgan, have taken time out of their already full schedules to help us as well.

Jeff Serena at Globe Pequot made this guide possible. The professional and gifted production team at Globe Pequot gave us all the help we could hope for—Shelley Wolf, Stephen Stringall, Laura Jorstad, and Elizabeth Taylor.

We thank our long-suffering families for holding our hands and cooking us dinner as we struggled to meet deadlines. Finally, we thank the Connecticut River for being such a wondrous friend through the years.

Preface

Just south of the Canadian border in the quiet mountains of New Hampshire, the Connecticut River trickles to life from spring-fed bogs and brooks. The river flows 410 miles and drains more than 11,000 square miles of land before its journey ends at Long Island Sound. Mostly meandering and at times rushing forcefully, the Connecticut River flows past a diverse landscape of rich agricultural lands, rural communities, urban centers, and tidal marshes. The river has often been admired for its ability to provide us with power, transportation, and food. In the last two decades, its ecological importance has also begun receiving wider acclaim. In 1997 the federal government designated the Connecticut River watershed as the Silvio O. Conte National Fish and Wildlife National Refuge to protect the resources of the region. In 1998 the river was also designated as one of only fourteen American Heritage Rivers in the country, an acknowledgment that its rich heritage, ecological importance, and natural diversity have national significance. The lower Connecticut contains one of the most pristine large-river tidal marsh systems in the Northeast, and is recognized as containing "Wetlands of International Importance" by the Ramsar Convention, an international treaty intended to help conserve valuable wetlands around the globe.

Unfortunately, the Connecticut River has not always been treated with such respect. In 1959, a few years after the Connecticut River Watershed Council was formed, Dr. Joseph Davidson and his wife took one of the earliest documented trips from the Connecticut River headwaters to the sea. The trip was designed to educate people about the river's polluted state and to inspire action for its preservation. Restoration efforts throughout our region have helped the river to recover. Now people have stopped turning their backs on the river and are diving in—literally— to experience and enjoy the wonderful natural resource we have flowing through our communities. At the Connecticut River Watershed Council, we still think the best way to protect the river is through you. We believe that once individuals experience firsthand the peacefulness and exhilaration the Connecticut has to offer, its value becomes clear and its protection, a priority.

It is this desire to share the Connecticut River with others that inspired the first *Complete Boating Guide to the Connecticut River* in 1986 and that, twenty years later, compels us to publish this revision. In addition to providing you with updated information, *The Connecticut River Boating Guide: Source to Sea* differs in several important ways from the earlier edition: We used GPS technology to create the maps and have provided mileage points to locate all major features and services; we have added sidebars to provide more in-depth information about the river and an appendix with contact information, Web sites, and other resources you can mine to expand your experience; and we have deleted the advertisements, allowing for the addition of some wonderful photographs.

It is our hope that this guide gives you the tools to make the most of your experiences on New England's longest and largest river, the beautiful Connecticut.

—Chelsea Reiff Gwyther, executive director
Connecticut River Watershed Council

There is great trout fishing above First Lake. Photo © Al Braden

Introduction

Authors' Welcome to the River

The Connecticut River runs through the heart of New England, through its geological beginnings, its Native American prehistory, and the founding of the United States. To travel from the Great North Woods at the New Hampshire–Canadian border to the sandbars on Long Island Sound—from source to sea—requires about a month of paddling. You will pass through New England's signature landscapes, such as its forests, farms, and mountains; you will see classic New England towns and industrial cities that date back to the Industrial Revolution; you will find run-down villages and thriving communities, sadly eroded banks and recovered waterfronts, surprising solitude right next to major cities and unexpectedly crowded motorboat traffic in some more rural reaches.

Great surprises await everyone who spends time on the Connecticut. You might see bears, moose, mink, otters, and weasels, not to mention eagles, ospreys, waterfowl, shorebirds, and two dozen species of warblers. Look for Indian petroglyphs and dinosaur footprints, or the remnants of a great glacial lake or a waterfall the river long ago abandoned. There will be what is left of bridges and ferries, and retainers for logs from upriver drives.

The river is waiting for you to discover it, so get into your kayak or canoe, gas up your motorboat, and get on the river. Above all, take your time, find the river's pace, and let it show you something you may have never known about yourself.

If nothing else, let the river connect you to the larger order of things. It has been around a long time, and you will gain much from knowing it more intimately. In connecting to the river, you enlarge yourself and find connections to the smaller and larger world around you.

Once you have gotten to know the river a bit better, please advocate for it. Join the many volunteer efforts in your community to get better access to it and keep its banks clean and stable, its fisheries healthy, and its communities vital. It's all of a piece, the river and its people.

Over our lifetimes we three authors have spent thousands of hours on this magnificent river and write this book to celebrate its existence, its resilience, and its global significance. Come, join us and enjoy the ride!

—John Sinton, Elizabeth Farnsworth, and Wendy Sinton

How to Use This Guide

The book is organized into the following sections:

- Introduction: How to use this guide and boating safety.
- The River: Essays on geography, history, and natural history.
- The Reaches: Overviews, reach descriptions, boating facilities charts, and maps from north to south.
- Appendixes: Contact information, bibliography of useful readings, and Web sites.

We describe twenty-eight reaches, which range in length from 9 to 21 miles. The beginning and end of each reach has a boat access area, and all reaches can be done in a single day. Each reach description has six elements: a map, a boating facilities table, at-a-glance information, an overview of the river with points of interest noted, a detailed reach description with mileage points, a sidebar highlighting a point of interest along the route. Wherever possible, we begin with a map and the boating facilities table on facing pages for easy navigation reference. River mileage is designated from the source at mile 410 to the sea at mile 0.

A Typical Reach Description

Here's the information you can expect to find within each reach:

Map

Each reach map includes large islands; significant tributary streams and rivers; bridges and dams; cities and towns; major roads; topography; and points of interest such as mountains, large wetlands, parks, or place-names. Numbered sites correspond to the numbers listing in the boating facilities table. All numbered sites were determined using a GPS to determine their locations as precisely as possible. Boat launches are indicated by numbered points, and campsites are indicated by triangular tent symbols.

Boating Facilities Table

The boating facilities table provides numbers that correspond directly to the numbers of launch sites and campsites on the maps. Driving directions from major roads to the site are given except where access is solely from the river. The table lists the type of ramp; its suitability for either car-top boats only or all types of boats; parking availability; the availability of supplies such as food; and whether there are fees for parking or services. It also lists public campsites, several of which are only accessible from the river by boat. We include information on private or semi-public marinas and yacht clubs, which charge fees or require membership, in a separate appendix.

Sample Boating Facilities Table

Access Point, Directions	Boat Type	Fee	Parking	Picnic	Toilets	Camping	Rentals	Supplies
❶ **Hoyt's Landing** VT 11 and US 5, Springfield, VT *At junction of US 5 and VT 11 just west of Cheshire Bridge.*	Improved ramp for all boat types	N	Y	Y	Y	N	N	N

At-a-Glance Information

Each reach begins with a brief list including mileage, difficulty based on water conditions, portages, campsites, special fishing regulations, and applicable USGS topographic or NOAA maps to consult for navigation.

Here's an example. Each entry is discussed further just below:

a. 24: HARTFORD TO MIDDLETOWN
b. Miles from mouth: 49–30 (19-mile span)
c. Navigable by: Kayak, canoe, powerboats
d. Difficulty: Flat water
e. Flow information: None
f. Portages: None
g. Special fishing/boating regulations: None
h. Camping: No established sites
i. USGS maps: Hartford North 7.5, Hartford South 7.5, Glastonbury 7.5, Middletown 7.5, Middle Haddam 7.5
j. NOAA charts: Connecticut River: Bodkin Rock to Hartford #12377

Key:

a. Each reach's name includes its beginning and end points.

b. River mileage is designated from the source at mile 410, down to the sea at mile 0. The length of the particular reach is also noted.

c. Here we tell you what type of boats are suitable for this section of the river; any restrictions on boat type are also noted.

d. The "Difficulty" category describes what type of water conditions you can expect. *Flat water* means smooth-surfaced water with a slight current. *Quick water* is faster-running water with some riffles and small waves. *Class I–VI* refers to the six difficulty classes from the International Scale of River Difficulty of the American Whitewater Association (see pages 6–8 in "Boating Safety").

e. Flow information is given only for those reaches affected by dam releases, namely reaches 1 through 9 and reaches 13, 16, 18, 19, and 22.

f. Under "Portages," we list the location and name of any dams or falls that require portaging, as well as the length of the portage.

g. Under "Special fishing/boating regulations," we list any rules specific to the particular reach under discussion. Also see the essay "Connecticut River Fisheries" on pages 21–25 for general fishing regulations. Marine police in each state establish its overall boating policies.

h. The "Camping" category gives the location—with mileage reference number—of all established campsites on the river, along with Web sites and phone numbers to check on their availability. We do not recommend camping anywhere except at established sites. Also, please note that we've used the word *campground* to indicate an area that is organized for that purpose and has a caretaker and (often) a fee. We've used the word *campsite* to indicate an informal place to pitch a tent, with no caretaker and no fee. *Boaters should never camp on private property without the permission of the landowner.* Wherever you camp, clean up afterward. Leave the site in the same condition in which you expect to find it.

The states of Massachusetts and Connecticut are trying to arrange for more camping spots, but there is only one established in Massachusetts and only two in Connecticut.

i. Here we list the United States Geological Survey (USGS) maps that cover the reach in question—both the name of the quadrant and the scale of the map.

j. National Oceanographic and Atmospheric Administration (NOAA) navigational charts covering the reach (applicable to Reaches 24 through 28 only) are listed here.

The Reach

This section gives a narrative overview describing the reach's general water conditions, the surrounding landscape, and pertinent background on historic or natural features on or near the river.

Miles and Directions

Under "Miles and Directions," we describe the significant landmarks on the river or its banks in the reach. Each landmark is designated by its mile point on the river; names of points illustrated on the map are indicated in **bold**. Points of interest on the river and on accessible tributaries or inlets will be described. To designate a bank of the river, we use *right bank* (*river right* in paddling guides) and *left bank* (*river left*), based on *looking downriver*. When the river clearly runs north and south, we may use the terms *east bank* and *west bank*. In the last three reaches (26–28) that describe the Connecticut River estuary, the terms *east shore* and *west shore* are used. Warnings about potentially dangerous conditions are prefaced with *Caution*.

Sidebar

Sidebars are short descriptions of notable historic, geological, cultural, or natural history features that you'll see along the reach. They give more detailed information than will be found in the reach description.

Boating Safety

Safety in boating is a combination of common sense and being well prepared with good information, including a map of the river area, weather and tide information, water-level fluctuations, and a float plan.

Since boating on the Connecticut River can involve kayaking or canoeing, motor cruising or sailing near the seacoast, and everything in between, we have included two sets of boating safety guidelines. Kayakers or canoeists should look carefully at the American Whitewater's International Scale of River Difficulty (pages 6–8). Power boaters and sailors should be familiar with the U.S. Coast Guard checklist for safe boating (page 8).

Tips for General Preparedness

- Be a competent swimmer.

- Wear a personal floatation device (PFD).

- Be practiced in self-rescue (for paddle boats).

- Do not boat alone.

- File a float plan with family members or friends, letting them know your route and estimated time of departure and arrival.

- Never drink alcohol while boating.

- Know the locations of dams and portages. This guide indicates the location of dams in the reach overview and on the map. Some dams must be portaged, and the reach description will provide that information. Some dams have been breached or dismantled, but that doesn't mean they're safe to run or boat through. Where there was once a dam, there are now almost certainly rapids or small falls. Look carefully at the description of breached dams and assess your skill level before considering running one. This guide does *not* recommend that you run breached dams unless you're a very skilled paddler. Do not overestimate your abilities. Respect the power of the river.

Monitor Changing River Conditions

Parts of the Connecticut River are notorious for rapidly changing river conditions, especially downstream of dams and during torrential rains. It is essential to monitor flows when you set out and during your trip.

The term *cfs* is a measure of river flow that indicates the river's condition. It stands for "cubic feet per second" and defines how many cubic feet of water (equal to about 7.5 gallons) are flowing over any one section at a given time. The average cfs on the Connecticut River depends on where you are; the farther downstream you go, the higher the average cfs you encounter since, of course, the river gets larger. At Pittsburg, New Hampshire, in Reach 2, 300 cfs is a moderate flow, 500 cfs produces Class II rapids, and 1,500 cfs is Class IV or V. At Reach 22 on the Massachusetts–Connecticut border, 11,000 cfs is considered a moderate flow, but during major floods the river carries more than 50,000 cfs.

Monitor river conditions before you set out. Scout the river from roads and from the bank. You should also check river flow levels with the U.S. Geological Survey. Visit http://water.usgs.gov/waterwatch, or the Waterline page at www.h2oline.com, or call (800) 452–1737. We provide contact information on flows for reaches that involve dams. To check tides, visit www.freetidetables.com.

Finally, note the weather conditions. NOAA weather is a good source, available on the radio at FM frequencies 162.40 to 162.55.

A Note on Strainers and Sweepers

Rivers carry a lot of debris, which can pose dangerous obstacles or create eddies and whitewater that boaters should avoid. *Strainers* are formed when an object, such as a fallen tree, blocks the passage of floating objects but allows the flow of water to continue. The flowing water can force a boat or body against the strainer, pinning it against the obstacle and pushing it down under water. *Sweepers* are still-rooted trees that lean low over the river and are not fully submerged. The trunk and branches may form an obstruction in the river like strainers. Although these above-water features usually do not increase turbulence, they are still hazardous and can "sweep" you right out of your craft if you are caught unaware. So stay alert and give strainers and sweepers a wide berth!

If You Get into Trouble

First, r*adio for help.* Use emergency VHF channel 16, or call 911.

Stay with your boat. In most capsizings, your chances of survival and being found are better if you stay with the boat.

International Scale of River Difficulty

This scale is a rating system produced by the American Whitewater Association (www.americanwhitewater.org) to classify river difficulty for nonmotorized boats such as canoes and kayaks. It's important to note what level of difficulty you'll encounter in order to be appropriately prepared. River difficulty changes seasonally and annually; you may find that an easy section of the river you've run in the past has become a roaring torrent later on. Get your information from a local source, and note the level of difficulty indicated in each reach overview.

- **Class I:** Fast-moving water with riffles and small waves. Few obstructions, all obvious and easily missed with little training. The risk to swimmers is slight; self-rescue is easy.

- **Class II—Novice:** Straightforward rapids with wide, clear channels that are evident without scouting. Occasional maneuvering may be required, but rocks and medium-size waves are easily missed by trained paddlers. Swimmers are seldom injured, and group assistance, while helpful, is seldom needed. Rapids that are at the upper end of this difficulty range are designated Class II+.

- **Class III—Intermediate:** Rapids with moderate, irregular waves that may be difficult to avoid and can swamp an open canoe. Complex maneuvers in fast current and good boat control in tight passages or around ledges are often required; large waves or strainers may be present but are easily avoided. Strong eddies and powerful current effects can be found, particularly on large-volume rivers. Scouting is advisable for inexperienced parties. Injuries while swimming are rare; self-rescue is usually easy, but group assistance may be required to avoid long swims. Rapids that are at the lower or upper end of this difficulty range are designated Class III- or Class III+ respectively.

- **Class IV—Advanced:** Intense, powerful, but predictable rapids requiring precise boat handling in turbulent water. Depending on the character of the river, Class IV rapids may feature large, unavoidable waves and holes or constricted passages demanding fast maneuvers under pressure. A fast, reliable eddy turn may be needed to initiate maneuvers, scout rapids, or rest. Rapids may require must-moves above dangerous hazards. Scouting may be necessary the first time down. Risk of injury to swimmers is moderate to high, and water conditions may make self-rescue difficult. Group assistance for rescue is often essential and requires practiced skills. A strong eskimo roll is highly recommended. Rapids that are at the lower or upper end of this difficulty range are designated Class IV- or Class IV+ respectively.

- **Class V—Expert:** Extremely long, obstructed, or very violent rapids that expose a paddler to added risk. Drops may contain large, unavoidable waves and holes or steep, congested chutes with complex, demanding routes. Rapids may continue for long distances between pools, demanding a high level of fitness. What eddies exist may be small, turbulent, or difficult to reach. At the high end of the scale, several of these factors may be combined. Scouting is recommended but may be difficult. Swims are dangerous, and rescue is often difficult even for experts. A very reliable eskimo roll, proper equipment, extensive experience, and practiced rescue skills are essential. Because of the large range of difficulty that exists beyond Class IV, Class V is an open-ended, multiple-level scale designated Class 5.0, 5.1, 5.2, and so forth, with each of these levels an order of magnitude more difficult than the last. That is, increasing the difficulty from Class 5.0 to Class 5.1 is similar to increasing from Class IV to Class 5.0.

- *Class VI—Extreme and Exploratory Rapids:* These runs have almost never been attempted and often exemplify the extremes of difficulty, unpredictability, and danger. The consequences of errors are very severe, and rescue may be impossible. For teams of experts only, at favorable water levels, after close personal inspection and taking all precautions. After a Class VI rapids has been run many times, its rating may be changed to an appropriate Class V rating. These conditions are unlikely to be found on the Connecticut River.

U.S. Coast Guard Safety and Survival Tips

Your water fun depends on you, your equipment, and other people who, like yourself, enjoy spending leisure time on, in, or near the water. These are your responsibilities:

- Make sure the boat is in top operating condition and that there are no tripping hazards. The boat should be free of fire hazards and have clean bilges.
- Safety equipment, required by law, must be on board, maintained in good condition, and you must know how to properly use these devices.
- File a float plan with a relative or friend.
- Have a complete knowledge of the operation and handling characteristics of your boat.
- Know your position and know where you are going.
- Maintain a safe speed at all times to avoid collision.
- Keep an eye out for changing weather conditions, and act accordingly.
- Know and practice the rules of the road (navigation rules).
- Know and obey federal and state regulations and waterway markers.
- Maintain a clear, unobstructed view forward at all times. Scan the water back and forth; avoid tunnel vision. Most boating collisions are caused by inattention.

About the Maps in This Book

The River section of this book includes an overview map of the entire Connecticut River Watershed, showing its major tributaries. Later sections of the book include state overview maps for Vermont and New Hampshire, Massachusetts, and Connecticut. These state maps show the river in greater detail as it passes through each state and indicate the approximate location of each numbered reach (or stretch) of river.

Within the state sections of this book, you will find twenty-eight individual reach maps that show optional put-in and take-out spots, including boating facilities such as boat ramps, and campgrounds. For the greatest possible accuracy, the authors paddled the entire river and verified the location of all of these put-in and take-out spots using a hand-held Global Positioning System (GPS) device. For your convenience, we have included longitude and latitude ticks on the maps, making them GPS-compatible. The authors also provided approximate mileages in the text of the book for key landmarks and directions along each reach route; these mileages, however, are estimates with an error possibility of plus or minus 1 mile.

MAP LEGEND

Boundary:

International Boundary

State Boundary

Transportation:

(15) Interstate

(89) U.S. Highway

(65) State Highway

Road

Unimproved

⊛ Capital City

◎ City, Town, Village

❼ Reach (Boat Launch)

Hydrology:

Rivers/Creeks

Lake

Dam

Marsh

Symbols:

△ Campground

⚱ Lighthouse

🏛 Museum

■ Point of Interest

⚑ State Park

✈ Wildlife

The River

Floodplain forests along the river harbor majestic trees and many rare plant and animal species.
Photo © Al Braden

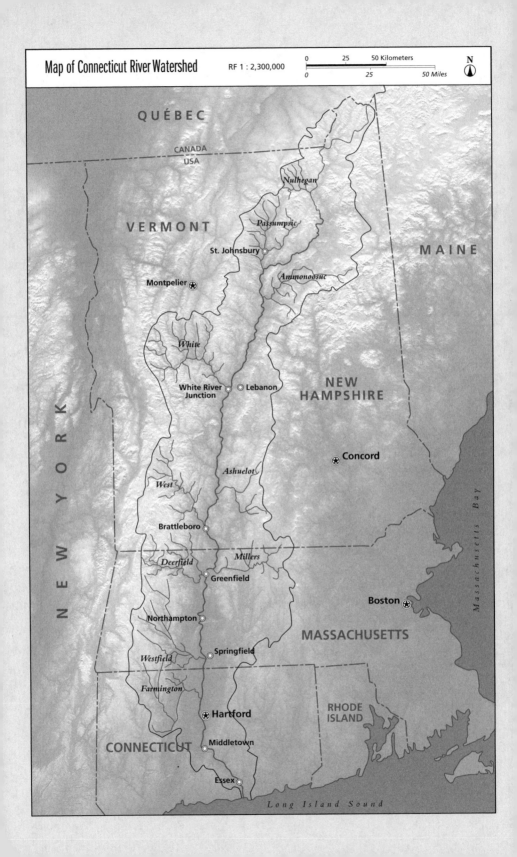

Map of Connecticut River Watershed   RF 1 : 2,300,000

0   25   50 Kilometers
0   25   50 Miles

N

QUÉBEC

CANADA
USA

Nulhegan

VERMONT

Passumpsic

St. Johnsbury

Ammonoosuc

MAINE

Montpelier

White

White River
Junction

Lebanon

NEW
HAMPSHIRE

Concord

Ashuelot

West

Brattleboro

Millers

Deerfield

Greenfield

Northampton

MASSACHUSETTS

Massachusetts Bay

Boston

Westfield

Springfield

Farmington

RHODE
ISLAND

Hartford

Middletown

CONNECTICUT

NEW YORK

Essex

Long Island Sound

The Four Geographic Regions of the Connecticut River Valley

History and geography have combined to divide the valley into the four regions whose names are in common use throughout the Connecticut River Valley. We will refer to them often throughout this guide:

- **The Great North Woods** stretch from the Connecticut Lakes to the Passumpsic River, from Reaches 1 through 7. The Vermont side of the watershed (Reaches 3–7) is generally called the Northeast Kingdom, while the New Hampshire section is the Great North Woods. Spruce-fir forests dominate this sparsely populated region, the last section settled by Europeans. The economy depends chiefly on the timber and recreation industries.

- **The Upper Valley** extends all the way from the Passumpsic River to the Massachusetts border, Reaches 8 through 17. Colonists established towns here only in the last third of the eighteenth century after the end of the French and Indian Wars (Seven Years' War) when the Native Americans were driven into Canada. It is a region with deep cultural ties among towns, and with an economy based on dairy farming, small industry, timber, and tourism.

- **The Pioneer Valley of Massachusetts and Tobacco Valley of Connecticut** from Northfield, Massachusetts, to Middletown, Connecticut (Reaches 18–24), was the first region settled by English colonists in the seventeenth century because of its extremely fine agricultural soils. The Pioneer and Tobacco Valleys are really a single entity, separated into two given local pride and historical use. The major centers, Hartford and Springfield, are old industrial cities, but industry is spread up and down the valleys, as are an extraordinary number of colleges and universities.

- **The Tidal River or Tidelands** (Reaches 25–28) is the section of the river that jogs east at Middletown and then south to Long Island Sound. The United Nations has recognized the Tidelands as Wetlands of International Importance under its Ramsar Convention. The Tidal River consists of small, mostly seventeenth-century towns that never became cities. It is a region that relied on fishing and shipbuilding until the mid–nineteenth century, but is now the province of summer homes, retired people, and many commuters to the New York metropolitan area. Tourism and recreation are the region's economic backbone.

Geology: Grand Events in the Making of a Great River

The Connecticut River cuts a swath through nearly 600 million years of the earth's turbulent geological history. The oldest rocks lining the Connecticut River Valley were laid down originally as sediments under a placid, tropical sea at a time when our part of the world was much closer to the equator. These sediments transformed into twisted and gnarly bedrock through the pressure and heating that accompanied a

These petroglyphs were carved by Native Americans who lived near the river's bank. Photo © Al Braden

series of three titanic continental collisions that took place between 500 and 245 million years ago.

About 430 million years ago, the North American continental plate collided with an island arc, culminating in the Taconic mountain-building event (*orogeny* in geological terminology), which built enormous mountains out of newly hardened volcanic rocks. Following this upheaval, a calmer period ensued in which these mountains were eroded, depositing new sediments into a shallow, warm sea.

Mountain building resumed around 360 million years ago when the mini continents of Nashoba, Merrimack, and Avalon, familiar place-names to New Englanders, slammed into North America. Proto–New England was becoming a lumpy mishmash of bedrock types from all over the world at this point. This orogeny gave rise to the northern Appalachian Mountains and converted the rich Taconic marine sediments into tortured metamorphic rocks—schists and gneisses—that can be seen today along the river from northern Massachusetts to central Vermont.

Following a final collision of North and South America with a portion of Africa in the Permian period about 260 million years ago, the supercontinent Pangea formed, incorporating all of the earth's landmasses. Some New England bumper stickers still exhort us to REUNITE PANGEA, reliving the days of geological unity. But

Pangea was to be only a flash in the pan; it would not hold together under the restlessness of plate tectonics.

In the earthquake-riddled middle Triassic, what is today's Atlantic Ocean began to widen and the land bordering it, including New England, began to tear raggedly apart. Great fissures opened in the fabric of the land, one of which created the enormous rift valley, called the Eastern Border Fault, that now holds the Connecticut River. The Connecticut Valley lies at the flank of the Eastern Border Fault, which is visible at its most dramatic at the French King Gorge in Turners Falls, Massachusetts. Lava flowing out of the Eastern Border Fault area built the layers of basalt rock that form the steep ridge of the Metacomet Range and constrain the course of the present-day river from Greenfield, Massachusetts, to Long Island Sound. These tilted bedrock layers were resistant to erosion, and effectively prevented the river at that time from taking a straight course south to the sea. Hence, the Connecticut River Valley hangs a sharp dogleg to the southeast near Middletown, Connecticut, seeking a path of least resistance through softer, older materials.

Under a climate of heavy rainfall, sediments streamed into the expanding rift valley. Dinosaurs moved across these vast, lush, muddy plains of towering tree ferns. We can still see the fantastic fossils of dinosaur footprints, whisk ferns, and bony fishes that predominated during the Triassic and Jurassic periods (245 to 200 million years ago) in redstone bedrock layers from Turners Falls, Massachusetts, to the coast of Connecticut. The fossils visible at Holyoke, Massachusetts, are a mere stone's throw from the Connecticut River main stem. The dinosaurs met their end about a hundred million years ago with the impact of a massive meteorite that severely altered world climate. Mammals would soon take center stage.

Gradually the earthquakes quieted while erosion began to deposit sediments into the valley, creating a wide, flat plain. Sixty million years ago a period of gentle uplift began, the ripple effect of distant orogenies that were creating the Rocky Mountains. As the valley rose, the unstoppable waters of the nascent Connecticut River worked their way down through it, capturing tributary streams along the way and carving the deep river valley that is recognizable today.

About two million years ago, a major climatic shift occurred, and New England would never again bask under tropical warmth. Glaciers made at least two advances over the Connecticut River Valley, with the most recent ice sheet finally receding from New England 11,000 years ago. Imagine an enormous bulldozer patiently moving billions of tons of New England's boulders, gravels, sands, and clays from northwest to southeast. Glaciers scoured and deepened the Connecticut Valley, sending its sediments southward. About 19,000 years ago glaciers dumped their southernmost load along a line stretching from New York City to Cape Cod. This load, called a terminal moraine, makes up Long Island, Martha's Vineyard, Nantucket, and the Cape. Glacial recession was a start-and-stop process, and many moraines were deposited at each successive ice-sheet terminus as it melted back northward. Large meltwater lakes formed behind these moraines. Glacial Lake Connecticut and Glacial Lake

Winter ice floes can intensify spring floods. Photo by Ruth Bergengren

Middletown formed in the south. The extensive Glacial Lake Hitchcock formed behind a bedrock spillway near New Britain and a jumbled dam of sediments left near Rocky Hill, Connecticut. For 4,000 years meltwaters flooded the Connecticut River Valley as far north as Littleton, New Hampshire, and St. Johnsbury, Vermont. We know there was a gigantic lake here because of the ubiquitous deep clays that only settle out and build up under calm, stillwater conditions. These clays show regular layers, called varves, which reflect the yearly sedimentation patterns of spring freshets that introduce coarse materials to the lake, interspersed with wintry periods, during which fine clays filter out of the water column. Look for varves anywhere valley clays are exposed in the cross section of a cutbank. Rich, fine glacial lake sediments underlie all the rich agricultural land of the Connecticut River Valley.

Upland sediments, washed in by raging side streams, hit the lake water and fanned out into large deltas that are visible today along much of the river. Look for steep sandy banks with exposures of regular horizontal or tilted layers. In places the under–

belly of the glacier melted as fast as its retreating front, leaving sinuous tumbles of gravels and cobbles, called eskers, 20 or more feet high. These snaky eskers are especially visible along the river from Windsor, Vermont, to Lyme, New Hampshire. Thousands of miles of stone walls throughout New England attest to the tons of rocky till that are also a legacy of the glaciers.

By around 15,000 years ago, the chain of glacial lakes in the valley was beginning to drain as waters forced their way through the earthen dams. Simultaneously, as the weight of the glacier gradually diminished, New England's southern coast rebounded upward, increasing erosion and hastening the process of lake drainage. By 13,000 years ago Lake Hitchcock had re-created the path of the Connecticut River in its valley for the first time since the breakup of Pangea, but it was a process that took several thousand years. In some places the river had to find its way through softer bedrock where remaining dammed sediments would not let it pass. In so doing the river carved beautiful waterfalls at the Lily Pond peninsula at Barton Cove in Turners Falls, Massachusetts. Today it has abandoned these waterfalls, which now remain as deeply incised coves that paddlers can explore.

· Spectacular waterfalls once punctuated the river at numerous points along its course. After all, the river drops about 2,700 feet from its source to where it meets sea level. Fifteen-Mile Falls at the Moore and Comerford Reservoirs (Reach 7) used to drop 350 feet over its length. Dozens of colonial and early American mills were erected at these falls, giving rise to hamlets and cities along the river. Dams at Beecher Falls, Lyman Falls, Guildhall, Gilman, Bellows Falls, Vernon, South Hadley Falls, and Enfield attest to the power inherent in water.

Today these dams regulate and exploit river flow, helping control violent flooding and generating electricity. Nevertheless, the river still flexes its muscles from time to time. The great flood of March 1936, caused by torrential spring rains and rapid snowmelt, left nearly half a million valley residents homeless and wreaked more than $6.5 billion worth of damage (in current dollars). Indeed, every spring the roaring tumble of ice and water displays the awesome power of the river, even as it presents kayakers with whitewater thrills. Over the course of decades and centuries, the river changes its path, abandoning meanders to oxbows, capturing new tributaries, replenishing floodplains, and creating and destroying islands.

The geological future will undoubtedly bring new surprises. Global climate change, wrought by a buildup of greenhouse gases, has occurred before and is occurring rapidly now due to human activity. This will bring rising temperatures and sea levels, and induce new weather patterns that will influence the river in as-yet-unknown ways. Meanwhile, over the longer haul, the great continental plates continue to jostle against each other. New meteors will hit . . . the possibilities are endless. But until it is digested by our own exploding sun, the earth will bear the evidence of this magnificent, changeable river.

River Dynamics and Natural Plant Communities

The Connecticut River traverses a dramatic gradient in elevation and climate as it travels from the high, chilly conifer forests at the Canadian border to the mild, maritime marshes on Long Island Sound. Cutting a north–south cross section through New England, the river encompasses the broadest possible variety of fascinating natural communities in the region. It is also a hot spot of botanical diversity, providing habitat for dozens of rare plant species. The source of all this diversity lies in the river's dynamism.

On a daily basis tides raise and lower water levels an average of 3.5 feet at the river's mouth and about 2 feet at Hartford, Connecticut, 50 miles upstream. Although salt water doesn't penetrate far north of Essex, Connecticut, the twice-daily fluctuations in water levels create changeable conditions that can only be tolerated by a specialized suite of wetland plant species. Near the river mouth salt-tolerant marshes take hold; farther inland to Haddam, Connecticut, spectacular freshwater tidal marshes line the river.

The Connecticut River annually rampages down its channel and spills over its banks, despite all the dams that would fetter it. Average daily flows swell to about twenty-nine billion gallons per day during the spring freshet—nearly five times the flow during the drier, more sluggish month of August. These floods carry rejuvenating soils into the backwater floodplain forests, where rich silts and clays settle out. Plying these calm reaches, a boater is treated to the sight of hauntingly beautiful floodplain forests interspersed with some of the most productive farmland in the Northeast. In other areas the river scours bedrock outcrops and erodes banks with its force, while the ice it transports southward favors what botanists call "fugitive" plant species that can survive, disperse quickly, and reestablish downstream in response to disturbance.

Over the course of decades, this dynamic river changes its course on a grand scale. Former bends are abandoned, becoming stillwater oxbow swamps. Old meander scars, looking like huge sidewinder trails from the air, create ridges and swales that support contrasting well-drained and waterlogged vegetation types. Sandbars and cobble deposits slowly accrete into islands, which further capture and build soils. Gradually, high and stable islands develop their own floodplain forests. Historic coastal storms have often breached and rearranged the barrier beaches at the river's mouth. Dune plants, adapted to fierce winds, salt spray, and sand burial, quickly reclaim these ephemeral shores.

Traveling north to south, a boater encounters a phenomenal, species-rich array of plant communities. Boreal forests of fir, spruce, tamarack, and birch surround the Connecticut Lakes and the whitewater Connecticut "stream" that links them. Look for cold-loving herbaceous species with berries that contrast with the cushiony sphagnum moss in the forest understory, including bunchberry, partridgeberry, and creeping snowberry. The Connecticut Lakes are graced with relatively pristine waters that

Carpets of graceful ostrich fern line the river and yield edible fiddleheads in early spring.
Photo by Elizabeth Farnsworth

foster the growth of delicate aquatic plants such as rare quillworts and spikerushes.

Between Comerford Dam (East Barnet, Vermont) and Walpole, New Hampshire, the river undergoes sudden changes in flow, due both to dam releases and to seasonal spikes in rainfall and snowmelt. In places the river scours a channel through steep bedrock, which in this region tends to be rich in calcium, magnesium, and other elements that favor the growth of specialized plant species. Some of these species have very restricted ranges; a few, like the rare milkvetch legumes, are known only from the Connecticut River and are federally endangered. These species depend on periodic river scour to sweep their habitats clear of potential competitors.

Seeps and ephemeral streams also nourish the river and are often home to botanical treasures. Look for fragile and bulblet ferns, spleenworts, and cliffbrakes with fronds that seem to drip from seepy bedrock crevices. In May and June glance uphill along the streams that tumble down steep ledges into the river to discover a wealth of herbaceous species such as American and dwarf ginseng, wild ginger, bloodroot, violets, and spring beauties.

Where they haven't been converted to farmland, floodplain forests line the river from northern Vermont and New Hampshire to south of Middletown, Connecticut. Here enormous sycamores, silver maples, ashes, and rare black maples festooned with grapevines and Virginia creepers grow. The understory of these magnificent forests can often comprise a noxious mix of poison ivy and stinging nettle. Hidden among the noxious plants, however, grow some rare gems like waterleaf and barren strawberry. Graceful, arching ostrich ferns, with edible fiddleheads, are common.

Cobble bars and sandbars form along islands and peninsulas of the river wherever flows are variable enough to transport and deposit heavier sediments. Especially lovely islands dot the river from Sunderland to Hadley, Massachusetts, near Suffield, Connecticut, and around the Mount Ascutney region of Vermont. In addition to the hardy willows, sand cherries, and young cottonwoods that first colonize this new ground, a few sparse, tough, herbaceous species such as dogbanes, horsetails, grasses, and sensitive fern may get a foothold.

From Haddam south to Essex, Connecticut, exceptional freshwater tidal marshes form in tributaries and embayments of the river. In midsummer these highly productive ecosystems are golden green with wild rice, providing essential fodder for waterbirds. Watch out for the razor-sharp stems of rice cut-grass and smartweed, aptly known as "tearthumb." Arrowhead and the purple-flowered pickerelweed send large, fleshy leaves up amid the mix. Yellow, daisy-like beggarticks and diminutive pipeworts with tiny white pom-pom flowers are some of the rare denizens of this very rich habitat.

Near the river mouth brackish marshes, dominated by salt-tolerant species such as salt marsh hay, smooth cordgrass, seaside goldenrod, narrow-leaved cattail, and the showy wild rose mallow form where tides raise soil salinities. All of these marshes have been ditched relentlessly in order to drain them and control mosquitoes, but tides and the river are slowly restoring many of these areas. The storm-battered barrier sand spit of Griswold Point at the river mouth is home to hardy beachgrass, evening primrose, beach plum, bayberry, and beach rose.

Peer underwater and you will notice that the river channel itself hosts a diverse assemblage of submerged aquatic vegetation, including the feathery coontail, tapegrass, and curly pondweed, which provide food for birds and habitat for fish and aquatic invertebrates.

Alas, the river also provides prime real estate for some unwelcome plants. Exotic invasive species have been spreading throughout the valley for the past few decades. Swards of Japanese knotweed with dense, bamboo-like stems are now a common feature on riverbanks. Toward the river mouth nearly impenetrable stands of the 14-foot-tall Phragmites reed have taken hold in brackish and freshwater areas, suppressing some of the native species. The aggressive, viny Asiatic bittersweet threatens to choke large trees of floodplain forests. And local residents constantly battle the invasive water chestnut, with its fearsomely spiky seeds and floating rosettes of leaves, yanking it out wherever it appears. These species tend to be symptomatic of deteriorating environmental conditions, such as artificially dampened flows, increased nutrient loading, and human-made disturbances of the riverbank. To reduce the spread and impacts of invasive species and restore the fabulous diversity of natural communities from source to sea, we need to foster a healthy and dynamic river ecosystem.

Connecticut River Fisheries

The Connecticut River, New England's greatest freshwater fishery, includes landlocked salmon at its headwaters and anadromous salmon at its mouth. In between is a fishery of unparalleled variety, from minnows and sculpin to trout, perch, sunfish, black bass, catfish, carp, pickerel, pike, and walleye to perhaps the river's greatest resource, the migrants from the ocean—striped bass, shad, sturgeon, salmon, lamprey, and eel.

The Fourth Connecticut Lake, at the very beginning of the Connecticut River, holds one of New England's only native trout (actually a char), the brook trout, which can be found throughout the Great North Woods and in tributaries throughout the watershed. The Connecticut Lakes are also home to native lake trout, another char, as well as landlocked salmon, originally transplanted from lakes in New Hampshire and Maine. Rainbow trout, originally from the West Coast, and the Eurasian brown trout join the brook trout in the upper reaches of the river, which has some of the most beautiful scenery and most productive trout fishing in the Northeast. Rainbow and brown trout can be found in much of the river's main stem except in summer, when they move into the cooler waters of the tributaries or into deep water.

Dyed-in-the-wool New England anglers, however, really love to go bass fishing, if you can judge by the number of bass tournaments throughout the watershed. In the last third of the nineteenth century, both large- and smallmouth bass, originally from the Great Lakes region, were planted or escaped into the Connecticut River

Though this old shad shack may be defunct, the fishery itself is still bountiful. Photo by Wendy Sinton

watershed, where they enjoy an extraordinary variety of habitats and food sources. From Reach 6 south you will find bass, mostly smallmouth in the faster water and largemouth in quieter spots. Besides bass, the warm-water fishery includes other planted species such as northern pike, walleye, bluegill, catfish, and carp, along with a few natives like yellow perch.

The great migratory fish runs make up the Connecticut River's most impressive fishery—alewives, blueback herring, American shad, shortnose sturgeon, sea lamprey, American eel, and Atlantic salmon. These were the runs that for thousands of years drew Native Americans to the river in springtime, the same runs that we lost in the nineteenth and twentieth centuries to dams and pollution (for information on river pollution and mitigation see pages 30-32).

Stephen Gephard, Connecticut state senior fisheries biologist, and Janice Rowan at the U.S. Fish and Wildlife Service's Connecticut River Atlantic Salmon Commission have had years of experience spearheading the restoration of Atlantic salmon to the river, efforts that have received overwhelming public support. Although unsuccessful salmon restoration projects began in the last quarter of the nineteenth century, the 1967 federal Anadromous Fish Restoration Act marks the beginning of modern salmon reintroduction. In 1985 a salmon tagged and released at the Holyoke Dam made its way to a pool in Vermont's White River, the first salmon in the Green Mountains in 200 years.

While biologists had originally hoped for a sportfishery for salmon by the 1990s, salmon counts at fishways and fish ladders have generally been fewer than 200 fish, most of which are captured and used for artificial spawning at fish hatcheries. The reasons for disappointing returns of salmon remain a mystery, but we do know that ocean fisheries in general are in trouble, some to the point of collapse.

The general public has become deeply involved in raising and releasing salmon fry, with public schools participating and volunteers working with fisheries staff to distribute fry in the far reaches of the Connecticut River tributaries. The salmon restoration project has recruited large numbers of local people in efforts to clean up the river, breach dams, build fishways, and even develop local, in-home hatchery projects.

Most important, perhaps, is that efforts to restore salmon have also restored other anadromous fish runs, chiefly the shad, which mostly spawn on the main stem and larger tributaries of the river and have now regained their historic stopping point at Bellows Falls, Vermont. Thousands of local residents gather at the Holyoke Dam's fish lift to watch hundreds of thousands of shad migrate upstream, while thousands more participate in springtime shad festivals and fishing derbies. The world-record shad, caught in 1986 near the Holyoke Dam, weighed in at eleven pounds, four ounces. If you want to catch sight of a bald eagle, go boating on the river during the shad run, when eagles regularly feast on the remains of spent shad.

The restoration of herring is of great biological importance to the river's health. Runs of blueback herring, unfortunately, have been disappointing; these fish at the lower end of the food chain are important in sustaining higher populations of larger predators, such as striped bass. The striped bass fishery in the river, all the way up to the Holyoke Dam, has been very healthy, with many twenty-pound stripers caught annually. The Tidelands of the lower river are critical to the spawning and growth of young striped bass, as well as for overwintering adults. Ironically, some have blamed the poor returns of salmon on the abundance of striped bass, which eat as many salmon smolts as they can on the smolts' run to the sea; data on this, however, are inconclusive.

Boyd Kynard of the Silvio O. Conte Anadromous Fish Research Center (USGS) in Turners Falls, Massachusetts, has been studying the federally endangered shortnose sturgeon for almost thirty years, trying to learn why they number only several hundred rather than several thousand. Is it natural or human factors that depress their numbers? Connecticut River shortnose sturgeon are diadromous—that is, they use both fresh and salt water—and have developed a complex pattern of up- and downstream migrations throughout their life. From early spring to late fall, there are always some young or older fish moving upstream and downstream, using the river as a superhighway. A sixty-million-year-old species, 4 feet long and twenty-five pounds, with a plated body and tail fin resembling a shark as well as a sucker-like mouth and barbels, these fish live thirty or more years and are an integral part of the river's fishery.

The sea lamprey and American eel complete the suite of native migratory fish in the Connecticut River. Totally unrelated to each other, equally repellent to most

Americans, admired throughout Europe and Asia as a taste treat (royalty would dine on lamprey pie), these two species form a substantial part of the food web in the river. The sea lamprey is a primitive cartilaginous fish with a round disk for a mouth that has rasping teeth and sucks blood and fluids from larger fish. It has a fascinating life history. Usually in June, spawning adults excavate 2- to 3-foot-wide egg nests in the main stem and in any tributary with fast stream flow and a gravelly to rocky bottom. Larvae in tributaries as far north as Vermont's White River burrow into sand or silt, filtering out tiny particles of food, then transforming into 6-inch-long migrant juveniles with eyes and teeth, which migrate downstream to the sea during fall to early spring. They spend up to four years in fresh water, then migrate to the ocean where they parasitize other fish for about two years, growing to 2 feet or more before returning to breed and die in the Connecticut River tributaries. Once sea lamprey enter fresh water in the Connecticut River, however, they stop feeding and are no threat to our fishery, unlike other areas in New England or the Great Lakes where they are not a native fish. Lamprey counts at the Holyoke Dam average 50,000 annually and have greatly increased over the past twenty years as adults have gained access to native spawning habitat provided by fish passages built at main stem dams for salmon and shad. Not only do the decayed bodies of the adults feed nutrients into the river system, but the larvae and juveniles are the most abundant fish in some of the tributaries and an important food source for sport fish.

Finally, we come to the American eel, just as extraordinary in its life cycle and biological importance as the sea lamprey. Unfortunately, eel populations have declined precipitously in the past decade, and the U.S. Fish and Wildlife Service has begun a study to try to ensure healthy populations and determine whether the American eel needs a threatened or endangered designation. The eel is our only catadromous fish—breeding in the ocean and maturing in fresh water. Eels begin life as tiny larvae born in the Sargasso Sea in the Gulf Stream north of the Bahamas. At less than 2 inches in size, the larvae drift for almost a year on ocean currents, transforming into 2- or 3-inch glass eels. In autumn and winter, when they reach the estuaries on America's East Coast, including the Connecticut River Tidelands, they transform into small gray juveniles, called elvers, that swim upstream and, sometimes with the help of artificial eelways at dam sites, find their way past seemingly insurmountable dams and waterfalls as far north as central New Hampshire and Vermont. They remain in the river for up to twenty years, females growing to 5 feet and males to 1 foot in length. They next transform into mature eels with dark backs and white bellies, stop feeding, and migrate on autumn nights back to the sea for their January spawning rendezvous in the Caribbean.

Fishing Regulations

A fishing license is required everywhere on the river except downstream of the Old Saybrook–Old Lyme Railroad Bridge at mile 3 near the mouth of the Connecticut River.

Be sure to check fishing regulations when you get your fishing license, or check them online at the following state Web sites:

- Connecticut: www.dep.state.ct.us/burnatr/fishing/fishinfo/angler.htm
- Massachusetts: www.mass.gov/dfwele/dfw/dfwrec.htm#FISH
- New Hampshire: www.wildlife.state.nh.us/Fishing/fishing.htm
- Vermont: www.vtfishandwildlife.com/fish_sportfish.cfm

Pay special attention to the following:

- **A New Hampshire fishing license is required in the Upper Valley.** While Vermont and New Hampshire jointly manage the fishery on their sections of the Connecticut River, New Hampshire regulations apply to both sides of the river. Therefore, *nonresidents of Vermont and New Hampshire require a valid New Hampshire license to fish the main stem of the river.* If you are fishing the Vermont side of the Moore or Comerford Reservoir or the mouths of tributaries in Vermont, you must have a Vermont license. However, resident Vermonters with valid Vermont licenses may fish the main stem of the Connecticut River to its mean low-water line without a New Hampshire license.

- **Lead sinker prohibition.** As of January 1, 2007, Vermont has prohibited the use of lead weights of half an ounce or less. Lead sinkers are responsible for almost 50 percent of loon deaths. Lead is deadly: Dispose of it properly, and use alternate material for weights.

- **Protect the fishery.** Practice catch and release whenever possible. While the Connecticut River has a productive fishery, it is not a bottomless resource. Specifically, adhere to catch regulations on anadromous fish. You will be heavily penalized for possession of anadromous Atlantic salmon, shortnose sturgeon, blueback herring, and alewives.

A Connecticut River Valley History

Prehistory

The first Native Americans came to the Connecticut River Valley at least 12,000 years ago, 4,000 years after the glaciers had receded and 2,000 years after Lake Hitchcock and Lake Middletown had drained into Long Island Sound. They lived as far north as Greenfield, Massachusetts, in scattered settlements on the tundra landscape, hunting mastodons, mammoths, deer, bears, beavers, and small animals. By about 9,000 years ago, the tundra and most of the boreal forest were fast disappearing, along with the mammoths and mastodons, replaced by deciduous woods of oak, beech, chestnut, ash, birch, butternut, and hickory. The new forest cover could provide for much larger populations of people, who also depended on the shad and other fish that seasonally ran upriver.

With the arrival of seed for growing corn, beans, and squash from southern tribes, agriculture became the principal means of subsistence, and a few decades before European contact, the population of Native Americans in New England had reached at least 90,000. The Connecticut River Native Americans had cleared and burned portions of the river valley of dense vegetation to improve agricultural land and deer browse and had long since settled into tribal homelands by the time the first Europeans arrived. All the New England tribes were part of the large linguistic group called Algonkians, who, through their stories, traced their lineage back to the arrival of the first people in New England. The Abenaki, or "people of the dawn lands," occupied the northern two-thirds of the watershed from Canada into northern Massachusetts, while the Pequot, Algonkian for "destroyers," occupied the state of Connecticut. The Native Americans of Massachusetts—the Pocumtuck, Norwottuck, and Agawam—were a mixed group of Abenaki, Pequot, and Nipmuk to the east.

Contact and Its Aftermath

Smallpox and other Eurasian diseases hit New England in the late sixteenth century with the first European trade contact prior to permanent white settlement. Epidemics laid waste to huge numbers of Native Americans; estimates run as high as 95 percent mortality for some Native American bands. When the first European, a Dutchman named Adriaen Block, explored the Connecticut River up to the Enfield, Connecticut, rapids in 1614, he would have found groups of Native Americans decimated by disease and many villages deserted. The Dutch later followed with trading posts in the 1620s at Saybrook and Hartford, Connecticut, but the Dutch presence was quickly overwhelmed by increasing numbers of English colonists and Pequot, who raided their outposts.

English settlers from Massachusetts Bay Colony in and around Boston, having heard of the river's extraordinarily rich valley lands, established towns in the valley in Massachusetts and Connecticut within a decade of their arrival in Boston. Their goals were clear. John Winthrop, one of the founders and the first governor of the Massachusetts Bay Colony, proclaimed on his arrival in Boston in 1630 that "wee must consider that wee shall be as a citty upon a hill. The eies of all people are uppon us."

In the generation between 1635 and 1665, nine colonial "citties upon a hill" had been established in the river valley: Saybrook, Middletown, Wethersfield, Hartford, Farmington, and Windsor in Connecticut; Springfield, Northampton, and Hadley in Massachusetts. Each town had a Congregational church; a self-governing body called town meeting, in which all male property owners could vote on town affairs, including the budget; a justice of the peace; a representative to the colonial legislature; and a local militia. Of these early features, the most lasting has been town meeting, which to this day is held in annually in the majority of towns in Massachusetts and the Upper Valley.

As white settlers worked to expand their territory and trade links, the Native Americans had quite different objectives, namely to recover from population loss and

Native American Nipmuks bless the river in an ancient ceremony. Photo by Tom Miner

maintain their way of life. Relying on ancient strategies, they used trade networks and shifting alliances to hold on to their hunting territories and village sites, resorting to war when necessary and taking prisoners to increase their numbers. Until the late seventeenth century, Native Americans had the advantage of numbers and knowledge to stave off the total loss of their homeland, but not for long; they were quickly losing ground to disease and the extraordinary demographic growth of the English.

From 1630 to 1763 the colonists and Native Americans endured periods of uneasy peace, punctuated by raiding wars that ultimately almost extirpated the Native Americans. The Pequot War of the mid–seventeenth century was followed by Sachem Metacom's War, or King Philip's War, in the late seventeenth century, after which ensued a series of raids until the 1760s. These last were part of the French and Indian Wars, or Seven Years' War, in which remnant bands of Pequot/Mohegan and Abenaki allied with other tribes and French soldiers in order to hold on to what little territory was left them. Prior to the French and Indian Wars, there were no permanent white settlements in the Upper Valley, except for the Fort at No. 4 at Charlestown, New Hampshire. The struggle for North America between England and France forced the French to cede northern New England to the British and opened up the whole Upper Valley to a flood of English settlers from Connecticut and Massachusetts, thus putting an end to significant Native American presence in the Connecticut River watershed.

The Connecticut River Valley at the Time of the American Revolution

By 1776 the Connecticut River Valley was becoming an agricultural and industrial center for the United States, providing agricultural products and a budding precision machine industry that produced armaments for George Washington's army. The Connecticut Valley would shortly become one of the four regional centers for the Industrial Revolution in America, along with the Schuylkill Valley in Philadelphia, the Blackstone Valley of Rhode Island, and the Merrimack Valley of eastern Massachusetts and southern New Hampshire. And in the middle of the eighteenth century, the valley had also become the center of America's first huge religious revival—the Great Awakening, led by Jonathan Edwards, one of America's first great intellectuals.

During the first 125 years of settlement, offspring from the original seventeenth-century towns had spread across the whole watershed, up into the hills of Litchfield County, Connecticut, and Berkshire County, Massachusetts. Then, a decade after the end of the French and Indian Wars, Massachusetts and Connecticut Yankees had established almost all the regional centers in the Upper Valley, from Brattleboro and Hinsdale to Windsor, Lebanon, and Hanover. New Englanders were changing their landscapes at great speed in a short space of time.

The Connecticut Valley witnessed no battles during the American Revolution, but shortly thereafter, rural discontent with the State of Massachusetts's strict monetary and tax policies resulted in riots that culminated in Shays' Rebellion. Debt-ridden local farmers, led by former army captain Daniel Shays, staged a series of riots that ended with 2,000 rebels storming the Springfield Arsenal in 1787; the state militia scattered the rebels, who were sentenced to death but later pardoned. The riots had a significant national impact because they occurred simultaneously with the Constitutional Convention in Philadelphia. Fear of popular uprisings played a central role in the convention's decision to create an indirectly elected republic rather than a directly elected democracy.

For all its industrial advantages and agricultural fertility, why does the Connecticut River have no great port? Why was it unable to challenge Philadelphia on the Delaware, New York on the Hudson, or even Boston on the Charles River? Geology prevented establishment of a major commercial center for the region; the river's mouth is notoriously filled with shoals and shifting sand islands, and its bed allows only shallow-draft vessels in its first mile or so from the mouth, north of which a series of unnavigable rapids begin at Enfield, Connecticut. While there was an important shipbuilding industry in the Tidal River until the mid–nineteenth century, it built only wooden, shallow-draft vessels.

The Industrial Revolution and Beyond

By the end of the eighteenth century, all the pieces were in place to welcome the Industrial Revolution: waterpower from thousands of mill dams on the tributaries; local capital to risk in developing industry; a highly trained and educated workforce with a strong, self-reliant work ethic; self-governing communities to provide social stability; a surplus of labor from burgeoning families; and rich agricultural lands with independent farmers to provide sufficient food for the population except in extreme circumstances, such as occurred between 1811 and 1817, for example. During that time New England experienced cold summers, the worst of which was the infamous "Year Without a Summer" in 1816 when it snowed every month of the year in the Upper Valley.

Inventors and engineers in the valley had already made considerable strides by 1800. There was David Bushnell's amazing *American Turtle*, a submarine torpedo that the Saybrook, Connecticut, native built to blow up England's warships during the American Revolution (unfortunately, the *Turtle* could submerge but was unable to blow up any British ships). In 1787 John Fitch of Windsor, Connecticut, built the first steam-propelled boat, followed five years later by Samuel Morey's steamboat in Orford, New Hampshire. The year 1784 saw the first bridge over the Connecticut between Bellows Falls, Vermont, and Walpole, New Hampshire, and the first dams on the river's main stem were built in the late 1790s at Bellows Falls and Turners Falls, Massachusetts. America's first canal was constructed in 1795 at South Hadley, Massachusetts, to transport goods past Holyoke Falls, followed in short order by canal systems at Turners Falls, Bellows Falls, and in Connecticut at Windsor Locks.

Heavy industry developed quickly in the valley, by midcentury prompting a major increase in population, principally through foreign immigration and the creation of industrial centers all the way from Middletown, Connecticut, to White River Junction, Vermont, and Lebanon, New Hampshire. Of these, perhaps the most interesting is Holyoke, Massachusetts, America's first planned city, constructed around a series of canals filled with water diverted from the Connecticut River that powered the mills. Holyoke became "the Paper City," manufacturing paper for the whole nation, chiefly made from cloth, although most mills up and down the river switched to wood pulp when the technology became available in the late nineteenth century. Holyoke was also the terminus for the great log drives from 1869 to 1915 that delivered logs cut in the Great North Woods almost 300 miles upstream.

The unique aspect of industrial life in the Connecticut River Valley turned out to be precision manufacturing, namely firearms. Local machinists were in the forefront of the race to develop interchangeable parts for industrial goods, and firearms were critical to the needs of the early republic. George Washington had chosen Springfield, Massachusetts, as the site for one of the country's first arms depots, which the government turned into the nation's first arms-producing arsenal in 1796. The center of gun manufacturing in the nineteenth century was in Connecticut, from Windsor to Hartford to New Haven. Techniques for making arms subsequently spread to other industries, making the valley a center for metalworking and machine tools in general. Its history can be retraced at the American Precision Museum in Windsor, Vermont.

By the 1820s the valley had become overpopulated. While residents of the valley proper generally flourished, people in the mountainous, rocky uplands on both sides became impoverished. Valley farmers continued to prosper by adopting intensive cultivation and specialty crops, particularly tobacco; in 1810 the nation's first cigar factory opened in Suffield, Connecticut. But settlers in the rest of the watershed had quickly depleted their farms' poor soil. Over the course of the nineteenth century, the upland regions lost their populations as young people emigrated west, and much of this region in Massachusetts and the Upper Valley still has fewer residents today than it did in the early nineteenth century.

The Connecticut Valley is now known for its institutions of higher education, but ironically, the only eighteenth-century college here was Dartmouth in Hanover, New Hampshire, near the frontier of European settlement. In the 1740s its founder, Eleazer Wheelock, had established the Moor Charity School to educate Native Americans in Lebanon, Connecticut, and twenty years later was hoping to turn it into a college. Despite the blandishments and bribes offered him by fellow ministers in Northampton and Hatfield, Massachusetts, he and his student, the Mohegan Samuel Occom, opened Dartmouth in 1769 in New Hampshire. In the 1820s and 1830s, Amherst, Mount Holyoke, Trinity, and Wesleyan Colleges opened their doors; Smith College, the University of Massachusetts, and the University of Connecticut followed later that century.

New England's Best-Landscaped Sewer and Its Recovery

The first half of the twentieth century saw continuing general prosperity in the river valley itself, but subsistence survival in most of the rest of the watershed. The cities flourished, developing parks and public spaces; Hartford and Springfield became cultural centers where people could watch New York theater and opera productions, stroll along the river, and visit museums. The poet Wallace Stevens and artist Alexander Calder found Hartford as welcoming as had Mark Twain in the previous century. Regional centers in the Upper Valley—Brattleboro, Windsor, Lebanon, St. Johnsbury—developed their own vital cultural lives, which continue to this day, attracting tourists with summer music festivals, autumn leaf-peeping, and winter skiing.

Industrialization, however, had significant, although easily explicable, environmental costs, which are still visible today. Since the early years of the republic, New England legislatures had passed a series of "Mill Acts" that favored mill rights over farming and fishing uses, judging that sawmills and gristmills performed a public service greater than the property rights of local landowners and fishermen. The New

England states fitfully tried to protect fisheries by barring commercial nets in most areas, demanding that industries provide fish ladders, and assuring public access to fish. However, state legislatures showed a clear bias toward industrial over rural uses of the river, not only for economic and political reasons, but also because during most of their history New Englanders have seen themselves as practical, inventive people with a strong attachment to industrial progress. From the mid–nineteenth to the mid–twentieth centuries, industries dumped increasing amounts of pollutants into the Connecticut, almost wiping out the shad runs and destroying what remained of the salmon runs. Valley residents born before 1950 can all tell stories of the multicolored plumes of effluent and strange smells from scores of paper companies along the river. Furthermore, forests in the Great North Woods and Upper Valley had been stripped bare, to the point that residents referred to logging sites as "skinned land."

In reaction to the loss of most of the Connecticut River fish runs and the mistreatment of forestlands, a backlash had already begun by the 1850s. In fact, the Upper Valley produced the first giant of America's environmental movement: George Perkins Marsh, born in Woodstock, Vermont, alumnus of Dartmouth, Vermont's first fish commissioner, and author of the nation's first environmental treatise in 1864, *Man and Nature, or Physical Geography as Modified by Human Action.* The Marsh-Billings-Rockefeller National Historical Park in Woodstock testifies to his standing as the father of the American conservation movement. In his 1857 report to the Vermont legislature, Marsh lamented "nature in the shorn and crippled condition to which human progress has reduced her."

A second critique of unfettered industrialization came simultaneously from public health advocates, who pressed the Massachusetts and Connecticut legislatures to reform industrial waste and municipal sewage dumping throughout the last third of the nineteenth century. Cities had been dumping their untreated sewage into the river. Holyoke, for example, dumped its above the Holyoke Dam, which allowed the sewage to flow back through the canals downstream and into the city center.

Today, despite the resurgence of a powerful environmental movement in the twentieth century and the passage of strongly enforced environmental laws, sewage dumping continues to prove intractable. At the time of this guide's publication, Hartford, Springfield, and Holyoke have still not solved their combined sewage overflow problem; they still use antiquated sewer systems that combine sewage and floodwater overflow, putting untreated sewage into the river during periods of heavy rain. Major financial help from the federal government in the 1970s, however, has helped alleviate smaller sewage problems throughout the watershed.

On the other hand, the river witnessed dramatic reductions in the dumping of industrial effluent during the last half of the twentieth century, chiefly due to the loss of all kinds of manufacturing. While the river has benefited enormously from the shuttering of factories, cities and towns have suffered dramatically, leaving the poorest citizens of Hartford, Springfield, and Holyoke in center cities while wealthier residents have moved to suburbs and hill towns. Towns up and down the valley have had to resort to Yankee ingenuity to stabilize their communities, turning industrial buildings into commercial sites and condominiums. In the last three decades, population numbers have remained stable, with cities losing people while suburbs and towns have increased their numbers.

The river has traversed an interesting road this past century, from the most beautiful sewer to one of the healthiest great rivers in America. The trick has always been to balance economic growth and environmental health. The Connecticut River watershed needs its cities as much as its wild areas; residents of the valley will have to find inventive ways to achieve that balance over the next century.

Animals Large and Small

The mountains, forests, and floodplains that surround the Connecticut River teem with birds and mammals that require extensive areas of continuous habitat for foraging and breeding. Once subject to decades of pollution and exploitation, the river is recovering and can once again support hordes of dragonflies and delicate aquatic invertebrates such as mussels; the return of a wide variety of animals to the river testifies to its resilience and robust ecological systems.

If you're interested in birding on the river, we suggest that before setting out you consult maps on the Web site for the Connecticut River Birding Trail (www.bird trail.org), based in White River Junction, Vermont. You can also contact local Audubon Societies for checklists and the latest sightings.

At its northern reaches the river is at its most wild. Thanks to recent conservation efforts, thousands of acres of the Great North Woods have been protected. Here the largest of New England's denizens still roam. You may be spellbound by the sight of a moose or a bear at the water's edge in northern New Hampshire. Spoor of coyotes and bobcats (hopes for a mountain lion spring eternal) can be seen along the rugged hiking trails that link the Connecticut Lakes with the nearby mountains. Boreal birds such as black-backed woodpeckers, spruce grouse, golden-crowned kinglets, pine grosbeaks, crossbills, and Cape May warblers frequent the deep woods, and the trill of the hermit thrush often echoes through the trees at dusk. The Connecticut Lakes themselves resound with the ethereal cry of the common loon.

Large areas of dense, mixed deciduous forests cloak the middle reaches of the river, home to an array of migratory bird species that split their years between New England and the tropics, including worm-eating, black-throated green, and cerulean warblers, scarlet tanagers, wood thrushes, rose-breasted grosbeaks, eastern towhees, and several species of flycatchers and vireos. In the more open lowlands of Massachusetts and Connecticut, the river still floods and ebbs on a yearly cycle, nourishing countless acres of wet meadows and floodplain forests. Here, from Deerfield, Massachusetts, to Cromwell, Connecticut, dozens of wading birds and ducks find crucial habitat. Mallards, American black ducks, wood ducks, common and red-breasted mergansers, blue-winged and American green-winged teal all paddle around these waters.

You'll find many moose in the north woods. Photo © Al Braden

Harder to spot amid the tall marsh grasses are the secretive sora, Virginia rails, clapper rails, and the very rare king and black rails; lucky bird watchers might see American or least bitterns. The aggressive mute swan is also becoming more common in these waters, and may vigorously "defend" its home coves from startled boaters; also look for native tundra swans in fall and winter months.

The muddy shoreline of the middle valley is a tableau of fascinating signs and footprints. The dexterous "hands" of raccoons mingle with the webbed toes and slide marks of river otters, alongside the tiny tracks of meadow voles, water shrews, and star-nosed moles. Riverbanks may be riddled with the holes of muskrats. Looking up at nearby hemlocks, you might see the telltale bark shreds and scattered twigs left by porcupines feeding high in the canopy or catch a rare glimpse of a fisher, the only predator that feeds on porcupines.

Where the river meets the sea, brackish marshes and tidal flats support a rich collection of shorebirds. Snowy and great egrets become increasingly common sights along the lower reaches from Middletown, Connecticut, south. A black-crowned night heron might peer out from below the trees. The saltmarsh sharp-tailed sparrow, seaside sparrow, and an occasional swamp sparrow inhabit the brackish tidal marshes. Diminutive marsh wrens will bob their tiny, expressive tails at you. Rich muddy flats are the favored feeding grounds of thousands of shorebirds: sanderlings and semi-palmated sandpipers, black-bellied plovers, willets, greater and lesser yellowlegs, and short-billed dowitchers, all of which need large stretches of clean habitat with a wealth of available food. The shifting sands of the point at the river's mouth are home to the endangered piping plover, where human volunteers assiduously take turns protecting their nests all summer long. The endangered least tern also finds critical nesting grounds here. Adventurous harbor seals even venture up the river a short way from their territories in Long Island Sound during winter and spring.

Certain charismatic species are found nearly throughout the river and are quite easy to spot. Once hunted nearly to extinction for their pelts, beavers now inhabit every accessible reach. Look for their lodges in quiet coves and tributaries of the river; they have even dammed a large former oxbow downstream of Guildhall, Vermont (see Reach 6), blocking it from the main stem. Ubiquitous great blue herons patiently ply the river shallows, hunting for anything that moves. Dozens of these graceful and startlingly large birds may be seen on a single paddle, rising pterodactyl-like at a boat's approach, only to settle again farther downstream. And perhaps you will spot the small, common, but shy green heron, especially in floodplain forests. Bank, barn, cliff, tree, and rough-winged swallows zip effortlessly along the water's surface, showing off their aerial acrobatics, while kingfishers rattle their calls up and down the river. Spotted sandpipers bob and weave, skirting the water in search of insects. In summer, rafts of temporarily flightless mergansers flee with their young in front of your boat. The piercing whistle of the osprey can be heard from the river's mouth to north-central Vermont, as this once declining bird recovers its former range. Emblematic of the river's resurgence, bald eagles have also begun to reclaim their extensive range on the river. Listen for the rude, raspberry buzz of red-winged blackbirds wherever they find cattails on which to perch. At dawn or dusk a white-tailed deer is highly likely to venture to the water's edge for a drink.

Amid all these showy species, however, don't overlook the smaller, slimier river dwellers. In spring and summer the wetlands and temporary pools near the river come alive with a chorus of amphibians: American toads, spring peepers, green and gray tree frogs, green, pickerel, and bullfrogs all join in the exuberant cacophony. A northern water snake may glide by your boat, hunting for frogs and fish. At 8 inches or longer, with flamboyant purple gills, the secretive mud puppy (a giant salamander) is quite a sight along the middle reaches. Beware the admirably prehistoric head of a snapping turtle if you decide to take a cooling dip in one of the lower river's many coves; it can sever a finger or toe if it is threatened. The southern brackish marshes

The American bald eagle has regained its habitat along the river.
Photo by U.S. Fish and Wildlife Service

are also home to the now rare diamondback terrapin. Painted turtles often clamber out onto logs and rocks to sun themselves by the river's edge.

The smallest inhabitants of the river are among its most colorful and among the world's rarest species. Several species of mussels are very common throughout the river's entire length, many of which need both clear waters and an abundance of fish to survive since mussel larvae actually disperse themselves by latching on to fish gills; therefore, the presence of certain specialized mussels can signal healthy water quality.

Dragonflies compete with swallows for the title of most gymnastic flier, especially the raucously colorful, powerful gomphids. Iridescent damselflies will perch delicately on your gunwhale, hitching a ride. Like mussels, damselflies and dragonflies need unpolluted, well-oxygenated waters in which to spend their fragile juvenile phases; hot spots of these insects indicate a clean stretch of river. Tiger beetles are fast and fearless predators of sandy and cobbly river shores. Less than an inch long and perfectly camouflaged for grayish gravels, they dig masses of tiny holes, often as deep as a foot or more, in unvegetated patches, where they lay their eggs. Because they nest in the raw, open sediments deposited with river floods, their habitats have been disappearing where dams dampen river action and vegetation takes over. Likewise, their beach habitats make popular picnic places; boaters can inadvertently trample their colonies. At least two species on the Connecticut River are globally endangered, but like all animals have a chance to make a comeback if river visitors treat them with care.

The river is still a brook trout stream above the Second Connecticut Lake. Photo © Al Braden

Vermont and New Hampshire

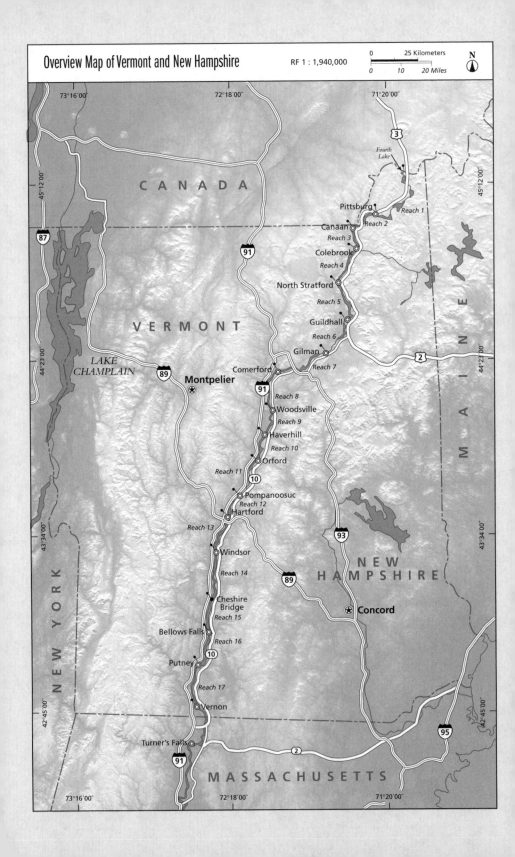

Overview Map of Vermont and New Hampshire

RF 1 : 1,940,000

0   25 Kilometers

N

0   10   20 Miles

CANADA

Fourth
Lake

Pittsburg   *Reach 1*

Canaan   *Reach 2*

Reach 3

Colebrook

Reach 4

North Stratford

Reach 5

Guildhall

Reach 6

Gilman

Comerford   *Reach 7*

VERMONT

Reach 8

Woodsville

Reach 9

Haverhill

Reach 10

Orford

Reach 11

Pompanoosuc

Reach 12

Hartford

Reach 13

Windsor

Reach 14

Cheshire
Bridge

Reach 15

Bellows Falls

Reach 16

Putney

Reach 17

Vernon

Turner's Falls

MASSACHUSETTS

LAKE
CHAMPLAIN

Montpelier

NEW
HAMPSHIRE

Concord

MAINE

NEW YORK

Reach 1 Fourth Connecticut Lake to Murphy Dam

Miles from mouth: 410–383 (27-mile span).
Navigable by: Kayaks, canoes, and small power-boats; sailboats on lakes only.
Difficulty: Flat water on lakes; quick water to Class V depending on river flow conditions.
Flow information: http://water.usgs.gov/water watch or www.h2oline.com; (800) 452-1737.
Portage: *Mile 383:* Murphy Dam, 1.5 miles.
Fishing regulations:
Third, Second, and First Connecticut Lakes, and Lake Francis: From April 1 through September 30, there is a combined daily limit of four fish, only two of which can be salmon or lake trout. Yellow perch cannot be used as bait on lakes or in the river.

Second Lake Dam to Magalloway Bridge: Fly fishing, catch and release only.
Magalloway Bridge to inlet at First Lake: Fly fishing only, limit of two brook trout per day.
First Lake Dam to Lake Francis: Fly fishing only, limit of two brook trout per day, minimum of 12 inches each. On river sections, the limit is 15 inches for salmon; there's a limit of two fish total per day, whether trout or salmon.
Camping: *Mile 409:* Deer Mountain State Park, Pittsburg, New Hampshire. *Mile 387.5:* Lake Francis State Park, Pittsburgh, New Hampshire.
USGS maps: Second Connecticut Lake 15, Indian Stream 15.

The Reach

The Connecticut River begins in New Hampshire, just a few hundred yards from the Canadian border. It will take at least two days to explore the headwaters of the river and Connecticut Lakes and, except for the lakes themselves, most of the Connecticut River in these uppermost reaches is *not navigable.* Take your time and enjoy the quiet of the Great North Woods.

The Connecticut Lakes are cradled in the Great North Woods of New Hampshire. This area is known for wild mountain streams and deep glacial lakes that hold indigenous lake trout and one of only two self-sustaining landlocked salmon populations in New Hampshire. The Connecticut Lakes region's signature animal is the moose, but you will also find plenty of deer, black bears and fishers, along with the rare pine marten.

The Connecticut River Birding Trail (www.birdtrail.org) has a list of north country birds you'll find here: snipe, woodcock, black-backed woodpecker, spruce grouse, white-winged crossbill, Bicknell's thrush, and a wealth of warblers. You will also see great blue herons—one of the few birds, along with ospreys and bald eagles, that nest from the Connecticut Lakes all the way down to Long Island Sound. A special note: Common loons, the most famous birds of northern lakes, nest on all these lakes. Enjoy their music, but please do not disturb them or come too close to them. Keep your wake low near their nests to avoid destroying them.

This is wild country, and, thanks to a landmark conservation project initiated by the State of New Hampshire, the Trust for Public Land, and The Nature Conservancy, it will remain so. Since 2003 the 171,500 acres of the Connecticut Lakes Headwaters

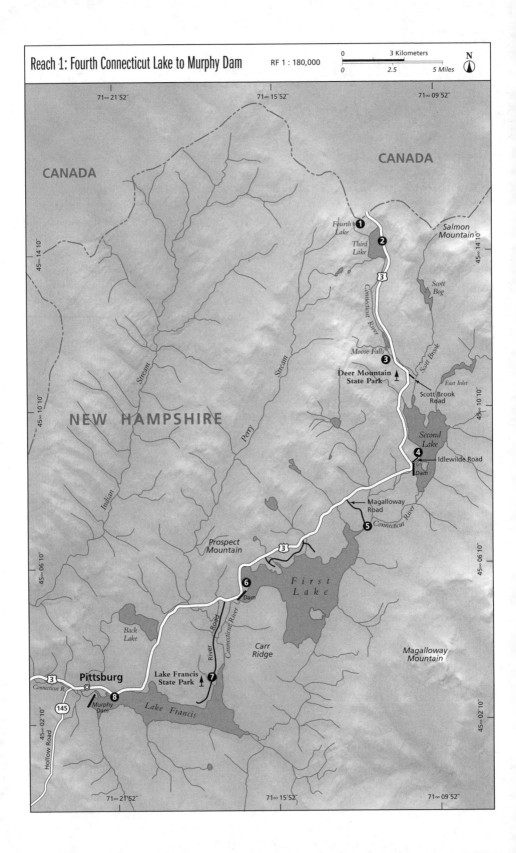

Reach 1: Fourth Connecticut Lake to Murphy Dam

RF 1 : 180,000

Forest, including all the Connecticut Lakes, are being managed by New Hampshire as a natural area for recreation and wildlife, with a timber company managing the forest for wildlife, recreation and sustainable forestry. The Nature Conservancy has a 25,000-acre conservation easement, which it manages as a nature reserve.

Boating Facilities Table for Reach 1

Access Point, Directions	Boat Type	Fee	Parking	Picnic	Toilets	Camping	Rentals	Supplies
❶ Fourth Connecticut Lake US 3 at Canadian border *Stop at border on US 3, let border officer know you are going to Fourth Lake, and climb trail marked near customs house.*	Foot access only	N	Y	N	N	N	N	N
❷ Third Connecticut Lake US 3, Pittsburg, NH *Halfway between north and south ends of lake.*	Unimproved ramp, car-top only	N	Y	Y	Y	N	N	N
❸ Deer Mountain Campground US 3, Pittsburg, NH *West side of US 3. Reservations: (603) 271-3628; www.nhparks.state.nh.us*	Car-top only	Y	Y	Y	Y	Y	N	N
❹ Second Connecticut Lake US 3, Pittsburg, NH *Turn east off US 3, 0.5 mile north of dam, onto Idlewilde Road.*	Improved ramp, all boats	N	Y	Y	Y	N	N	N
❺ Magalloway Bridge Access US 3, Pittsburg, NH *Off US 3 at northeast end of First Connecticut Lake; turn southeast onto Magalloway Road.*	Car-top only	N	Y	N	N	N	N	N
❻ First Connecticut Lake US 3, Pittsburg, NH *Directly off US 3 just north of dam.*	Improved ramp, all boats	N	Y	Y	Y	N	N	N
❼ Lake Francis State Park River Road, Pittsburg, NH *Turn right onto River Road just south of First Lake dam off US 3. Reservations: (603) 271-3628; www.nhparks.state.nh.us*	Improved ramp, all boats	Y	Y	Y	Y	Y	N	N
❽ Lake Francis Ramp US 3, Pittsburg, NH *South side of US 3.*	Improved ramp, all boats	N	Y	Y	Y	N	N	N

Miles and Directions

Mile 410: Fourth Connecticut Lake. You will find the headwaters of the Connecticut River a few hundred yards from the Canadian border. It's worth the 0.75-mile walk to this shallow pond with its floating bog simply to contemplate the beginning of this great river and look for birds and wetland plants. The Nature Conservancy owns this seventy-eight-acre parcel.

Miles 410–409: Fourth to **Third Connecticut Lake.** No boating possible. The Connecticut River begins here as a small brook trout stream, and only avid anglers are willing to wade through the overhanging alders and past beaver ponds.

Miles 409–407.5: Third Connecticut Lake. This small, crystalline lake, 100 feet at its deepest, is generally used only by anglers with or without motors.

Miles 407.5–403: Third Connecticut Lake to **Second Connecticut Lake.** This section of the river is not navigable except for a quiet paddle on Moose Falls Flowage just upstream from **Deer Mountain State Park.** You can get to **Moose Falls** on a short path at the upper end of the campground. A small dam holds back just enough water to create a pretty wetland and pond that is excellent for birding and botanizing. Deer Mountain, with exceptional views of the north country, is a fine two- to three-hour hike that starts at the campground. The wet forest on both sides of U.S. Route 3 in this northern section of the lakes is prime moose habitat; the best chance for a sighting is early morning or late afternoon into the evening. Moose, however, are a major cause of nighttime car accidents, so drivers should take care.

Miles 403–399: Second Connecticut Lake. This is big, open, sometimes choppy water, excellent for sailing but often dangerous for canoes. Many consider that Second Lake has the most beautiful setting of all the lakes, with its views toward the Salmon Mountains in Quebec and Diamond Ridge to the south. North and east of the lake are two lovely ponds for paddling and fishing—**East Inlet** and **Scott Bog**—accessible from East Inlet Road, which runs east of US 3 just south of Deer Mountain Campground. These are part of The Nature Conservancy's conservation easement.

Miles 399–396: Second Connecticut Lake to **First Connecticut Lake.** The river drops 200 feet between these two lakes, and its cascades are extremely dangerous as the river carves its way down through granite. Paddlers and anglers can access the river at **Magalloway Bridge**, where a group from Americorps has stabilized the banks and installed a stone stairway down to the river. Experienced paddlers can run the river below the bridge, where the current ranges from quick water to Class IV, depending on the flow. Anglers must be aware that special fishing restrictions apply. Magalloway Road takes you to the base of **Magalloway Mountain**, where, after about a mile hike, you gain a fine view of the Connecticut Lakes and some nearby Maine lakes from the fire tower on the mountaintop.

Land Trusts, Land Preservation, and the Conte Refuge

The purchase of the 171,500-acre Connecticut Lakes Headwaters Forest is the largest purchase of land for conservation in this 11,000-square-mile watershed, but it's only one of thousands of efforts to preserve land from development in exchange for natural flood control, wildlife habitat, nature reserves, recreation, agriculture, and timber harvesting. As you work your way downriver, remember that much of your delight derives from the wild and rural qualities of most reaches, often thanks to the work of land trusts.

For most river reaches, there is a local, regional, or national land trust ready to partner with government agencies to ensure the pleasure of your river experience. Groups such as the Upper Valley Land Trust depend almost solely on local residents for funding and work in close cooperation with national nongovernmental organizations and government agencies. A national network, Land Trust Alliance, provides contact information for more than 1,500 local land trusts in America.

The Silvio O. Conte National Fish and Wildlife Refuge works with land trusts and state agencies throughout the watershed and is unique because it deals with both fish and wildlife, it covers the entire river in all four states, and it's charged with protecting the watershed's natural diversity, not just particular species. The refuge has identified roughly 180,000 acres of "special focus areas" that contribute substantially or in unique ways to supporting natural diversity in the watershed. Recognizing that land acquisition alone cannot meet this challenge, the Conte Refuge also involves the people of the watershed, especially landowners and land managers, in environmental education programs and cooperative management projects. The Conte Refuge may become the model for refuges of the future.

Miles 396–391: First Connecticut Lake. The largest and deepest of the Connecticut Lakes, this lake can provide a fine outing in beautiful weather or a brutal experience in wind and rain. Be sure to check the weather forecast before venturing out. As with the other lakes, shorelines, water levels, and boating and camping facilities are the province of the hydropower company, while the forest lands are all part of the Connecticut Lakes Headwaters Forest. This lake holds the largest populations of trout and salmon, but only the most experienced anglers know the seasons and methods to find them.

Miles 391–388: First Connecticut Lake to **Lake Francis**. Back on the Connecticut River once again, you'll reach a beautiful, wooded stretch of *unnavigable* water, which is simply too dangerous even for experts to run. On the other hand, this is a

Fourth Lake is the source of the Connecticut River. Photo © Al Braden

prize section of blue-ribbon water for trout and salmon. It begins at a splash pool at the base of the dam, followed by a steep, bumpy section, then some rapids, ending with a long whitewater drop into Lake Francis. The section from First Lake to Lake Francis is a trophy section for anglers; special fishing regulations apply.

Miles 388–383: Lake Francis. With its state park and campgrounds, Lake Francis has the busiest boat traffic of all the Connecticut Lakes, especially on weekends. The long, narrow lake acts as a wind funnel, so try to paddle with a fair wind from the stern. Lake Francis is oriented east–west, unlike the other lakes, and it used to be a steep, winding section of river before the 100-foot-high Murphy Dam was built in 1940. This lake has the most complete boating and camping facilities in the lakes region. Take out at the **Lake Francis Ramp** and portage 1.5 miles to the Pittsburg (Bacon Street) Covered Bridge. *Caution:* The section of river between Lake Francis and the Bacon Street Bridge is too dangerous to run.

Reach 2 Murphy Dam to Canaan Dam

Miles from mouth: 383-373 (10-mile span).
Navigable by: Kayaks, canoes.
Difficulty: Class II to Class IV.
Flow information: http://water.usgs.gov/water watch/ or www.h2oline.com; (800) 452-1737.

Portages: *Mile 374.5:* Beecher Falls, 2 miles. *Mile 373:* Canaan Dam, 0.25 mile.
Camping: No established sites.
USGS maps: Indian Stream 15, Averill 15.

The Reach

These 10 miles are what anglers consider classic trout water and boaters wish were more navigable. Cold water (generally fifty to fifty-five degrees Fahrenheit) is released from the bottom of Murphy Dam at Lake Francis and remains cold for 10 miles downstream, fed by multiple springs and Indian Stream about 4 miles south of Pittsburg.

The river is narrow and rocky with heavily forested banks, perfect for several days of fishing or a couple of hours of paddling—but only if the water levels are optimal. In general, however, this section of the river is simply too shallow to paddle. Below 200 cubic feet per second (cfs) is low water, and you must often get out to drag your craft. The best boating levels are from 200 to 500 cfs; water releases of more than 500 cfs are considered very dangerous. As it is, only paddlers with extensive whitewater experience should attempt to run this section. Be constantly aware of water releases and especially rain and thunderstorms.

Miles and Directions

Miles 383-382.5: Not even whitewater enthusiasts should attempt the water between **Murphy Dam** and the Pittsburg Covered Bridge (locally called the **Bacon Street Bridge**), 0.5 mile downstream. The first few hundred yards of the river below Murphy Dam are disarmingly calm, but once **Crawford Stream** enters from the south at the juncture of New Hampshire Route 145 and U.S. Route 3, it becomes very rough.

Mile 379.5: Indian Stream enters from the right bank about 4 miles south of Pittsburg and, in thunderstorms or springtime high water, can double the size of the river. High water levels attract experienced whitewater paddlers, who can put into Indian Stream 5 miles up from its mouth. Most of the lower sections of Indian Stream are agricultural, so please respect the property rights of local farmers.

Miles 379.5-374.5: Given sufficient water you can paddle from Indian Stream to Stewartstown, New Hampshire, or on the opposite bank Beecher Falls, Vermont, on the 45th parallel at the Canadian–Vermont border. This is a lovely forested stretch of 5 miles. Beecher Falls boasts the Ethan Allan Furniture Company's original factory, which has been here since 1936. **Hall Stream** comes in on the right bank just before

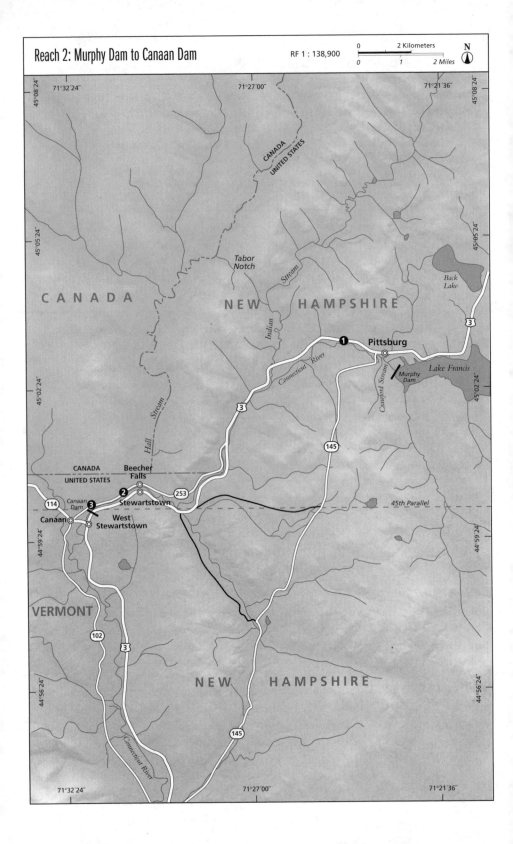

45°08'24"   71°32'24"   71°27'00"   71°21'36"   45°08'24"

CANADA
UNITED STATES

45°05'24"   45°05'24"

Tabor
Notch   Stream   Back
Lake

CANADA   NEW   HAMPSHIRE

Indian   3

Pittsburg
1   Lake
Francis

45°02'24"   Connecticut River   Murphy
Dam   45°02'24"

Stream

3   145

Hall   Stream

CANADA   Beecher   45th Parallel
UNITED STATES   Falls   2   253
114   Canaan   Stewartstown
Dam   3
Canaan   West
Stewartstown

44°59'24"   44°59'24"

VERMONT

102

3   NEW   HAMPSHIRE

44°56'24"   44°56'24"

145

Connecticut River

71°32'24"   71°27'00"   71°21'36"

Pittsburg Covered Bridge (known locally as the Bacon Street Bridge) is the first of several covered bridges in the Upper Valley. Photo © Al Braden

Boating Facilities Table for Reach 2

Access Point, Directions	Boat Type	Fee	Parking	Picnic	Toilets	Camping	Rentals	Supplies
❶ Bacon Street Bridge Bridge Road, Pittsburg, NH *Take short dirt road on south side of US 3, 1 mile south of the center of Pittsburg.*	Unimproved ramp, car-top only	N	Y	N	N	N	N	N
❷ Beecher Falls VT 253, Beecher Falls, VT *Take out 200 yards above Beecher Falls Bridge on right bank. Portage 2 miles to Canaan–West Stewartstown Bridge on VT 253.*	Unimproved ramp, car-top only	N	Y	N	N	N	N	N
❸ Canaan Dam US 3 and VT 114, Canaan, VT *Take 0.25-mile portage on paved road to VT 114 bridge in Canaan–West Stewartstown.*	Car-top only	N	Y	N	N	N	N	N

the falls at Beecher Falls. *Caution:* These falls are *dangerous,* and only whitewater experts should run them. The takeout at Beecher Falls is difficult to find; it's 200 yards above the Beecher Falls Bridge on the Vermont side, and you must ask permission from the landowner to take out your canoe or kayak. It's a 2-mile portage down Vermont Route 253 to the put-in below Canaan Dam.

Miles 374.5–373: If you are sufficiently experienced to run Beecher Falls, you will find a pleasant 2-mile stretch to Canaan or West Stewartstown, New Hampshire. Take out your boat on the Vermont side just above the **Canaan Dam**.

New England's Independent Republic

Americans have come to imagine the borders of New England as set in stone by the time of the American Revolution in 1776, but when it comes to northern New England, that's not so. Vermont, for example, was up for grabs prior to the Revolution; the New Hampshire colonial governor began selling grants for land in the mid-eighteenth century on both sides of the Connecticut River. Then, abruptly, King George allowed the governor of New York to claim land from the colony of New York eastward across the Green Mountains—this at a time when France and England were arguing over that same region. In addition, the Abenaki claimed the northern Connecticut Valley as their birthright.

From western Vermont came Ethan Allen to demand Vermont's independence. Whether you consider him "rather an overbearing, loud-mouthed braggart," as did some, or a man "about whom there is an original something that commands attention," as did George Washington, it was clear to all that Allen had established his personal militia—the Green Mountain Boys—to ensure Vermont's independence.

From the east came the governor of New Hampshire to claim the whole of Vermont to the New York border. Caught in the middle of these boundary disputes were the towns of the Connecticut River Valley, which gathered in 1778 in Cornish, New Hampshire, to consider creating the independent state of New Connecticut. The end result, of course, was Vermont's 1791 entry into the United States as the fourteenth state.

Yet even in the 1830s, English Canada and the Abenaki still claimed territory on the northern boundaries from the Connecticut Lakes south to the current border of Vermont. Arguments centered on which streams were the actual headwaters of the Connecticut River. The residents of the region around Pittsburg, tired of the wrangling, simply declared themselves the United Inhabitants of Indian Stream Republic, complete with a constitution and a forty-one-man militia. While the Indian Stream citizens argued whether to form an alliance with Canada or the United States, the New Hampshire legislature finally got them to agree to incorporate into the state of New Hampshire in 1840.

Reach 3 Canaan Dam to Colebrook

Miles from mouth: 373–363 (10-mile span).
Navigable by: Kayaks, canoes.
Difficulty: Class I to Class III, depending on flow conditions.
Flow information: http://water.usgs.gov/water watch or www.h2oline.com; (800) 452-1737.

Portages: None.
Camping: No established sites.
USGS maps: Averill 15, Dixville 15.

The Reach

This reach stretches from Canaan, Vermont, to Colebrook, New Hampshire. Most boaters begin their north country Connecticut River trip on the Vermont side of the Canaan–West Stewartstown Bridge, where there is sufficient water year-round for floating the river. This is almost the last reach of pure mountain stream on the Connecticut, with alternating fast and quiet stretches and water that remains cold and pure enough to support good numbers of brook, brown, and rainbow trout, both stocked and wild. This reach, however, will take a bit longer to paddle than you might think, since it winds back and forth through the first of a number of agricultural valleys with oxbows.

Bird-watchers can look for a host of birds, from warblers and thrushes to hawks and turkeys. That small bird you see flying in quick bursts along the shore, stopping and bobbing on a rock, is a spotted sandpiper, a common companion from the Connecticut Lakes all the way to Hartford, Connecticut. Don't be surprised if you spot bald eagles and ospreys almost every day that you're on the water.

You end your trip at Colebrook with its beautiful view of Monadnock Mountain. Protection of this area is another successful example of work by conservation groups and local government: the Trust for Public Land, the Green Mountain Club, and the Town of Lemington. Here you will also find the northernmost waypoint center of the Connecticut River Byway, a cooperative effort of Vermont, New Hampshire, and the Connecticut River Joint Commissions to preserve, protect, and enhance the Connecticut River Valley from the Great North Woods to the Massachusetts line. At byway centers you will find information on culture and history, natural history and scenic areas, and tips on travel and recreation.

Miles and Directions

Mile 373: Begin your trip at the town-owned access point just below the Vermont Route 114 **Canaan–West Stewartstown Bridge**. There is quick water at the put-in. Exercise caution around the many little cobble islands and riffles. *Caution:* Take care near the heads of islands; trees often fall in the water and become sweepers that can trap your boat.

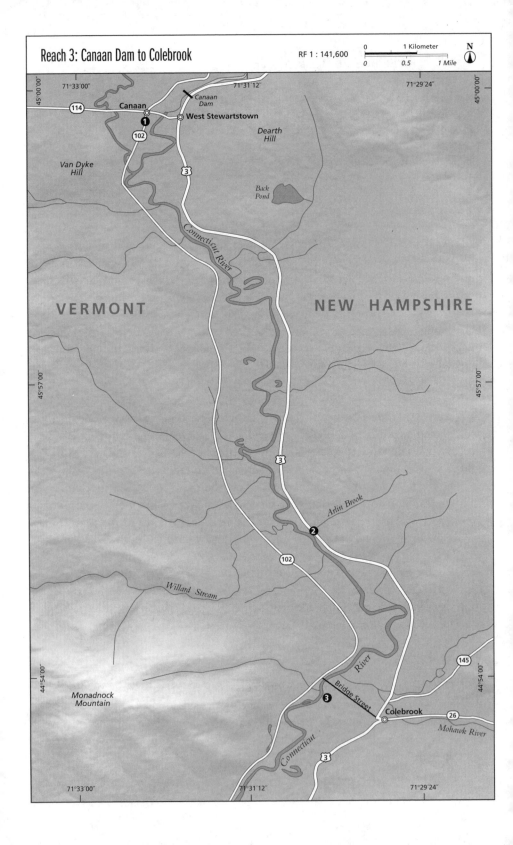

Reach 3: Canaan Dam to Colebrook

RF 1 : 141,600

0   1 Kilometer
0   0.5   1 Mile

N

71°33'00"   71°31'12"   71°29'24"
45°00'00"

114   Canaan   Canaan Dam
West Stewartstown

102

Dearth Hill

Van Dyke Hill

3

Back Pond

Connecticut River

VERMONT   **NEW HAMPSHIRE**

45°57'00"

3

Arlin Brook

2

102

Willard Stream

River

145

44°54'00"

Monadnock Mountain

Bridge Street

3

Colebrook   26

Mohawk River

Connecticut

3

71°33'00"   71°31'12"   71°29'24"

The fishing is great on the upper river and lakes. Photo by Lopstick Outfitters, Pittsburg, New Hampshire

Boating Facilities Table for Reach 3

Access Point, Directions	Boat Type	Fee	Parking	Picnic	Toilets	Camping	Rentals	Supplies
❶ **Canaan–West Stewartstown Bridge** VT 114 (Main Street), Canaan, VT *Put in on Vermont side of river just down-stream from bridge; loop road is public, all land downstream of it is private.*	Improved ramp	Y on week-ends	Y	N	N	N	N	Nearby
❷ **Arlin Brook** US 3, Colebrook, NH *Dirt road leading west off US 3 across from rest area.*	Unimproved ramp, car-top only	N	Y	N	N	N	N	N
❸ **Bridge Street Access** Bridge Street, Colebrook, NH *Put in just downstream of bridge on New Hampshire side.*	Unimproved ramp, car-top only	N	Y	N	N	N	N	Nearby

Mile 366: After several miles of flat water and pleasant meanders with farms on both banks, **Willard Stream** will enter from Vermont 3 miles upstream of Colebrook. At this point you will have a fine view of **Monadnock Mountain**, also called Mount Monadnock, but not to be confused with the more famous Mount Monadnock near New Hampshire's border with Massachusetts. (*Monadnock* is the generic term that geologists use for an isolated mountain surrounded by a relatively flat area.) If you are on the river at sundown, you will get a beautiful sunset behind the mountain. Immediately after this, **Arlin Brook** comes in from New Hampshire; here you'll find a

Natural Valley Flood Storage

The broad, 12,000-acre floodplain stretching from Canaan–West Stewartstown to Lancaster–Guildhall plays a vital role in protecting downstream cities and towns from flooding. Like all floodplains and wetlands, this northernmost one acts as a sponge, storing floodwaters for slow release over days and weeks. During floods, water spills over the adjacent valley, which acts as a second riverbed, dissipating the force of the current and depositing nutrients in the soil. Some water soaks into the ground, while the rest is temporarily stored until floodwaters recede. The effect is to reduce the flood peak as it progresses downstream toward the towns and cities on the flatlands of Massachusetts and Connecticut.

Watershed associations and regional planning commissions up and down the river have led a decades-long struggle to preserve floodplains and wetlands in the face of increasing development pressures. Unfortunately, as houses and malls move onto the floodplains, dikes are built to protect them, thus preventing the floodplain from performing its natural job of storing floodwaters and enriching farmlands. While the dikes temporarily protect adjacent development, they actually endanger other residents downstream by increasing the force of the current, which must find some other area to flood, such as low-lying cities. A recurrence of the great flood of 1936 on the Connecticut would wreak untold damage.

Furthermore, filling the floodplain with structures and pavement makes the ground incapable of holding water, which increases the rate of runoff and potential for flooding. Town planning boards and zoning commissions all along the river must decide how to protect their towns' natural valley flood storage as they deal with the demands of economic growth and the rights of private property owners.

state fish and game access point. Across U.S. Route 3 from this access, in the rest area, is the Connecticut River Byway Waypoint Center for Colebrook, with an exhibit and history of the area.

Miles 366–363: The last 3 miles are a pleasant run through rural New England to Colebrook Bridge. Just before the bridge the **Mohawk River** makes for fast water as it comes in from New Hampshire. From the Colebrook Bridge you can access a trail that climbs 2,100 feet up to the restored fire tower atop the mountain, where you have a marvelous view of the north country. Birders will find a variety of boreal forest birds on Monadnock Mountain, similar to those found in the lakes region.

Mile 363: There is a steep uphill takeout on the downstream New Hampshire side of the Colebrook Bridge. The town of Colebrook, New Hampshire, is 0.5-mile east of the river at the crossroads of New Hampshire Route 26 and US 3.

Reach 4 Colebrook to Bloomfield-North Stratford

Miles from mouth: 363–349 (14-mile span).
Navigable by: Kayaks, canoes.
Difficulty: Class I to Class II.
Flow information: http://water.usgs.gov/water watch or www.h2oline.com; (800) 452-1737.
Portage: Mile 351.5: Lyman Falls Dam (breached), 400 yards.

Fishing regulations: From 250 feet below Lyman Falls Dam to 1,600 feet above Bloomfield–North Stratford Bridge: Catch and release, flies and artificial lures only.
Camping: Mile 351.5: Lyman Falls State Park, Bloomfield, Vermont; river access only.
USGS maps: Averill 15.

The Reach

This reach takes you from Colebrook, New Hampshire, to two optional take-outs: one in Bloomfield, Vermont, and the other in North Stratford, New Hampshire. In this reach you will begin to see the river's transition from mountain stream to rural river. It's a very pretty stretch, with classic northern New England landscapes of dairy farms and riparian woodlands. You will pass under a covered bridge and, if you are an experienced paddler, over a breached dam. The fishing is excellent through much of the reach; this is trout territory and maintained as such by the State of New Hampshire. And, of course, you will find great blue herons, ospreys, and bald eagles.

There are a number of straight stretches in this reach. Recent research by the Connecticut River Joint Commissions has discovered that several areas from Murphy Dam to Gilman Dam were straightened, with the State of New Hampshire's permission, between 1867 and 1925 to help log drivers. The river is now working to regain its meandering form, which will decrease erosion in the long run.

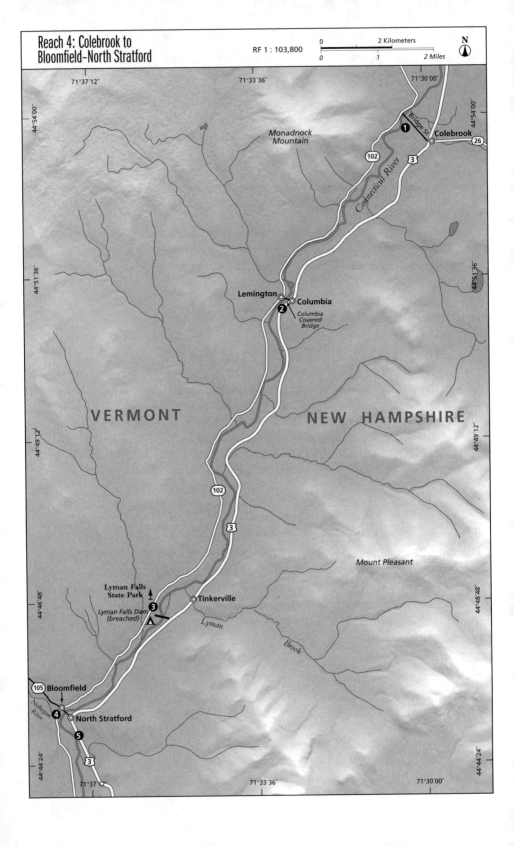

0   2 Kilometers

0   1   2 Miles

N

71°37′12″   71°33′36″   71°30′00″

44°54′00″

Monadnock Mountain

①

Bridge St.

Colebrook

102

Connecticut River

3

26

44°51′36″

Lemington ○—○ **Columbia**

②

Columbia Covered Bridge

VERMONT   **NEW HAMPSHIRE**

44°49′12″

102

3

Mount Pleasant

Lyman Falls State Park

○ **Tinkerville**

③

Lyman Falls Dam (breached)

Lyman

Brook

44°46′48″

105 **Bloomfield**

Nulhegan River

④

○ **North Stratford**

⑤

3

44°44′24″

71°37′12″   71°33′36″   71°30′00″

Miles and Directions

Mile 363: The access is on the downstream New Hampshire side of the **Colebrook Bridge**, which crosses the river from Vermont Route 102 to Bridge Street. You immediately encounter fast water and a couple of twists in the river for the first mile. *Caution:* Beware of sweepers at the head of the island just downstream from the bridge. There is some good fishing from shore in this fast water, and the first 5 miles are reminiscent of the mountain stream character in Reach 3, Canaan Dam to Colebrook.

Mile 359: Before you approach the Columbia Covered Bridge, you will see that the river skirts an island on the left bank, which is rapidly becoming a classic example of an oxbow. A group of large downed trees have forced the river to shift toward the right bank, which over time will leave the left bank cut off from the main stem, a fine example of how oxbows are created.

Boating Facilities Table for Reach 4

Access Point, Directions	Boat Type	Fee	Parking	Picnic	Toilets	Camping	Rentals	Supplies
❶ Bridge Street Access Bridge Street, Colebrook, NH *Put in just downstream of bridge on New Hampshire side.*	Unimproved ramp, car-top only	N	Y	N	N	N	N	Nearby
❷ Columbia Covered Bridge VT 102, Lemington, VT, and US 3, Columbia, NH *Access is easier on Vermont side of river.*	Unimproved ramp, car-top only	N	Y	N	N	N	N	N
❸ Lyman Falls Dam and State Park Campground VT 102, Bloomfield, VT *At breached dam on right bank. Boat and foot access on trail off VT 102. No reservations.*	River and foot access only	N	N	N	N	Y	N	N
❹ Bloomfield Access River Street, Bloomfield, VT *Turn south off VT 105 onto River Street next to DeBanville Country Store; go under railroad underpass. Park on right in parking area. On left side, cross grassy field to access.*	Unimproved path, car-top only	N	Y	N	N	N	N	Nearby
❺ North Stratford Access Main Street, North Stratford, NH *At bridge, turn south onto Main Street, then onto dirt road at Riverside Park playing fields.*	Unimproved path, car-top only	N	Y	Y	N	N	N	Nearby

Bank swallows carve communal nesting holes in high, sandy banks. Photo by Elizabeth Farnsworth

Miles 359-358: Stay to the right bank to avoid being trapped in flat water on the New Hampshire side. You will find access on either bank at the **Columbia Covered Bridge**—the upriver side of the left bank and downriver side on the right bank.

Miles 358-351.5: There is quiet water here, but as you approach a high sand bank on the Vermont side, you will come to a flat pool that quickly turns into shallow, fast water over Rainbow Rocks—so named for the paint scraped off the bottoms of hundreds of kayaks and canoes. You are now approaching **Lyman Falls Dam** and portage, which used to present extreme difficulty until the Connecticut River Joint Commissions had most of the rebar and all the metal spikes removed from the remains of the dam that was breached on both sides. You will not see the 3- to 4-foot drop from upstream. Look for a house on the Vermont side and paddle immediately over to the New Hampshire bank. *Caution:* Avoid the Vermont side, because there may still be remains of the dam that could pin your boat. Check locally to see if you can scout this section from U.S. Route 3. **Lyman Falls State Park Campground**, on the Vermont side, is accessible from the water and by foot off VT 102; it's located on the Vermont side at the breached dam immediately downriver of the old dam.

Miles 351.5–349: Below the dam there is "bony" bottom that can scrape your boat on rocks, but it's fast water on a quick run to the Bloomfield–North Stratford Bridge. The access on the New Hampshire side is 400 yards below the bridge, at a town-owned playground and picnic area. The Vermont access is 100 yards south of the bridge at the mouth of the **Nulhegan River** on an easement that the owner has granted the public.

Log Drives

The Connecticut River log drives, America's longest in terms of distance, began in 1869 and were over by about 1915, although local log drives continued north of Gilman until the 1940s. Every year river men drove over a quarter million spruce logs 300 miles from the river's headwaters near Quebec to sawmills in Massachusetts. The clear-cutting of the virgin red spruce forests at the headwaters was so thorough that by the 1900s, the countryside was described by contemporary observers as having been "skinned." By 1915 this land could no longer be profitably cut for sawlogs, and the era ended. Subsequent Connecticut River drives mainly provided pulpwood for north country paper mills.

Beginning in April each year, loggers started driving 30- to 40-foot-long logs to sawmills at Turners Falls, Northampton, and Holyoke, Massachusetts, reaching these mills in late summer. The drives, involving hundreds of loggers and accompanied by all sorts of ancillary craft, including floating cookshacks and rafts carrying horses and supplies, were extraordinarily arduous and hazardous. Logs had to go over 60-foot falls, through narrow gorges, and under bridges. Logs became stuck on any number of obstacles and collected into huge logjams, where as many as a dozen men could drown in a single drive trying to untangle the mess.

The last of the long log drives took place about a hundred years ago. In many places the riverbed of the Connecticut remains a museum of log drive artifacts: Divers have found lost tools, whiskey bottles, boom chains, log cribs that anchored booms, sunken bateaux, and even the occasional spruce log.

Reach 5 **Bloomfield–North Stratford to Guildhall**

Miles from mouth: 349–326 (23-mile span).
Navigable by: Kayaks, canoes.
Difficulty: Quick water, Class I to Class III, depending on flow conditions.
Flow information: http://water.usgs.gov/water watch or www.h2oline.com; (800) 452-1737.
Portage: *Mile 326:* Wyoming Dam (breached), 500-yard portage on the Vermont side on a private easement.

Boating regulations: *"Natural Segment" from mouth of Wheeler Stream to Maidstone Bridge:* No motorized craft allowed.
Camping: *Mile 344:* Railroad Trestle Campsite, Brunswick, Vermont; river access only.
USGS maps: Averill 15, Guildhall 15.

The Reach

From optional put-ins in Bloomfield, Vermont, or North Stratford, New Hampshire, the river meanders south to Guildhall, Vermont. Here the river completes its transition to a large, placid water body feeding the farmland of the valley. By the time you get to Guildhall, you will know what to expect for much of the next 200 miles—a predominantly agricultural river interrupted by rapids, dams, and reservoirs that cover former cascades.

In this stretch you might see almost every type of North American raptor, save kites: bald eagles, turkey vultures, ospreys, broad-winged and red-tailed hawks, kestrels, sharp-shinned and Cooper's hawks, and northern harriers. With luck, you may catch sight of mink, muskrats, beavers, and otters, all with the backdrop of Vermont's Bear Mountain and New Hampshire's Percy Peaks as you paddle downriver.

Miles and Directions

Mile 349: The access at North Stratford, New Hampshire, is a town-owned playground and picnic area. The Bloomfield, Vermont, access is at the mouth of the **Nulhegan River** on an easement from the owner.

Mile 349: The Nulhegan River enters from Vermont near the Vermont Route 105 bridge and leads upstream into one of the finest wilderness areas in the whole watershed, with more than 200,000 of its 360,000 acres protected for rare plants and animals as well as for recreation; it lies in the heart of what's known as Vermont's Northeast Kingdom, which extends from the Canadian border south to St. Johnsbury.

Miles 349–348: Immediately after you put in, watch for rapids and quick water (from Class I to Class III in spring flood). About a mile below the put-in is the Horse Race, a stretch of exciting water that novices with some experience can handle without problems. Watch for strainers and sweepers in this part of the river. *Caution:* Do not

Bear Mountain in Vermont is a beautiful backdrop for 10 miles in the Upper Valley. Photo by Elizabeth Farnsworth

take side channels, but stick to the main channel of the river. You may well find yourself dragging your craft over rocky river bottom on the side channels.

Miles 347–340: The 7-mile stretch from **Wheeler Stream**, 2 miles south of the VT 105 bridge, to the **Maidstone Bridge** is the only section of the Connecticut River designated as a Natural Segment (by State of New Hampshire). Motorized craft are prohibited and no fish stocking takes place here, although fishing is permitted. The mountain to the south is Vermont's **Bear Mountain**. As you paddle farther down this winding, rural stretch, look east for a fine view of the **Percy Peaks**. It almost feels like you are running an Alaskan river. Note how the river has cut down through a very high, sandy, gravelly bank on the right in this section. This is an esker—a long, winding ridge of sediment deposited by meltwater from glaciers. Small brown and white bank swallows nest in holes in these banks, safe from fox and raccoon predation. Also look for the osprey nesting platform below a ruined bridge stanchion and 1.3 miles upstream from the Maidstone Bridge.

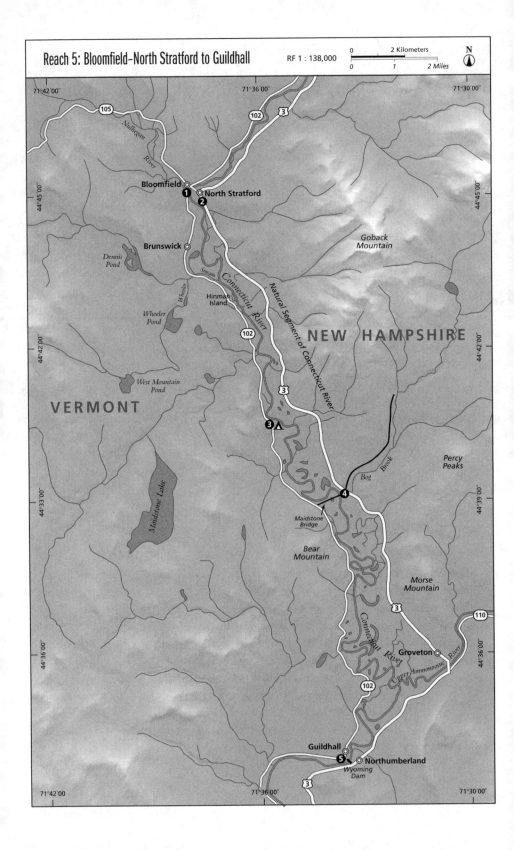

Reach 5: Bloomfield–North Stratford to Guildhall

RF 1 : 138,000

0   2 Kilometers
0   1   2 Miles

N

Mile 340: At the Maidstone Bridge there is an unimproved access on the New Hampshire side. After you pass this pretty, restored iron bridge, you will begin the long, twisting journey to the next access point; do not be surprised if your compass points true north from time to time as the river meanders widely through farmland.

Mile 330: The **Upper Ammonoosuc River**, which provides good paddling both above and below Groveton, enters from New Hampshire 4 miles from the Guildhall access. At this point you will get a glimpse of the White Mountains.

Mile 326: The **Wyoming Dam** is breached. *Caution:* Do *not* try to run the breach; rebar is still sticking up through the old concrete. It should be portaged unless there is high water and you are an experienced paddler; local emergency crews have had to rescue many boaters at this spot. The portage access is a steep, worn, and clearly marked path just past an island on the Vermont side above the Wyoming Dam between Guildhall, Vermont, and Northumberland, New Hampshire. The portage is on private land, donated by the owners and the Vermont Agency of Transportation.

Boating Facilities Table for Reach 5

Access Point, Directions	Boat Type	Fee	Parking	Picnic	Toilets	Camping	Rentals	Supplies
❶ **Bloomfield Access** River Street, Bloomfield, VT *Turn south off VT 105 onto River Street next to DeBanville Country Store; go under railroad underpass. Park on right in parking area. On left side, cross grassy field to access.*	Unimproved path, car-top only	N	Y	N	N	N	N	Nearby
❷ **North Stratford Access** Main Street, North Stratford, NH *At bridge, turn south onto Main Street, then onto dirt road at Riverside Park playing fields.*	Unimproved path, car-top only	N	Y	Y	Y	N	N	Nearby
❸ **Railroad Trestle Site Campground** Brunswick, VT *River access only.*	River access only	N	N	N	N	Y	N	N
❹ **Maidstone Bridge Access** US 3, Stratford, NH *Maidstone Bridge Road, off US 3.*	Unimproved path, car-top only	N	Y	N	N	N	N	N
❺ **Wyoming Dam** VT 102, Guildhall, VT *At Guildhall-Northumberland Bridge, VT 102 and US 3 in Guildhall, on north side of bridge and breached dam. Marked path.*	Unimproved path, car-top only	N	Y	N	N	N	N	N

Be aware that the river's current increases before the takeout, so stay near the right bank. Take a short walk around the delightful historic town of Guildhall, a village of fewer than 300 people with classic upper Connecticut Valley architecture.

The Connecticut River Joint Commissions

In 1989 the states of Vermont and New Hampshire created the Connecticut River Joint Commissions (CRJC) to promote the ecological health of the river, develop a river plan through grassroots efforts, preserve the region's cultural heritage, and help develop the agricultural and tourist economy in the north country and Upper Valley. The organization is the principal partner of the Connecticut River Watershed Council (CRWC) in New Hampshire and Vermont. The CRJC and CRWC work together for the health of the river, attending meetings with government agencies to ensure good water quality and to coordinate efforts such as federal designation of the Connecticut as an American Heritage River and the restoration of habitat for migratory fish.

The CRJC is an advisory, not regulatory, body; as such it has been particularly effective in developing a series of river corridor management plans that local residents up and down the river helped create. The CRJC has been the lead agency in gaining federal status for a scenic byway program in the Upper Valley, providing economic development initiatives for tourism in the region. This boating guide mentions all the byway centers in the appropriate reach descriptions.

We urge boaters interested in detailed descriptions of each river section in the north country and Upper Valley to go to the CRJC Web site (www.crjc.org) and read the "River Plan." The CRJC will also provide you with details on the culture and history of the region as well as travel itineraries.

Reach 6 Guildhall to Gilman Dam

Miles from mouth: 326–302 (24-mile span).
Navigable by: Kayaks, canoes, small motorboats.
Difficulty: Quick water, Class I.
Flow information: http://water.usgs.gov/water watch or www.h2oline.com; (800) 452-1737.

Portage: *Mile 302:* Gilman Dam, 0.5 mile.
Camping: *Mile 302:* Gilman Dam (on the New Hampshire side), Dalton, New Hampshire.
USGS maps: Guildhall 15, Whitefield 15.

The Reach

From Guildhall, Vermont, to Gilman Dam, the river is slow, wide, and rural with big oxbows and long, quiet stretches. It belongs to great blue herons, beavers, and the occasional boater. The two oxbows contain excellent birding habitat, and the warm waters in summer will reward anglers with bass, yellow perch, and northern pike.

Through much of this stretch, you will see the struggle to prevent farmland from eroding into the river. At least one farmer has carefully lined the banks with cars, all interior parts and engine removed, but, as you will see, the river shoves the cars into disorderly ranks. The water becomes more brown and turbid here, witness to the ineffectiveness of most attempts to halt erosion. As the river regains its meanders, which were straightened for the sake of log drives, the erosion will attenuate.

The reach ends at the Vermont town of Gilman, which has a long history of papermaking. Here you will find the first large campsite on the river.

Miles and Directions

Mile 326: The access below the **Wyoming Dam** (breached) is a steep, clearly marked path on the Vermont side of the Guildhall–Northumberland Bridge.

Miles 326–324.5: The flow is pleasantly quick before the river slows going into the first wide curve, with **Washburn Brook** entering from Vermont. Beavers have dropped trees across the mouth of the brook, making it impenetrable. Note the pretty old stone railroad bridge at the confluence.

Mile 323: After passing **Jones Brook** on the right bank, you will see the ruins of old log cribs that helped control logs during log drives (see the "Log Drives" sidebar in Reach 4).

Mile 318.5: After **Sheridan Brook** enters from Vermont, you will see on the New Hampshire side what remains of a farmer's attempts to stabilize the banks with the chassis of cars, emptied of their engines and interiors.

Mile 317: Shortly after, you will come to the first oxbow in this reach, a beaver pond with remnants of a floodplain forest at its mouth; it's an excellent birding spot with a number of wood duck boxes and fine habitat for waterbirds and warblers.

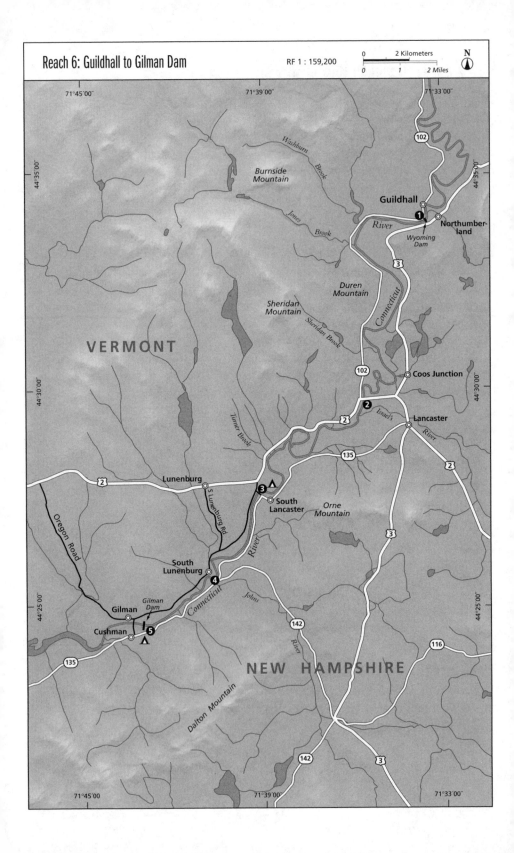

Reach 6: Guildhall to Gilman Dam

RF 1 : 159,200

0   2 Kilometers
0   1   2 Miles

N

71°45'00"   71°39'00"   71°33'00"

102

Washburn Brook

Burnside Mountain

Jones Brook

Guildhall
①
Northumber-
land

River

Wyoming Dam

3

Duren Mountain

Sheridan Mountain

Sheridan Brook

VERMONT

102

Coos Junction

②

Israel's

River

2

Lancaster

135

2

Turner Brook

2   Lunenburg

③ Λ

South Lancaster

Orne Mountain

3

S Lunenburg Rd

River

South Lunenburg

④

Connecticut

Johns

142

116

Gilman Dam
Gilman

I⑤

Cushman   Λ

River

NEW   HAMPSHIRE

135

Dalton Mountain

142   3

71°45'00   71°39'00"   71°33'00"

44°35'00"
44°30'00"
44°25'00"

Mile 315.5: A mile south of the oxbow, you come to Lancaster, a town of about 3,300 with the biggest fair in New Hampshire's north country. The town has built a greenway along the **Israel's River**, which enters the Connecticut 0.25 mile below the U.S. Route 2 bridge. The boat access is at the bridge, where you will find a store, gas station, and campground. Ask at the store where you can park in the parking lot. Lancaster is the southernmost point on the Connecticut River where New Hampshire Fish and Game stocks trout in the river. Since the water warms considerably in the summer, only brown trout are released. The fishery at this point is a mix of warm- and cold-water species.

Mile 311: The second oxbow is 4 miles downstream from Lancaster, accessible over a small muddy berm, but generally too shallow to allow paddling. This is another excellent birding and botanizing site.

Miles 310–308.5: A mile south of the oxbow, **Turner Brook** enters from a culvert on the right bank, and after another mile, past two sets of log crib remains, you will see the beautiful **Mount Orne Covered Bridge** at the junction of New Hampshire

Boating Facilities Table for Reach 6

Access Point, Directions	Boat Type	Fee	Parking	Picnic	Toilets	Camping	Rentals	Supplies
❶ **Wyoming Dam** VT 102, Guildhall, VT *At Guildhall–Northumberland Bridge, VT 102 and US 3 in Guildhall, on south side of bridge and breached dam. Marked path.*	Unimproved path, car-top only	N	Y	N	N	N	N	N
❷ **US 2 Bridge Access** Lancaster, NH *At junction of US 2 and VT 102.*	Improved ramp, all boats	N	Y	N	Y	N	N	Y
❸ **Mount Orne Covered Bridge** Lancaster, NH/Lunenburg, VT *NH 135 and River Road off US 2.*	River access only	N	Y	N	N	Y	N	Spring water
❹ **Johns River Ramp** Dalton, NH *Westerly turn directly off NH 135.*	Improved ramp, all boats	N	Y	N	N	N	N	N
❺ **Gilman Dam Portage** VT 102, Gilman, VT *NH side of Gilman-Cushman Bridge Road. Emergency access number for portage area: (802) 892-9043. Campsite operated by hydropower company.*	River access only	N	Y	Y	N	Y	N	N

The remains of log cribs are reminders of the river's historic log drives. Photo by Elizabeth Farnsworth

Route 135 and US 2 between South Lancaster and Lunenberg; there is an access point just below the bridge on the Vermont side.

Mile 305: You will encounter quick water as you continue downstream, and after another 3 miles, **Johns River** enters from the left bank. Johns River and Israel's River in Lancaster were named for two brothers in the eighteenth century. Just downstream of the confluence is the **Johns River Ramp** on NH 135, maintained by the power company at Gilman Dam.

Mile 302.5: After 2 more miles of flat water, you will see the orange boom that marks the approach to Gilman Dam, where a hydropower plant and paper company are located. The 0.5-mile portage is on the New Hampshire shore at the end of a small cove; the trail is well marked, leading up a hill. There is a dirt road, but *there is no vehicular access to this road except for emergencies.* Camping is permitted at a large field, but open fires are not allowed without a permit from the Town of Dalton, New Hampshire.

The White Mountains and the Presidential Range

In this and Reach 7, you'll be treated to views of the White Mountains and the Presidential Range that frame the east side of the Connecticut River. When first created by the great Appalachian mountain-building event from 350 to 300 million years ago, the Whites were the size of the Himalayas, but water and wind eroded them down from more than 20,000 feet to their current heights of 5,000 to 6,000 feet; even so, they are the second highest mountains east of the Mississippi River.

At the northern end of the White Mountains are its highest peaks, the Presidential Range: Mount Washington at 6,288 feet, followed by Adams (5,805), Jefferson (5,725), Monroe (5,385), and Madison (5,363). Mount Washington is notorious for having the worst climate in North America, with killing cold, heavy snow, and the world record for the highest wind speed ever recorded—231 miles an hour on April 12, 1934. During summer, however, the Whites are crowded with hikers who walk from hut to hut, enjoying the hospitality of the Appalachian Mountain Club hut keepers who cook meals and provide entertainment for tired travelers.

The White Mountain National Forest, one of the nation's first national forests when it was established in 1918, is almost 800,000 acres. It is one of eastern North America's most popular outdoor recreational destinations, and certainly worthwhile for any person who enjoys hiking, skiing, ice and rock climbing, or fishing. If you have the good fortune to hike on a clear day, you can climb Mount Washington; at the summit look east to the Atlantic Ocean and imagine what early travelers might have seen when sailing along the Maine coast as they spied the snowy peaks of the Whites.

Reach 7 Gilman Dam to Comerford Dam

Miles from mouth: 302–282.5 (19.5-mile span).
Navigable by: Kayaks, canoes, motorboats.
Difficulty: Flat water, quick water, Class I and II
Flow information: http://water.usgs.gov/water watch or www.h2oline.com; (800) 452-1737.
Portages: *Mile 289:* Moore Dam, 300 yards.

Mile 282.5: Comerford Dam, 0.25 mile.
Camping: *Mile 302:* Gilman Dam (on the New Hampshire side), Dalton, New Hampshire; at portage, river access only.
USGS maps: Whitefield 15, Miles Pond 7.5, Littleton 7.5, Lower Waterford 7.5.

The Reach

From Gilman Dam to Comerford Dam, you are entering the Fifteen-Mile Falls section of the river, as it is still known locally. Before there was a Comerford Dam in 1930 and a Moore Dam in 1957, this was Class IV and V whitewater, plunging 350 feet over ledge rock and huge boulders for 15 miles. Now most of this reach is a reservoir and the province of motorboats and anglers. The area formerly supported a logging industry. With the construction of the dams, the towns and residents, including their cemeteries and churches, were all moved to nearby locations. Still, during the summer when the water is lowered, the stone walls that marked the pastures of early settlers are clearly visible.

This is a beautiful part of the river—the 3,500-acre Moore Reservoir and 1,100-acre Comerford Reservoir are surrounded by mixed evergreen–deciduous woods with a view of the Presidential Range of the White Mountains to the east. Fishermen love these lakes; fishing derbies draw anglers from all over New England to go after salmon, trout, pike, pickerel, perch, bass, and even sunfish. Hardly a day passes without seeing ospreys and bald eagles. There are loon nesting platforms, too (please avoid disturbing nesting loons).

Motorboats, paddlers, campers, and hikers are all welcome here, and, except on July and August weekends, the boat traffic is moderate to light. Picnic areas and launch sites are scattered along both the Vermont and New Hampshire shores. Numerous tributary streams enter from both sides and are worth exploring on foot. The streams, arising from seeps and springs, are critical native brook trout habitat. The presence of brook trout indicates healthy stream habitat, but many of these waterways are seriously compromised by human impacts and support few brookies. The streams and adjacent land need restoration.

Caution: Water levels vary up to 10 feet. While Moore Dam produces electricity year round, flow changes are greatest during winter in preparation for spring runoff when the reservoir is dramatically lowered. It is the largest conventional hydro station in New England with a 192-megawatt generating capacity.

Caution: Beware of floating debris. Moore Reservoir has a serious problem with drifting stumps and logs, and you may find yourself almost crawling through the debris. The problem usually occurs when there is a wind shift.

Caution: Do not anchor at the base of Moore Dam or you could end up either on the rocks or swamped if the water rises quickly and your anchor line is too short. Also, beware of submerged rocks and other objects during drawdown; they could leave your boat stranded.

Furthermore, this is big water, so watch for notoriously changeable weather. Strong southerly winds produce whitecaps, so the calmer water of early morning is the best time for canoeing or kayaking.

Miles and Directions

Mile 302: Paddlers begin at the end of the portage trail on the New Hampshire side just downstream from the **Gilman–Cushman Bridge**, where it's too shallow for motorized boats. About 500 yards downstream, as the water begins to slow, motorboats become common. During major drawdowns from Gilman Dam, however, the rapids extend a mile downstream.

Mile 301: The northernmost access point for motorboats is the **Gilman Boat Launch** on the Vermont side, although it is rather difficult to find. The reservoir widens just west of the Gilman site, and, after a few miles, the full 3,500 acres of **Moore Reservoir** becomes apparent as you turn south.

Mile 295: The **North Littleton Access** is a convenient launch site on the New Hampshire side with several amenities.

Mile 292.5: Dodge Hill Boat Launch, a larger site just 2.5 miles south of North Littleton Access, has a large parking area and improved boat launch. West of the Dodge Hill launching site on the Vermont side is the **Waterford Boat Launch**.

Miles 291–289: There are three more access sites on the New Hampshire side, starting with the **Pattenville Boat Launch**, which has parking and picnic areas plus a private campground next to it. Across the inlet from Pattenville is the **Pine Island Boat Launch**, just off New Hampshire Route 135, and finally a launch site at the **Moore Dam Portage**. The visitor center at the portage is closed.

Mile 289: While Moore Dam has a portage on both the Vermont and New Hampshire sides, most paddlers use the Vermont side, which is accessible only by water. Paddle to the open sandy area at the north end of the dam and portage your boat along the well-marked path to a put-in below the dam. The New Hampshire side has a large picnic area and improved launch. *Caution:* Paddlers, take care and do not anchor here! Check for water release schedules; there's a lot of turbulence below the dam at high water and dangerous rocky areas at low water.

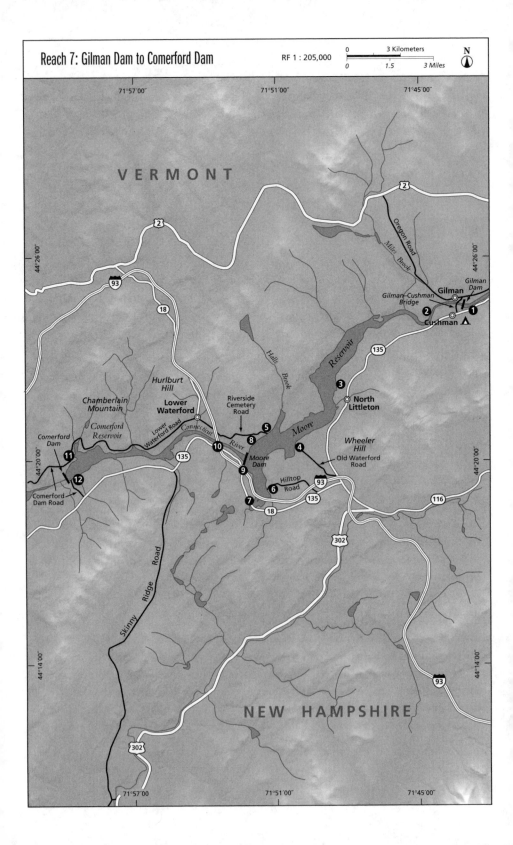

RF 1 : 205,000

0   3 Kilometers
0   1.5   3 Miles

N

VERMONT

Oregon Road

Miles Brook

2

2

93

18

Gilman Dam

Gilman

Gilman–Cushman Bridge

Cushman

1

2

135

Halls Brook

Reservoir

3

North Littleton

Hurlburt Hill

Chamberlain Mountain

Lower Waterford

Riverside Cemetery Road

5

Moore

Wheeler Hill

Comerford Reservoir

Comerford Dam

Lower Waterford Road

Connecticut River

8

10

135

Moore Dam

4

Old Waterford Road

11

12

9

6

Hilltop Road

93

135

Comerford Dam Road

7

18

116

Skinny Ridge Road

302

302

NEW HAMPSHIRE

93

Boating Facilities Table for Reach 7

Access Point, Directions	Boat Type	Fee	Parking	Picnic	Toilets	Camping	Rentals	Supplies
❶ **Gilman Dam Portage** NH side of Gilman–Cushman Bridge Road. Emergency access number to portage area: (802) 892–9043. Camping operated by hydropower company.	River access only	N	N	Y	N	Y NH side	N	N
❷ **Gilman Boat Launch** Cozy Nook Road, Gilman, VT Go west on East Concord Road in Gilman; after 2 miles, just after crossing brook, turn left onto Cozy Nook Road; take road to second cemetery on left. Area can be shallow and muddy in low water.	Unimproved ramp for all boat types	N	Y	N	N	N	N	N
❸ **North Littleton Boat Launch** NH 135, North Littleton, NH Take road going west off NH 135 just north of North Littleton.	Improved ramp for all boat types	N	Y	Y	Y	N	N	N
❹ **Dodge Hill Boat Launch** Old Waterford Road, Littleton, NH Two miles west off NH 135 at junction of I–93.	Improved ramp for all boat types	N	Y	Y	Y	N	N	N
❺ **Waterford Boat Launch** Riverside Cemetery Rd, Waterford, VT Easterly turn from VT 18 onto Riverside Cemetery Road; bear right onto TH 13 and go to end of road.	Improved ramp for all boat types	N	Y	Y	Y	N	N	N
❻ **Pattenville Boat Launch** Hilltop Road, Littleton, NH Westerly turn onto Hilltop Road from NH 135/18; 2 miles to end.	Improved ramp for all boat types	N	Y	Y	Y	N	N	N
❼ **Pine Island Boat Launch** NH 135/18, Littleton, NH On north side of NH 135/18, 2 miles south of Moore Dam.	Improved ramp for all boat types	N	Y	Y	Y	N	N	N
❽ **Moore Dam Portage** North side of Moore Dam Well-marked, 150-yard portage trail.	River access only	N	N	N	N	N	N	N
❾ **Moore Dam Portage and Boat Launch** South side of Moore Dam Well-marked, 400-yard portage trail. Turn east at Moore Dam sign off NH 135/18.	Improved ramp for all boat types	N	Y	Y	Y	N	N	N
❿ **Waterford Bridge Boat Launch** NH 135, Littleton, NH On north side of NH 135 just after NH 135 and 18 split.	Improved ramp for all boat types	N	Y	Y	Y	N	N	N

Boating Facilities Table for Reach 7 continued

Access Point, Directions	Boat Type	Fee	Parking	Picnic	Toilets	Camping	Rentals	Supplies
⓫ Pine Grove Boat Launch Comerford Dam Road, Barnet, VT *Off Comerford Dam Road on Vermont side,* *3 miles east of East Barnet.*	Improved ramp for all boat types	N	Y	Y	Y	N	N	N
⓬ Comerford Dam *Northwesterly turn onto Comerford Dam Road* *from NH 135. Steep but groomed portage trail.*	Improved ramp for all boat types	N	Y	Y	Y	N	N	N

Mile 288: Motorboats can put in at the **Waterford Bridge Boat Launch** in New Hampshire, which has parking and amenities. **Comerford Reservoir** is a much smaller, quieter, and narrower reservoir than is Moore. Whereas the power company currently allows water levels to fluctuate more frequently in Moore Reservoir, exposing much of its banks, Comerford remains consistently high and the banks are heavily forested; you'll have a much more enclosed boating experience. You will also notice that, unlike Moore, most of the banks at Comerford are privately owned, with numerous docks and second homes on the steep hillsides.

Mile 283: The **Pine Grove Boat Launch** is the only other access point at Comerford and is located near the lower end of the reservoir on the Vermont side.

Mile 282.5: Comerford Dam is the end point of this reach for boaters. You will find the access to the portage on the New Hampshire side. The 0.5-mile portage is clearly marked.

Damming and Fragmenting the River

Upper Valley residents still call the section of the Connecticut River from Gilman to below Comerford Dam "Fifteen-Mile Falls." Before the dams were built, the river fell almost 350 feet over 15 miles here, cascading over large boulders and ledge rock. In 1930 Comerford Dam created a reservoir at the downstream end of the falls, and Moore Dam backed the water up to Gilman, Vermont, in 1957. The purpose of the sixteen dams on the river's main stem is to help prevent flooding and, in most instances, to produce hydropower for electricity or manufacturing.

Most residents of the Connecticut Valley want the large dams to remain, because they provide some flood protection and a source of renewable energy. But this comes at a cost, namely fragmentation of the river's ecosystems. A dam prevents the constant, natural transport of soil, nutrients, and fish downstream by storing soil and nutrients for habitats above the dam while starving reaches downstream of it.

Stanley Swaim, a longtime resident and volunteer in the Upper Valley, has studied this phenomenon from the perspective of a trout. After years of fishing the section of the river between Comerford Dam and McIndoe Dam 6 miles downstream, he rarely catches a trout smaller than a foot in length, and, while there are some extremely large trout here, their numbers are fewer than you'd expect in a reach with plenty of available food. This section does not receive heavy fishing pressure, and, since the New Hampshire Fish and Game Department does not stock the area—nor should it—these may be fish that have somehow gotten past Comerford Dam during big floods or have drifted down from the tributaries.

Most data we currently have about the river's fishery come from anecdotal evidence. Funding for fish studies is scarce, although some scientific evidence was gathered in 2005 in preparation for a fisheries management plan. If, however, you look at the Comerford to McIndoe stretch from the trout's vantage point, the problem may well be lack of spawning habitat. The river bottom contains either large stones or fine silt, neither of which fills spawning needs for trout, which very specifically need clean gravel a bit smaller than marbles. From immediately below Comerford Dam down to the confluence with the Passumpsic River, the river is starved of sediment, and the only available spawning gravel is in small tributaries blocked by steep cascades that trout cannot navigate. Therefore, the few trout that drift downstream into this section are anglers' prizes. This is only one of many reaches that needs serious efforts at fish restoration.

Dams also isolate fish populations, segmenting the river and fragmenting their habitat. This happens throughout the watershed, and is most egregious when it isolates federally endangered species such as shortnose sturgeon upstream of the Holyoke Dam; these fish are barely maintaining their population of a few hundred adults. For this reason, government agencies, universities, and nongovernmental organizations work closely with power companies to improve river habitat.

The river deserves to be connected again, so the trout between Comerford and McIndoe can reach spawning grounds and the sturgeon can run to the sea once more. It is not a question of destroying dams, but of finding ways to balance competing uses—constructing fish ladders, breaching or eliminating "deadbeat dams" that are no longer useful, modifying culverts, and regulating flows for recreational uses and healthy ecosystems. For further information, contact the Connecticut River Watershed Council.

Reach 8 Comerford Dam to Woodsville

Miles from mouth: 282.5-268 (14.5-mile span).
Navigable by: Kayaks, canoes, motorboats.
Difficulty: Class I and II, quick water, flat water.
Flow information: http://water.usgs.gov/water watch or www.h2oline.com; (800) 452-1737.
Portage: *Mile 282.5:* Comerford Dam, 0.25 mile. *Mile 276:* McIndoe Falls, 200 yards. *Mile*

272: Ryegate Dam, Dodge Falls, 0.25 mile.
Camping: *Mile 273:* Fiddlehead Island Campground, East Ryegate, Vermont. *Mile 273:* Dodge Falls Campground, Bath, New Hampshire.
USGS maps: Lower Waterford 7.5, St. Johnsbury 15, Woodsville 7.5 or 15.

The Reach

This portion of the river extends from the New Hampshire side of Comerford Dam to Woodsville, New Hampshire. An extremely interesting and adventurous reach with two short portages after Comerford Dam, the stretch begins with quick water (Class II in high water), then proceeds down a narrow rocky section, past the mouth of the Passumpsic, and onto the flat water above the McIndoe and Ryegate Dams. The first section is solely for canoes and kayaks, while motorized boats are most common between Barnet, Vermont, and McIndoe Falls.

The Nine Islands section near the confluence of the Connecticut and Passumpsic were particularly important to the local Abenaki Indians. It was a crossroads for Native Americans that led into Vermont's Northeast Kingdom and up into the St. Lawrence region, also part of the Abenaki homeland. The number of visible islands will vary according to the height of the water, but the largest—high, flat Indian Island—is always in sight, a commanding place on the river from which you can see movement up and down both the Connecticut and Passumpsic. You will find the remnants of an ancient floodplain forest here, with marshy areas that harbor wetland plants and shorebirds.

The Upper Valley Land Trust has its northernmost campsite below McIndoe Falls Dam, and from here down to the Massachusetts line you will find the group's river access campsites. It's a partner with the Connecticut River Joint Commissions, local land trusts, and private landowners to give boaters access to these resources.

The reach ends with an excellent run down some rapids and narrows to Woodsville and the mouth of the Ammonoosuc. It is easy to confuse the three Ammonoosuc rivers. The Upper Ammonoosuc enters at Groveton, north of Guildhall in Reach 5; the Wild Ammonoosuc enters the Ammonoosuc from the south just west of Woodsville in Bath. The Ammonoosuc proper enters the Connecticut at Woodsville.

The lower two-thirds of this reach should yield sightings of bald eagles and ospreys, and, of course, the ubiquitous great blue herons. These last are so numerous because they are so adaptable: They tend to nest in colonies of up to thirty, high in woodlands not far from water, but they will also nest alone, on or near the ground.

They will eat anything from large carp to large insects, and they don't mind human company.

Miles and Directions

Mile 282.5: The **Comerford Dam Access** for canoes and kayaks should only be used by whitewater enthusiasts who can handle water levels that can rise up to 6 feet and Class III rapids at high water. The going is also difficult at low water because of boulders and shallows.

Mile 281: A mile and a half downriver, you will find more accessible water—though still limited to canoes and kayaks—below a dam at East Barnet, on the **Passumpsic River**, just north of its confluence with the Connecticut. From here you paddle quickly in fast water to the **Nine Islands** area, which is worth exploring for its botany and wildlife. Remember, you are now in the heart of historic Abenaki territory.

Mile 278.5: Just south of the town of Barnet, Vermont, where the Stevens River enters and below **Stevens Island**, is a bridge connecting U.S. Route 5 and New Hampshire Route 135. There is a small car-top boat launch where kayaks and canoes can put in at a pretty section of the river with generally gentle current. The river here slows considerably due to the influence of the McIndoe Dam and becomes almost lake-like after you pass through a narrow stretch and get a glimpse of **Gleason Island**. You then take a sharp turn northeast and then south, approaching McIndoe Falls.

Mile 276: **McIndoe Falls and Dam** marks the first portage on this reach. The short, easy portage is on the New Hampshire side. Now the water begins to run more quickly through a relatively shallow section for about 3 miles as you approach the next dam.

Mile 273: The first of the Upper Valley Land Trust's primitive camping sites is **Fiddlehead Island Campground**, the third and largest of three wooded islands about halfway between McIndoe and Ryegate Dams. The second site is the **Dodge Falls Campground** on the New Hampshire shore at the portage of Ryegate Dam.

Mile 272: From the right bank you will see the smokestack of the **Ryegate Paper Company Dam** at Dodge Falls portage well before you reach it. *Caution:* Do not run these falls unless you are an experienced paddler and have scouted the stretch. At Dodge Falls you will find a well-marked short portage on the New Hampshire side. The paper company is inactive and the dam has always been "run of river," which means that it was never intended to impound water, only to hold some in reserve during low flows to power the mill. In summer the river below Dodge Falls is quite shallow, but swift for about 3 miles.

Mile 269: A mile before Woodsville, you enter tricky currents and bends, and the river quickens as it goes through the **Narrows**, veering through faults in the folded

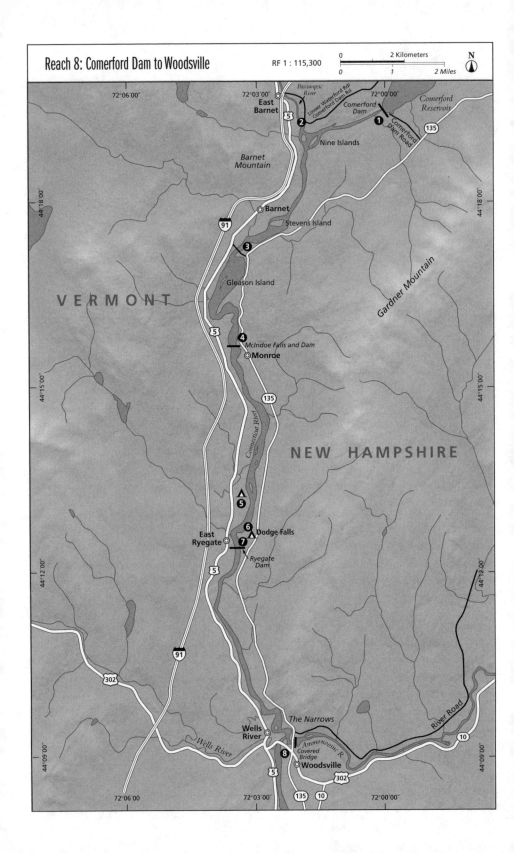

Boating Facilities Table for Reach 8

Access Point, Directions	Boat Type	Fee	Parking	Picnic	Toilets	Camping	Rentals	Supplies
❶ Comerford Dam Access & Picnic Area Comerford Dam Road, Monroe, NH *Turn west off NH 135*	Improved ramp, all boats	N	Y	Y	Y	N	N	N
❷ Passumpsic River Access Lower Waterford Road, East Barnet, VT *Take US 5 to East Barnet, turn east at dam, cross Passumpsic River, turn right onto Lower Waterford Road. Access is 400 yards on riverside. Steep trail down riprapped bank.*	Unimproved ramp, car-top only	N	Y	N	N	N	N	N
❸ Barnet–Monroe Bridge Access Barnet Road, Monroe, NH *At base of bridge that connects US 5 (Barnet) and NH 135 (Monroe) on New Hampshire side.*	Unimproved ramp, car-top only	N	Y	N	N	N	N	N
❹ McIndoe Falls Portage Connecticut River Road and Plains Road, Monroe, NH *Found 200 yards on New Hampshire side. West of NH 135 in town of Monroe; turn onto Plains Road.*	Car-top only	N	Y	N	N	N	N	N
❺ Fiddlehead Island Campground East Ryegate, VT *Third of three wooded islands in middle of river halfway between McIndoe and Ryegate Dams.*	River access only	N	N	N	N	Y	N	N
❻ Dodge Falls Campground Bath, NH *On New Hampshire side 0.5 mile from Ryegate Dam/Dodge Falls, west off NH 135 on Dodge Falls Road. Essex Hydro: (603) 747-8015.*	Foot and river access only	N	N	Y	Y	Y	N	N
❼ Ryegate Dam Portage Dodge Falls Road, Bath, NH *West off NH 135.*	Unimproved ramp, car-top only	N	Y	N	N	N	N	N
❽ Woodsville Access Connecticut Street, Woodsville, NH *Turn south off US 302/NH 10 right after bridge over Connecticut River onto Connecticut Street in Woodsville; access is below bridge on right side.*	Unimproved ramp, car-top only	N	Y	N	N	N	N	N

The portage at Dodge Falls is one of several on the upper river. Photo by Wendy Sinton

schist bedrock. As you approach the Narrows, and just after the river bends sharply east, then south, you will see an island owned by Connecticut River Watershed Council where paddlers often picnic or camp. *Caution:* Paddlers, take care! You should scout the Narrows in high water because just below the rapids, as the **Ammonoosuc River** enters from the left bank, you will encounter a tricky whirlpool. The oldest surviving covered bridge in New Hampshire is found near the mouth of the Ammonoosuc.

Mile 268: Two bridges close together cross the Connecticut at Woodsville, and the **Wells River** enters inconspicuously from the Vermont side at the town of Wells River. Paddle to the New Hampshire shore right after the bridges; you'll find an access point there at a small, sandy spot. If you stay over in Woodsville, you'll find very good paddling on the Ammonoosuc River. Woodsville was once a booming Upper Valley center, the head of navigation in the nineteenth century with locks and canals around rapids on the two rivers; it was particularly important in the history of logging in the Great North Woods. There is a Connecticut River Byway Waypoint Visitor Center in Wells River between US 5 and the Wells River–Woodsville Bridge.

People of the Dawn

The homeland, or Ndakinna, of the Abenaki (Wôbinaki or "people of the dawn" in the Native language) encompassed the region from Lake Champlain (Bitawbakw or "waters in-between") to the ocean and from southern Quebec into Massachusetts. Western Abenaki, who lived west of the Maine–New Hampshire border, spoke a different dialect from their eastern counterparts, such as the Kennebec and Penobscot. As the Abenaki anthropologist Margaret Bruchac has written, some of the Abenaki's oldest oral traditions recount how, in ancient times, ice pushed the land into mountains before melting away to water (see the "Lake Hitchcock" sidebar in Reach 10), and how Odzihozo, a creature made of ice and dust, formed Petowbowk, or Lake Champlain. Farther south in Massachusetts, a giant beaver, who built a dam to flood the valley, was turned to stone, his body becoming the mountain of Pemawatchuwatunck, now called the Pocumtuck Range, with his head at Mount Sugarloaf in Sunderland, Massachusetts.

In 1600 some ten thousand Western Abenaki lived in Ndakinna in scattered family bands, the Abenaki's basic social unit. Within bands lived not only family members but also captives and visitors from other tribes, all of whom moved often, traveling long distances to seasonal territories and sometimes settling for longer periods in villages where agriculture could support denser populations. Family bands were members of larger communal groups. At the time of European contact, the northern group in the Connecticut River Valley were the Cowasuck ("people of the pines") in the north, centered at the Oxbow near Newbury, Vermont; later English versions of the name Cowasuck included Coos, pronounced *cowass*, a geographic term still in general use. The southern group were the Sokoki ("the people who separated"), whose village, Squakheag, was at a site near Northfield, Massachusetts.

Although devastated by disease that came from European traders in the sixteenth century, Abenaki were able to hold on to their territory and traditions until the late eighteenth century, when the French and Indian Wars ended, and English settlers flooded the Upper Valley beginning in the 1760s. Most of the remaining few Abenaki from Ndakinna fled to the village of St. Francis on the St. Lawrence River halfway between Quebec City and Montreal.

The People of the Dawn did not, however, succumb to complete assimilation. Once again they are recovering their language and traditions, and 2,500 "Vermont Abenaki" live in Vermont and New Hampshire, concentrated near Lake Champlain. In 1982 they applied for federal recognition as a tribal entity; their application is still pending.

Reach 9 **Woodsville to Haverhill**

Miles from mouth: 268-255 (13-mile span).
Navigable by: Kayaks, canoes, motorboats.
Difficulty: Class I, quick water.
Flow information: http://water.usgs.gov/water watch or www.h2oline.com; (800) 452-1737.

Portages: None.
Camping: *Mile 265.5:* Howard Island, Woodsville, New Hampshire. *Mile 259.5:* Harkdale Farm, Newbury, Vermont.
USGS maps: Woodsville 7.5 or 15.

The Reach

This stretch of the Connecticut River runs from Woodsville to Haverhill, New Hampshire. This reach begins with fast water, but the current slows considerably within a few miles, and by the time you reach South Newbury you'll be paddling on flat water in the company of a few motorboaters and fishermen. Since this is a quiet stretch with two campsites, it's a great place for rest and recreation, watching birds, and casting a fishing line. Vermont's much-photographed Placey Farm will be visible from the river halfway down this reach. North Haverhill, one of New Hampshire's prettiest historic towns, is found along this reach, east of the river. As you paddle down this section, you will be following the historic retreat from Wells River of Major Robert Rogers, commander of Rogers' Rangers, during the French and Indian Wars.

Miles and Directions

Mile 268: The **Wells River–Woodsville Access** is at a small, sandy spot on the New Hampshire shore just downstream from the bridge. You will be paddling in quick water for about a mile after you put in, but before long the river slows.

Mile 265.5: Howard Island and **Campground** is attached to New Hampshire at low water and, thus, is generally navigable only on the Vermont side. Land your boat on the north end of the island near the gravel bar that connects to the New Hampshire shore. Howard is a large island that is worth exploring, but expect to meet large groups of campers in summer. New Hampshire's Grafton County maintains the site.

Miles 263–259.5: The current continues to carry you over a shallow stretch 1.5 miles past Howard Island until the river turns sharply northeast at the beginning of the **Great Oxbow** at Newbury, Vermont, and Haverhill, New Hampshire, where large bands of Cowasuck and Sokoki from the Abenaki tribe congregated in the late 1600s. Placey Farm, a lovely and much-photographed site, can be glimpsed on the right bank here as the river turns east. There is a second oxbow further south where you will find the **Harkdale Farm Campsite** on the Vermont side. From here on, the river begins to back up behind the Wilder Dam more than 40 miles downstream.

This round barn in Newbury, Vermont, is a beauty. Photo by Wendy Sinton

Miles 259.5–257.5: The river slows as it becomes deeper and wider, heading downstream through rich farmland toward the **Newbury–Haverhill Bridge**, where you will find an access point on the Vermont side just upstream from the bridge.

Miles 257.5–255: From here it's a short trip to the end of the reach. Just past **Oliverian Brook** on the left bank is **Bedell Bridge State Park** in Haverhill, New Hampshire, a premier birding site. You will see stone abutments, which are all that remain after a freak windstorm destroyed the reconstructed bridge in 1979, just months after it reopened. There is a boat ramp and picnic area here; you can access the park from New Hampshire Route 10 in Haverhill. *Caution:* Do not park where you might interfere with farm vehicles.

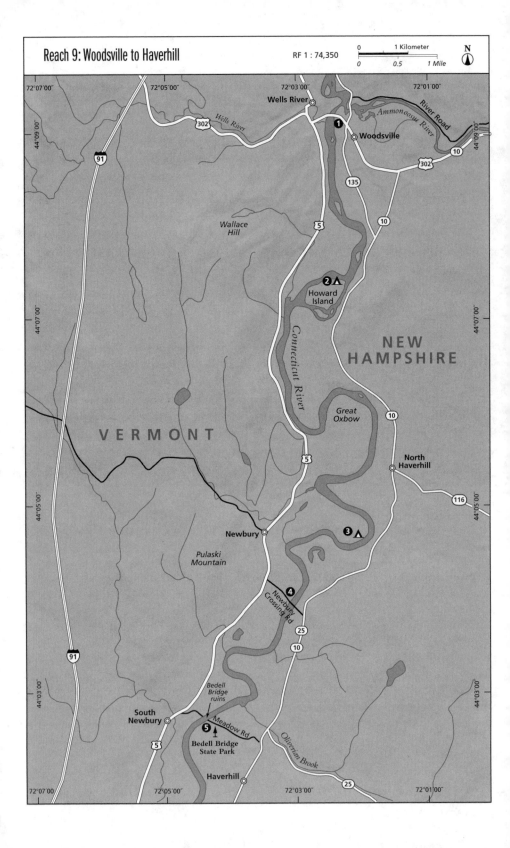

Reach 9: Woodsville to Haverhill

RF 1 : 74,350

0   1 Kilometer
0   0.5   1 Mile

N

Wells River

302 *Wells River*

Wells River

Ammonoosuc River

River Road

1

Woodsville

302

10

135

10

Wallace Hill

5

2 ⛺
Howard Island

Connecticut River

NEW HAMPSHIRE

Great Oxbow

91

VERMONT

5

10

North Haverhill

116

Newbury

3 ⛺

Pulaski Mountain

4

Newbury Crossing Rd

25

10

91

Bedell Bridge ruins

South Newbury

5

5

Meadow Rd

Olivarian Brook

Bedell Bridge State Park

Haverhill

25

Boating Facilities Table for Reach 9

Access Point, Directions	Boat Type	Fee	Parking	Picnic	Toilets	Camping	Rentals	Supplies
❶ Woodsville Access Connecticut Street, Woodsville, NH *Turn south off US 302/NH 10 right after bridge over Connecticut River onto Connecticut Street in Woodsville; access is below bridge on right side.*	Unimproved ramp, car-top only	N	Y	N	N	N	N	N
❷ Howard Island Campsite Woodsville, NH *River access only at northern tip of Howard Island south of Woodsville. Upper Valley Land Trust; www.uvlt.org.*	River access only	N	N	Y	Y	Group	N	N
❸ Harkdale Farm Campsite Newbury, VT *River access only on Vermont side at second large oxbow downstream of Howard Island, across from high, eroding sand bank that meets small brook with fallen trees. At low water you will see campsite sign at edge of brush above sandy beach. Upper Valley Land Trust; www.uvlt.org.*	River access only	N	N	Y	Y	Y	N	N
❹ Newbury–Haverhill Bridge Access Newbury Crossing Road, Newbury, VT *On bridge road between US 5 and NH 10.*	Improved ramp for all boat types	N	Y	N	N	N	N	N
❺ Bedell Bridge State Park Meadow Road, Haverhill, NH *Turn west onto Meadow Road at state park sign on NH 10 in Haverhill. Do not park in farmers' fields.*	Improved ramp for all boat types	N	Y	Y	Y	N	N	N

Rogers' Rangers

Robert Rogers, born in 1731 and raised in southeastern New Hampshire, was attracted early to soldiering, briefly becoming a colonial scout by the age of twenty. In 1756 the English government asked him to establish one of the first special forces regiments in modern history—Rogers' Rangers, guerrillas fighting an unconventional war against the French and Indians in the Upper Valley, Lake Champlain region, and the St. Lawrence Valley.

Rogers is famous in the Upper Valley for his 1759 exploits. General Jeffery Amherst ordered Rogers to take the Native American village of St. Francis on the St. Lawrence River. In a surprise attack the rangers destroyed the village, killed about forty Abenaki, and took several prisoners. The French and their Native American allies were immediately on Rogers's trail as the rangers fled south to Vermont's Northeast Kingdom and the Connecticut River Valley. Rogers broke his rangers into several groups, telling them to reassemble at Coos (Cowass) Meadow where the Ammonoosuc and Connecticut Rivers meet (Woodsville, New Hampshire) and where they expected emergency supplies to await them.

Supplies from Fort at No. 4 at Charlestown, New Hampshire, had indeed arrived at Woodsville, but, thinking that Rogers was the enemy, the supply soldiers fled, leaving the rangers starving. Rogers and three of his men floated a raft downriver to get provisions for the others, but almost lost the raft when they were caught in the currents at White River Junction. After patching together another raft, Rogers almost lost his life at Sumner Falls before finally reaching the Fort at No. 4.

Robert Rogers led a checkered career after his later victories with Amherst in the French and Indian Wars. George Washington, thinking Rogers a spy and calling him "the only man I was ever afraid of," spurned Rogers's offer to enlist with the Americans in the Revolution. Rogers then became a lieutenant colonel in the Queen's Rangers, was captured at Mamaroneck near New York City, escaped, and went to England, where he died penniless in 1800.

Rogers is best remembered for establishing the first ranger regiment in America, soldiers who "ranged" between fixed forts on the frontier. The first of his famous Standing Orders for his rangers was, "Don't forget nothing." Unfortunately, those orders are apocryphal, although the well-educated Rogers did indeed write a set of formal ranging rules. It is likely the modern myth derives from Kenneth Roberts's 1936 novel, *Northwest Passage,* which resurrected his exploits, long forgotten by 1900. Now, however, you can join any number of reenactment activities in which twenty-first-century rangers participate.

Reach 10 **Haverhill to Orford**

Miles from mouth: 255-239 (16-mile span).
Navigable by: Kayaks, canoes, motorboats.
Difficulty: Class I, flat water.
Portages: None.
Camping: *Mile 254:* Vaughan Meadow, Newbury, Vermont; river access only. *Mile 248:* Bugbee

Landing, Bradford, Vermont. *Mile 245:* Underhill Camp, Newbury, Vermont; river access only. *Mile 239:* The Pastures Campground, Orford, New Hampshire.

USGS maps: Woodsville 7.5 or 15, Mt. Cube 15.

The Reach

This leg of the river meanders from Haverhill to Orford, New Hampshire. Boating this lovely, winding, rural reach, you may find your mind drifting along with the slow current. There is good birding here, especially around the oxbows, and fine fishing for warm-water species—pike, bass, perch, and walleye. Furthermore, you will have a choice of three campsites. At the beginning and end of this stretch are two nesting pairs of peregrine falcons, so this may be your best chance to spot one while hunting its favorite prey—pigeons, doves, and ducks. The reach ends at one of the most beautiful villages in the Upper Valley, Orford, New Hampshire, and across from its pretty Vermont neighbor, Fairlee.

Miles and Directions

Mile 255: The reach begins in New Hampshire at **Bedell Bridge State Park**, located downstream from the Newbury–Haverhill Bridge between U.S. Route 5 and New Hampshire Route 10. The stone abutments are all that remain from the reconstructed bridge that a windstorm destroyed in 1979.

Mile 254: You will shortly reach the first campsite, **Vaughan Meadow**, on the right bank just as the river makes a mild turn from south-southeast to south-southwest.

Mile 251.5: As **Roaring Brook** enters from the right bank, you will see above it the sheer rock wall of **Sawyer's Ledge** where there is an active peregrine aerie. Watch for a medium-size bird that looks like a speeding boomerang with a tail attached; peregrines have been clocked at 200 miles per hour in a dive. Directly across from the ledge is an oxbow, a good spot for fishing and birding.

Mile 248: The **Waits River** now enters from Vermont at the town of Bradford, where you can replenish your provisions. The mouth of the Waits River has various inlets and dead ends to explore, and, just as you head north up the Waits itself, you will find **Bugbee Landing and Campsite**, with a small dock and unimproved ramp.

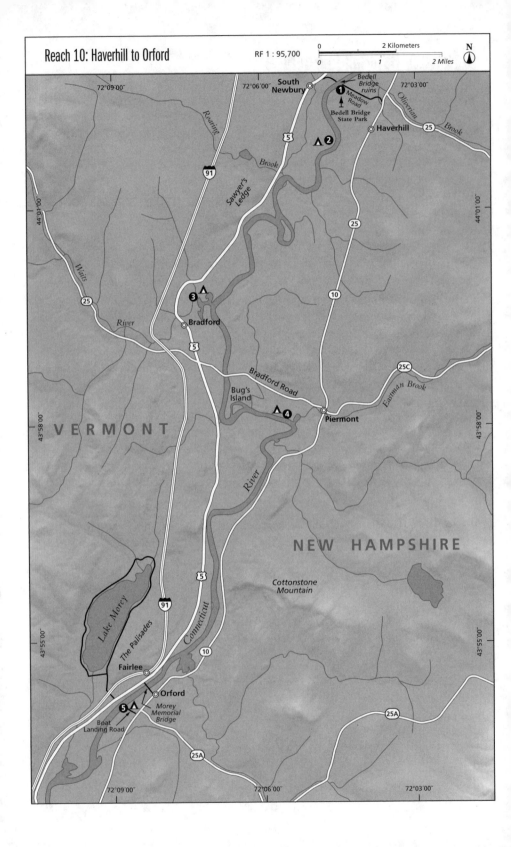

Miles 246–245: After a straight southerly stretch, the river turns sharply northeast as you pass **Bug's Island**, on the New Hampshire side. You will now be going directly toward the town of Piermont, New Hampshire, and, before the river makes a sharp west turn, you will see the mouth of **Eastman Brook** where the **Underhill Campsite** is located.

Miles 245–239: As you continue through farmlands on a southwesterly course, you will notice the mountains beginning to close in as you approach Orford, New Hampshire, and Fairlee, Vermont. **The Palisades**, rising directly behind Fairlee, host a peregrine aerie. The town itself, a Connecticut River Byway Waypoint, has a historic district and a weekend flea market at the site of Vermont's earliest railroad depot. The

Boating Facilities Table for Reach 10

Access Point, Directions	Boat Type	Fee	Parking	Picnic	Toilets	Camping	Rentals	Supplies
❶ **Bedell Bridge State Park** Meadow Road, South Newbury, VT *Turn west onto Meadow Road at state park sign on NH 10 in Haverhill. Do not park in farmers' fields.*	Improved ramp for all boat types	N	Y	Y	Y	N	N	N
❷ **Vaughan Meadow Campsite** Newbury, VT *One mile below old Bedell Bridge abutment, on wooded bank as river turns from southeast to south on Vermont side. Upper Valley Land Trust: www.uvlt.org.*	River access only	N	N	Y	Y	Y	N	N
❸ **Bugbee Landing** Bradford, VT *Turn east off US 5 onto Doe Meadow Road; go through fairgrounds to access. Campsite is managed by Bradford Elementary School. Phone ahead: (802) 222-4077.*	Improved ramp for all boat types	N	Y	Y	Y	Y	N	N
❹ **Underhill Campsite** Newbury Crossing Road, Newbury, VT *Just before river takes sharp turn west-southwest, within view of Piermont village to east on New Hampshire bank and just above mouth of Eastman Brook. Managed by Piermont Conservation Commission: (603) 272-4359, rabenest@together.net.*	River access only	N	N	Y	Y	Y	N	N
❺ **Orford Boat Landing and Pastures Campground** Boat Landing Road, Orford, NH *Turn west off NH 10 onto Boat Landing Road. Camping: www.thepastures.com.*	Improved ramp, dock	Y	Y	Y	Y	Y Fee	Y	Y

This is all that remains of the rebuilt Bedell Bridge after a 1979 windstorm. Photo by Wendy Sinton

Lake Hitchcock

Seventeen thousand years ago the Connecticut River Valley from Rocky Hill, Connecticut, to St. Johnsbury, Vermont, lay under the great, elongated Lake Hitchcock. The lake was a product of melting glaciers in the north and the resulting huge earthen dams south of Hartford, Connecticut, at Rocky Hill and New Britain. As the glaciers retreated, sometimes slowly, sometimes quickly, sometimes even returning for a while, they sent huge amounts of eroded material from boulders as large as a garage to silt as fine as mud into Lake Hitchcock. As the pressure of the water built up behind the earthen dams south of Hartford, the dams slowly gave way, draining the lake and leaving the eroded materials from nearby hills and mountains in the valley through which the river now runs.

It's hard to imagine such a lake, surrounded by melting glaciers as deep as 2 miles, something like coastal Alaska, but there are some indications in Abenaki stories that remnants of the lake did exist when the first Americans arrived 10,000 to 11,000 years ago. When Native Americans first planted seeds in the valley soils, they must have quickly discovered how easily crops grew in the dark earth, a gift of Lake Hitchcock. Four thousand years of rocks and mud from the mountains had poured into the lake, which, when it drained, left the fertile valley soils we have been using for agriculture these past thousand years. For more information on Lake Hitchcock, see the introductory essay "Geology" and consult the appendix.

Morey Memorial Bridge, which is on the National Historic Register, links Fairlee to the more famous historic district of Orford, with its extraordinary line of "Ridge" houses. The takeout is on the New Hampshire bank just downstream of both the Morey Bridge and a private campground. The State of New Hampshire and the Town of Orford plan a significant upgrade of this facility in the near future.

Reach 11 Orford to Ompompanoosuc River

Miles from mouth: 239–225 (14-mile span).
Navigable by: Kayaks, canoes, motorboats.
Difficulty: Flat water.
Portages: None.
Camping: *Mile 236.5:* Birch Meadow, Ely, Vermont; river access only. *Mile 234:* Roaring

Brook, Ely, Vermont; river access only. *Mile 231:* Esther Salmi, East Thetford, Vermont; river access only.
USGS maps: Mt. Cube 15.

The Reach

Like the previous reach, Orford, New Hampshire, to the Ompompanoosuc River in Vermont is flat water with little current, due to the backup from Wilder Dam in Reach 12. There is a lot of motorboat traffic, but also excellent birding and camping. You will pass several wetlands, excellent habitat for waterfowl, rails, and shorebirds. You will end up at the Ompompanoosuc River. Its mudflats provide excellent shorebird viewing as well as fine bass, perch, and pike fishing.

Caution: You can only access the campgrounds in this reach from the river. Do not walk through farm fields! Trespassing and abuse of private property rights can lead to withdrawal of camping rights for everyone.

Miles and Directions

Miles 239–237: After taking one last look at the peregrine aerie on the Palisades above Fairlee, launch your boat at the Orford ramp on the New Hampshire bank just downstream of the Morey Bridge off New Hampshire Route 10 and below a private campground. About 1 mile downstream you will spot the **Reeds Marsh Wildlife Management Area** on the New Hampshire bank, the first of several excellent birding and fishing spots.

Mile 236.5: At the mouth of the unnamed stream that leads north to **Lake Morey**, Vermont, you will find an inlet and marshy areas with good birding and fishing. Just before the inlet is the **Birch Meadow Campsite** on the downstream side of the private campsites on the right bank. Make sure you camp at Birch Meadow; do not

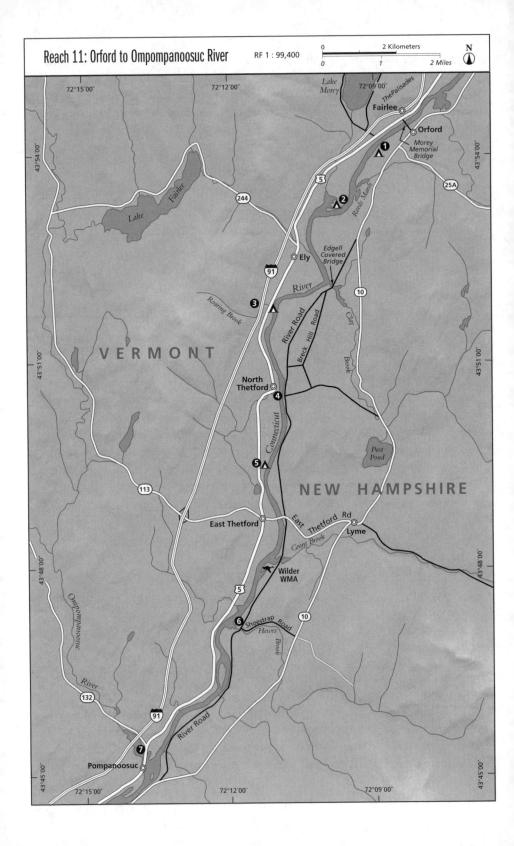

Reach 11: Orford to Ompompanoosuc River

RF 1 : 99,400

0   2 Kilometers
0   1   2 Miles

N

Boating Facilities Table for Reach 11

Access Point, Directions	Boat Type	Fee	Parking	Picnic	Toilets	Camping	Rentals	Supplies
❶ Orford Boat Landing Boat Landing Road, Orford, NH *Turn west off NH 10 onto Boat Landing Road.*	Improved ramp, dock	Y	Y	Y	Y	Y	Y	Y
❷ Birch Meadow Campsite Ely, VT *Two miles below Fairlee–Orford Bridge on low wooded point on Vermont bank just above wetland at outlet of stream leading north to Lake Morey. Upper Valley Land Trust: www.uvlt.org.*	Unimproved, river access only	N	N	N	N	Y	N	N
❸ Roaring Brook Campsite Ely, VT *River turns sharply south as it approaches railroad tracks; Roaring Brook enters from VT bank. Campsite is on grassy site between two brooks. Upstream one is unnamed; downstream one is Roaring Brook. Upper Valley Land Trust: www.uvlt.org.*	Unimproved, river access only	N	N	N	N	Y	N	N
❹ North Thetford Landing Bridge Street, North Thetford, VT *Off US 5 on Bridge Street.*	Improved ramp for all boat types	N	Y	Y	Y	N	N	N
❺ Esther Salmi (formerly Thetford) Campsite East Thetford, VT *On straight stretch of north–south river, on Vermont bank across river from white house on left bank, 2 miles south of Roaring Brook Campsite. Managed by Bill Bridge: (802) 785-2964. No fires permitted.*	Unimproved, river access only	N	N	N	N	Y	N	N
❻ Hewes Brook Boat Launch River Road, Lyme, NH *South of intersection of River Road and Shoestrap Road. Maintained by Lyme Conservation Commission.*	Unimproved, car-top only	N	Y	N	N	N	N	N
❼ Ompompanoosuc Boat Launch Pompanoosuc, VT *Turn west onto Old Bridge Road off US 5.*	Unimproved ramp for all boat types	N	Y	N	N	N	N	N

trespass on private land or try to access the campsite from the road. Lake Morey is one of Vermont's most visited recreation areas, popular with boaters and fishermen, and particularly with skaters; it's the site of the U.S. long-distance speed-skating championships. The Hurlbert Outdoor Center, with a host of outdoor adventure programs, is also located here.

Mile 235: Heading south toward Lyme, New Hampshire, you will spot the **Edgell Covered Bridge** in a small cove on the left bank near the mouth of **Clay Brook**. Assuming there is sufficient water in the brook, this makes another fine side trip for birding.

Miles 234–232.5: The river now turns southwest. As it makes its turn south, on the Vermont side you will find **Roaring Brook Campsite** near the mouth of **Roaring Brook**. A mile and a half south of the campsite, as you approach some stone abutments, you will see the **Vermont State Landing at North Thetford**.

Miles 231–230: Another mile south of the landing is the last campsite on this reach, **Esther Salmi** (formerly called the Thetford site), after which is the East Thetford–Lyme Bridge on Vermont/New Hampshire Route 113. Lyme is a pretty town just north of Hanover, New Hampshire. From here south to Wilder Dam, however, you may have to dodge water-skiers, especially on weekends.

Miles 229.5–228: Half a mile south of the VT/NH 113 bridge, **Grant Brook** enters from the New Hampshire side and the **Wilder Waterfowl Management Area**, which harbors good numbers of rails and waterfowl, surrounds the brook; there is an osprey nesting platform here. Another 1.5 miles south on the New Hampshire side is the **Hewes Brook Boat Launch**.

Mile 225: The end of the reach is at the **Ompompanoosuc River**, which flows into the Connecticut from Vermont at the **Ompompanoosuc Launch**, managed by the State of Vermont. This is a shallow area with mudflats that can be used by canoes and kayaks and is suitable for small motorboats. The Ompompanoosuc mudflats are important shorebird habitat, especially during migration.

The New England Town

Reaches 9 through 11 boast some of the prettiest towns in the Upper Valley: North Haverhill and Orford in New Hampshire and Vermont's Thetford and Norwich. New England towns draw tourists to their inns and stores, complete with "shoppes for Olde AuntTeaks" and the endless wheels of cheese and cans of maple products.

Residents of historic towns are rightly proud of their handsome residences and churches, their town commons, and their orderly mix of fields and woods. In fact, the Maine geographer Joseph Wood has argued that present-day town centers only developed after the American Revolution. Early New England towns had scattered homesteads with only the Congregational church as a central gathering place; the Industrial Revolution increased economic development, transportation, and trade, leading to a demand for more centralized locations, which in turn led to the development in the early nineteenth century of the "traditional" New England town. What you currently see, therefore, is a nineteenth- and twentieth-century creation, a successful attempt to clean up the remnants of a muddy working landscape in which many residents were often in dire poverty, especially in the last half of the nineteenth century after the timber gave out and the vast farmlands of the Middle West drew young New Englanders toward new riches, leaving the old behind.

Actually, the town's external appearance masks the remarkable significance of the town as a community center and the last outpost of direct democracy in America. Colonial governments in New England allowed settlers to establish self-governing communities (John Winthrop's famous "cities upon a hill") in which male property holders could vote annually to elect town leaders and fund items in the town budget. To this day residents of most New England towns attend town meeting to carry out the town's business, elect the select board (the town's governing body), and vote on budget items. If you wish to participate in the essence of New England town life, attend an annual town meeting in spring; then go have a cup of coffee at the general store and listen to the local gossip.

Reach 12 Ompompanoosuc River to Wilder Dam

Miles from mouth: 225-215.5 (9.5-mile span).
Navigable by: Kayaks, canoes, motorboats.
Difficulty: Flat water.
Portage: *Mile 215.5:* Wilder Dam, 400 yards.

Camping: *Mile 217.5:* Gilman Island, Hanover, New Hampshire; river access only.
USGS maps: Mascoma 15, Hanover 7.5.

The Reach

This short reach takes you down the most populated section of the Upper Valley from Ompompanoosuc River to Wilder Dam, an area of the river that is the region's recreational center. Local residents use the river heavily, and you're likely to see an extraordinary variety of craft—motorboats large and small, fast and slow; kayaks and canoes; and a great many rowing sculls and shells. Because of the heavy river traffic, especially on weekends, motorboaters and paddlers need to be mindful of each other.

Dartmouth College and Dartmouth-Hitchcock Medical Center dominate the area's culture, but you will find a mix of blue-collar New Englanders, a few farmers, wealthy retirees, perpetual students, and artists, writers, and musicians of the first rank. It will be worth your while to spend time around Hanover, New Hampshire, or Norwich, Vermont, both handsome New England towns. In particular, consider visiting the Montshire Museum of Science in Norwich, a 0.5-mile walk from Dartmouth's Ledyard Boathouse. In cooperation with the Silvio O. Conte National Fish and Wildlife Refuge, the museum has established a rich collection of exhibits on the natural history of the Connecticut River watershed, including a nature trail. It also has excellent displays for children.

Miles and Directions

Mile 225: Begin your boating at the mouth of the **Ompompanoosuc River**, which flows into the Connecticut from Vermont at the **Ompompanoosuc Launch**, managed by Vermont Fish and Game. This is a shallow area with mudflats that can be used by canoes and kayaks and small motorboats. It is an important shorebird site.

Miles 223.5-219: **Wilson's Landing** soon appears on the New Hampshire shore, a boat launch managed by the town of Hanover. Both boat and vehicular traffic increase rapidly in this area as you approach the center of Hanover, and within sight of **Ledyard Bridge**, you will reach Dartmouth College's **Ledyard Canoe Club** on the New Hampshire side. This facility is open to the public; kayak and canoe rentals are available. Next door is the Dartmouth College boathouse for its crew teams. *Caution:* There's a no-wake zone from Ledyard Bridge to 1,000 feet upstream. Watch for shells and sculls, as well as canoes and kayaks; it gets very busy here.

Mile 218.5: Ledyard Bridge is the Appalachian Trail link between Vermont and New

Wilder Dam hydroelectric facility was built across Olcott Falls south of Hanover, New Hampshire. Photo © Al Braden

Hampshire, so you will find many backpackers crossing the river here in summer. On the Vermont side of the river between Interstate 91 and Ledyard Bridge you'll find the **Montshire Museum of Science**. The museum has many interactive exhibits for adults and children as well as several nature trails (see "Museums" sidebar, page 99).

Mile 217.5: Not far downstream from Ledyard Bridge, you will come to **Gilman Island**, one of the most welcoming sites on the river with its group campsite and a rental cabin that belongs to the Ledyard Canoe Club. You can reserve the ten-person **Titcomb Cabin** on the northeast side of the island by contacting the canoe club. The cabin was built in response to the construction of Wilder Dam in 1950, which raised the level of the Connecticut by 15 feet and submerged Johnny Johnson Island, Chase Island, and Occum Island, on which the club had cabins. The power company manages a campsite on the southeast end of the island.

Miles 216.5–216: A mile south of Gilman Island on the Vermont shore is **Wilder Picnic Area** with a small dock and picnic area, and about 0.25 mile south of this is the **Wilder Dam Boat Launch** on land owned by the power company. The town of Hartford, Vermont, is working with the power company to construct an expanded boating facility and public recreation area here in the near future. Just across from the Wilder Dam Boat Launch is the **East Wilder Boat Launch** managed by the City of Lebanon, New Hampshire.

Mile 215.5: Just downriver you will see **Wilder Dam**, built in 1950 to take advantage of Olcott Falls for producing electricity. The portage is on the New Hampshire side just before the orange buoys marking the dam. From the portage parking lot, there's a nice side trip on a trail that leads to small, lovely **Boston Lot Lake**.

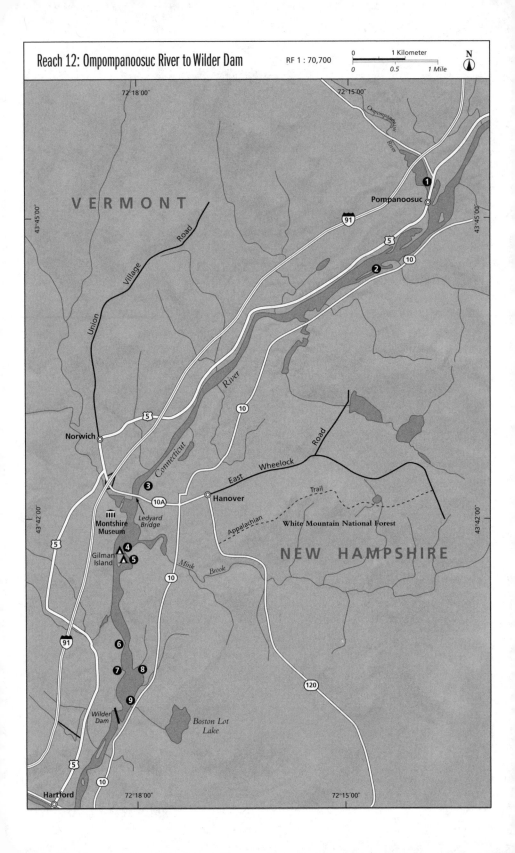

Reach 12: Ompompanoosuc River to Wilder Dam

RF 1 : 70,700

0   1 Kilometer

0   0.5   1 Mile

N

72°18'00"   72°15'00"

Ompompanoosuc River

VERMONT

43°45'00"   43°45'00"

Pompanoosuc ❶

91   5   10   ❷

River

Village

Union   *Road*

10

Connecticut   10

Norwich   5

East   Wheelock   Road   *Trail*

❸   10A   **Hanover**   *Appalachian*   **White Mountain National Forest**

43°42'00"   43°42'00"

5   **Montshire Museum**   *Ledyard Bridge*

NEW HAMPSHIRE

△❹
Gilman Island   △❺   *Mink*   *Brook*   10

❻

91   ❼   ❽   120

❾

Wilder Dam   *Boston Lot Lake*

5

Hartford   10   72°18'00"   72°15'00"

Boating Facilities Table for Reach 12

Access Point, Directions	Boat Type	Fee	Parking	Picnic	Toilets	Camping	Rentals	Supplies
❶ Ompompanoosuc Boat Launch Pompanoosuc, VT *Turn west onto Old Bridge Road off US 5.*	Unimproved ramp for all boat types	N	Y	N	N	N	N	N
❷ Wilson's Landing Hanover, NH *Turn west off NH 10, 3 miles north of center of Hanover.*	Improved ramp and dock for all boat types	N	Y	Y	N	N	N	N
❸ Ledyard Canoe Club Hanover, NH *Turn north off West Wheelock Street at eastern end of Ledyard Bridge between brick pillars; keep left, then bear right to back of parking lot; take path to left of small boathouse. Managed by Dartmouth College Outing Club: (603) 643–6709.*	Unimproved, car-top only	N	Y	Y	Y	N	Y	Nearby
❹ Titcomb Cabin, Gilman Island Hanover, NH *Northeast corner of island. Downriver from Ledyard Bridge and just below Mink Brook on New Hampshire side of island. Managed by Ledyard Canoe Club (Dartmouth Outing Club). Reservations required: (603) 643–6709.*	River access only	Y	N	Y	Y	Y	N	N
❺ Gilman Island Campsite Hanover, NH *Southeast corner of island. Managed by power company.*	River access only	N	N	Y	N	Y Groups	N	N
❻ Wilder Picnic Area Gilette Street, Hartford, VT *Turn east off US 5 onto Gilette Street just north of center of Wilder, Vermont. Follow road to picnic site.*	Unimproved path, car-top only	N	Y	Y	Y	N	N	N
❼ Wilder Dam Boat Launch Passumpsic Street, Wilder, VT *Turn east off US 5 in center of Wilder onto Chandler Street; go one block. Turn right onto Passumpsic Sreet, follow to end.*	Improved ramp for all boat types	N	Y	N	Y	N	N	N
❽ East Wilder Boat Launch East Wilder Road, Lebanon, NH *Turn west off NH 10 halfway between Hanover and West Lebanon at Cole Park Boat Launch sign onto East Wilder Road.*	Improved ramp for all boat types	N	Y	N	N	N	N	N

Boating Facilities Table for Reach 12 continued

Access Point, Directions	Boat Type	Fee	Parking	Picnic	Toilets	Camping	Rentals	Supplies
❾ **Wilder Dam Portage** Lebanon, NH *Go ashore on New Hampshire side before orange buoys at set of wooden steps. Walk along NH 12A guardrail to grass and gravel road on right; pass power company building; continue down road to series of granite steps to river.*	Unimproved path, car-top only	N	Y	Y	N	N	N	N

Reach 13 Wilder Dam to Cornish–Windsor Bridge

Miles from mouth: 215.5-199 (16.5-mile span).
Navigable by: Kayaks, canoes, small motorboats.
Difficulty: Class I through IV.
Flow information: http://water.usgs.gov/water watch or www.h2oline.com; (800) 452-1737.
Portage: *Mile 205:* Sumner Falls (0.25 mile).
Fishing regulations: No fishing the first 150 feet below Wilder Dam.

Camping: *Mile 209:* Burnap's Island, Plainfield, New Hampshire; river access only. *Mile 201:* Burnham Meadow, Windsor, Vermont; river access only.
USGS maps: Hanover 7.5, North Hartland 7.5, Hartland 7.5, Claremont 15.

The Reach

This section of the river flows from the Wilder Dam to the Cornish–Windsor Bridge, with the first put-in and last take-out both on the New Hampshire side of the river. This reach is the halfway point between the Connecticut River's source and Long Island Sound. As if to mark the event, the character of the river changes dramatically below Wilder Dam: The valley narrows, the current speeds up, and you encounter interesting rapids up to Class IV during periods of high water at Sumner Falls. Many sections of this reach are suitable only for kayaks and canoes, and the only ramp for small motorboats is at Cornish, New Hampshire.

The reach is notable for the large number of rare and endangered species on the islands in the river (see the sidebar). Please *do not* disturb the cobbles on the upstream end of islands, do not make campfires, and do not trample the vegetation.

You begin at Wilder Dam and almost immediately come to the urban centers of White River Junction, Vermont, and West Lebanon, New Hampshire. The region was originally a major trade route for Indians and European colonists. For the last 150 years, it has been a significant railroad center; these two cities have shared an

Museums Devoted to the Connecticut River

Just north of this reach, across the river from Hanover, New Hampshire (Reach 12), you will find the first of three museums devoted to the Connecticut River. The Montshire Museum of Science in Norwich, Vermont, focuses on science exhibits that feature the Connecticut River, along with a 2-acre science park and a trail system, on its 110-acre site. Children will especially love the museum's hands-on material. The Montshire Museum is also an official visitor center for the Silvio O. Conte National Fish and Wildlife Refuge. If you want to know something about the natural history of the river, this is the place to visit.

At the end of Reach 13 in Windsor, Vermont, the American Precision Museum is located in a nineteenth-century armory that houses America's largest collection of historically significant machine tools. In its 1998 study of the historical significance of the Connecticut River Valley, the National Park Service pinpointed precision manufacturing as the region's unique historical contribution to the nation. This was the seedbed of the American System of Manufacturing, which used accurate cutting machines in the early nineteenth century to produce machines and products, particularly armaments, of unparalleled quality. If the firearms, machine tools, measuring devices, typewriters, and sewing machines don't overwhelm you, find time to watch master craftsmen use the old tools at special exhibits.

Near the mouth of the river in Essex, Connecticut, the Connecticut River Museum sits on a pretty piece of land overlooking the river. Devoted chiefly to maritime history, this is a great place to look at oddities such as a model of the *Turtle*, America's first submarine (see the "Boatbuilding" sidebar in Reach 27) or the finer points of netting and boning shad. Under its RiverQuest program, the museum runs boat tours on the river, including special eagle cruises.

While not devoted exclusively to the Connecticut River, the Fairbanks Museum and Springfield Science Museum are well worth visiting, and they often have exhibits related to the watershed. The Fairbanks Museum in St. Johnsbury, Vermont, has the most comprehensive collection of New England flora and fauna north of Boston. It is also the regional center for arts and crafts with wonderful year-round activities and exhibits for all ages on New England and Native American lifeways. If you're in Springfield, Massachusetts, stop by the Springfield Science Museum with its planetarium, dinosaurs, and an exhibit on the underwater world of the Connecticut River.

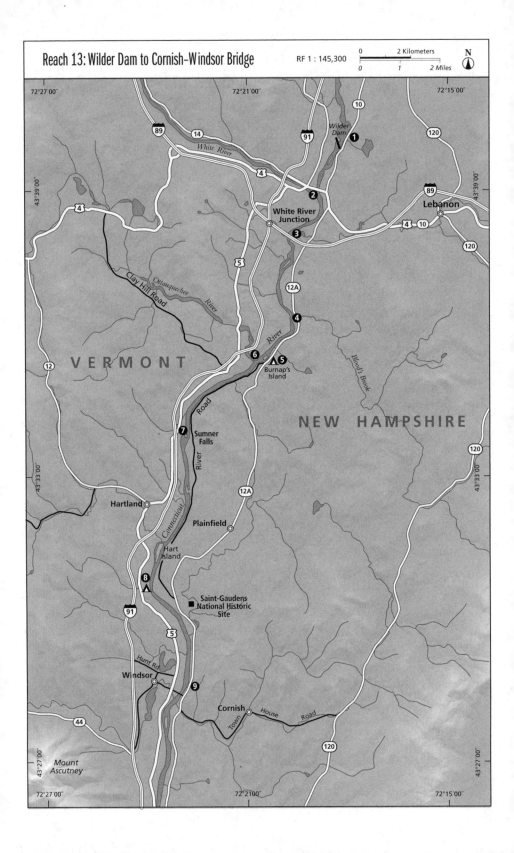

Reach 13: Wilder Dam to Cornish-Windsor Bridge

RF 1 : 145,300

0   2 Kilometers

0   1   2 Miles

N

72°27'00"   72°21'00"   72°15'00"

43°39'00"   43°39'00"

89   14   White River   91   Wilder Dam   ❶   10   120

4   ❷   89   Lebanon

White River Junction   ❸   4   10   120

5   12A   120

Clay Hill Road   Ottauquechee River   ❹

12   V E R M O N T   ❻   ❺   Blood's Brook   N E W   H A M P S H I R E

Burnap's Island

Connecticut River   ❼   Sumner Falls

River Road   120

Hartland   43°33'00"   43°33'00"

Plainfield   12A

Hart Island

❽   Saint-Gaudens National Historic Site

91   5

Hunt Rd   Windsor   ❾   Cornish   House Road   Town

44   120

Mount Ascutney

43°27'00"   43°27'00"

72°27'00"   72°21'00"   72°15'00"

Boating Facilities Table for Reach 13

Access Point, Directions	Boat Type	Fee	Parking	Picnic	Toilets	Camping	Rentals	Supplies
❶ Wilder Dam Portage Lebanon, NH *Go ashore on New Hampshire side before orange buoys at set of wooden steps. Walk along NH 12A guardrail to grass and gravel road on right; pass power company building; continue down road to series of granite steps to river.*	Unimproved path, car-top only	N	Y	Y	N	N	N	N
❷ Lyman Point Park Launch Hartford Township, VT *At corner of Bridge Street and VT 14, turn into town hall parking lot; park entrance is at back right corner. Check in at town manager's office for overnight parking.*	Unimproved path, car-top only	N	Y	Y	Y	N	N	Nearby
❸ Lebanon Public Boat Launch NH 12A, Lebanon, NH *West side of NH 12A at junction with I-89. Difficult to spot from river; just above wastewater treatment plant outfall.*	Unimproved ramp, car-top only	N	Y	N	N	N	N	N
❹ Blood's Brook Launch Lebanon Wildlife Management Area, NH NH 12A, Lebanon, NH *West side of NH 12A near Lebanon–Plainfield town line; turn west onto unmarked dirt road just north of farm near Trues Brook Road.*	Unimproved path, car-top only	N	Y	N	N	N	N	N
❺ Burnap's Island Campsite Plainfield, NH *Land on west side of island. Managed by Upper Valley Land Trust: www.uvlt.org.*	River access only	N	N	Y	Y	Y	N	N
❻ Ottauquechee Launch North Hartland, VT *From US 5 in North Hartland, take Evart Road just south of I-91 overpass; left onto Mill Road, then left onto dirt road before covered bridges.*	Unimproved ramp, car-top only	N	Y	N	N	N	N	N
❼ Sumner Falls Portage Hartland, VT *Well-marked portage trail on Vermont side. On unmarked road east off US 5, 2 miles south of church in center of North Hartland. Endangered plants here; please avoid trampling!*	Unimproved path, car-top only	N	Y	Y	Y	N	N	N

Boating Facilities Table for Reach 13 continued

Access Point, Directions	Boat Type	Fee	Parking	Picnic	Toilets	Camping	Rentals	Supplies
❽ Burnham Meadow Campsite Windsor, VT *One mile below Hart Island, 2 miles above Cornish–Windsor Bridge on elevated site where river bends southeast.*	River access only	N	N	N	N	Y Groups	N	N
❾ Cornish Boat Landing NH 12A, Cornish, NH *West turn off NH 12A, just north of covered bridge.*	Unimproved ramp for car-top and small trailers only	N	Y	N	N	N	N	N

extraordinary railroad history at the junction of five rail lines constructed between the 1840s and 1860s. White River Junction's historic railroad district is up for nomination to the National Historic Register. White River Junction is a byway community with a visitor center at the Amtrak railway station.

The White River, one of the largest tributaries to the Connecticut River, is one of the few large free-flowing rivers in New England. Originating northwest in the Green Mountains not far south of Montpelier, it has a famous trout fishery.

Immediately below White River Junction, the river regains its rural landscapes, dominated by farms and woodlands. You will find no oxbows or sinuous stretches in this north–south reach. It ends at the regional center of Windsor, Vermont's first capital (1791–1805) and the site of one of New England's premier covered bridges. This famed bridge connects with Cornish, New Hampshire, home of the Cornish Art Colony, where you will find Augustus Saint-Gaudens's wonderful house and grounds. Windsor is a Connecticut River Byway Waypoint Community with a waypoint center at the railroad station.

Miles and Directions

Mile 215.5: Kayaks and canoes can put in below **Wilder Dam** on the New Hampshire side at the end of the portage around the dam. From here to White River Junction and West Lebanon is a short paddle that is unnavigable for motorboats. The speed of the current depends on releases from Wilder Dam, so check by phone or Internet for flow information. At low flows the going can be bony, while high flows make for good Class I or II water.

Mile 214: The **White River** enters from Vermont at White River Junction, the transportation center for the Upper Valley. Across the river are West Lebanon and Lebanon, site of the Dartmouth-Hitchcock Medical Center. The town of Hartford, Vermont,

The Cornish–Windsor Bridge is the longest covered bridge in the United States. Mount Ascutney rises in the background. Photo © Al Braden

has made significant efforts to develop the White River for recreation. There are five car-top boat launches with picnic areas on the lower White River, so it is very worth-while to spend a day on the river, which is also a fine trout fishery. The boat launch at the confluence of the White and Connecticut Rivers adjacent to the Hartford–West Lebanon Bridge is on the north shore of the White River behind the Hartford town offices in **Lyman Point Park**. *Caution:* the put-in is steep and the current is dangerous during periods of high water.

Miles 214–211.5: Just downstream from the Hartford–West Lebanon Bridge, the river bends westward, and you will hear the traffic on the Interstate 89 bridge even before you see it. Before you reach the I–89 bridge, however, there is **Lebanon Public Boat Launch** on the New Hampshire side, above the water treatment facility at the mouth of the Mascoma River. The river then turns south, and you will pass two small islands before you get to Johnston Island. *Caution:* Do not land at the head of any island or disturb the cobbles. The globally endangered cobble tiger beetle lives on this island, as do several rare plant species. When you paddle this reach in late summer, banks of brilliant cardinal flower will greet you.

Miles 210–208: At **Blood's Brook Launch** on the New Hampshire bank, the river narrows and the current increases as you head toward **Burnap's Island Campsite**

in the middle of the river. Within sight of Burnap's Island is the mouth of the **Ottauquechee River** on the Vermont side. It is worth a paddle 0.5 mile up this river to two old dams, both topped by pretty covered bridges. This is the site of an old woolen mill and another industry that now lies in ruins. There is a car-top access on the right bank. Just below the Ottauquechee stay toward the middle of the river as you paddle past several large and small boulders near the New Hampshire side called the Hen and Chicks; from here on, the river has shallow spots to watch for as you head toward a major rapids.

Mile 205: Congratulations! You have now reached the halfway point between the Connecticut River's source and Long Island Sound. Very near this point is **Sumner Falls**, a favorite "park and play" stop for whitewater enthusiasts in the Upper Valley. *Caution:* Do not run these falls unless you're an experienced whitewater paddler and have first scouted them. You will hear the falls well upriver, and 200 yards above the falls you can pull over to the Vermont side and portage your boat up the well-marked trail. If you can handle the water, run it down the New Hampshire side, but be sure you get over toward that bank well upstream of the falls, where kayakers play almost every day in summer. It's a favorite training spot for the sport; different flows produce standing waves in different spots in the rapids. But do not overestimate your abilities. People have recently died in these rapids, and a log driver is buried near the portage trail. Sumner Falls has a lovely setting with beautiful rocks and plants, some of which are rare and endangered, so please take care not to trample them.

Miles 204–201: Below the falls the river runs with a moderate current between steep walls until you approach **Hart Island**, an endangered species site, near the Vermont shore. *Note:* The island is closed to public use! A mile below Hart Island, you will arrive at the **Burnham Meadow Group Campsite**, on the Vermont side, as the river bends southeast.

Mile 199: Take out on the New Hampshire side at the **Cornish Boat Landing** just north of the covered bridge. As you approach the end of this reach, you will get some beautiful views of Mount Ascutney, which dominates the landscape of two of the most interesting Upper Valley towns: Windsor, Vermont, and Cornish, New Hampshire. The 460-foot-long covered bridge that connects these two towns is the longest covered bridge in the United States. Within walking distance of the boat landing is the **Saint-Gaudens National Historic Site**. Cornish was the home of the nineteenth-century Cornish Arts Colony, while Windsor was Vermont's first capital.

The Connecticut River Macrosite

Plainfield, New Hampshire, on the river's eastern shore, may be one of the only towns in the world to have proclaimed an official "town bug." That's right: The diminutive but feisty cobblestone tiger beetle (*Cicindela marginipennis* is its formal Latin name) is the celebrated insect of this proud mid-Connecticut River town. What is so special about this critter? Less than an inch long, it's a fearsome predator of other insects, a strong flier, and, if caught by an unsuspecting human, a vigorous biter. Its coppery wing covers are delicately calligraphed with white filigree. Although its ecological role in the river scheme of things is not yet fully appreciated, the species is emblematic of the river's unique, dynamic habitats. It's one of the rarer species in the world, with scattered, small populations restricted to a handful of cobbly river islands east of the Mississippi. It walks a fine line in its preferences for habitat, preferring rocky shores that are well scoured by Connecticut River floods, while being vulnerable to floods that last too long. But the tiger beetle is not the only choosy and exceptional resident of this reach of the river.

Several islands on this reach are home to a number of rare, threatened, and endangered species. In fact, the reach has become known to conservation professionals as the Connecticut River Rapids Macrosite, because the highest concentration of globally rare species in all of Vermont and New Hampshire occurs in this reach. The endangered dwarf wedgemussel enjoys the relatively clear and well-aerated waters along this stretch. A rare plant, the Jesup's milkvetch, is known *only* from three populations in this area. So when you are boating in this area, celebrate the unique wildlife with the enthusiasm of a Plainfield native. Tread carefully, avoiding the upper parts of cobble beaches and slippery bedrock outcrops, and, to pass the time, hum to yourself the anthem of the cobblestone tiger beetle (to the tune of "Battle Hymn of the Republic"):

The cobblestone tiger beetle's coat is black and bronzy, too.
We deem it far more beautiful than those of emerald hue.
If you think our beetle homely, well, we think the same of you.
Our beetle crawls right on.
Glory, glory, it's the bug we like to see.
Glory, glory it's the bug for you and me.
I'd do anything to find one, even climb up in a tree.
Our beetle marches on . . .

For more information or additional verses, contact the Plainfield Tiger Beetle Fund, Box 78, Plainfield, NH 03781.

Reach 14 Cornish-Windsor Bridge to Cheshire Bridge

Miles from mouth: 199–181 (18-mile span).
Navigable by: Kayaks, canoes, small motorboats.
Difficulty: Quick water to Class I.
Portages: None.

Camping: *Mile 192.5:* Wilgus State Park, Ascutney, Vermont. *Mile 185:* SCA Campsite, Charlestown, New Hampshire.
USGS maps: Claremont 15.

The Reach

This span of the river begins on the New Hampshire side of the Cornish–Windsor Bridge and ends on the Vermont side of the Cheshire Bridge. This is another quiet, rural reach of river that generally runs straight south past several large islands. Vermont's 3,150-foot Mount Ascutney dominates a landscape that was home to the artists of the Cornish Art Colony (see the sidebar). In the last half of the reach, look for flocks of swallows that nest colonially in the sand banks. You will find good opportunities for fishing in this reach, although there is only one access ramp for motorboats; in any case, much of this reach is too shallow for large boats. North Star Canoe Rentals (see Appendix C) provides kayak and canoe rentals as well as guided tours from its center at Cornish.

Miles and Directions

Mile 199: Put in on the New Hampshire side at the **Cornish Boat Landing** just north of the covered bridge. If you have time, be sure to visit Windsor, Vermont, and Cornish, New Hampshire. Immediately after putting in you'll pass two **Mill Brooks**, one entering from New Hampshire, the other from Vermont, shortly after which you pass under the railroad bridge and skirt either side of **Chase Island** in the middle of the river. From here it is an almost straight run due south for 5 miles with views of 3,150-foot Mount Ascutney on the Vermont side.

Mile 192.5: Vermont's **Wilgus State Park** is a pleasant stop with its small park and campgrounds just past the mouth of the **Sugar River** on the New Hampshire side. The takeout here, however, is rather steep and muddy.

Mile 190: The river makes only one wide turn in this reach, at **Jarvis Island**, with its thick wetland forest. You can pass the island on either side, but take care not to clamber up the New Hampshire bank opposite the island; there are a significant number of endangered species there, mixed in with the poison ivy.

Mile 189: At the end of Jarvis Island, you can see **Ashley Ferry State Park** on the New Hampshire bank at the bend of the river as it turns south. Ashley Ferry is the only improved boat ramp on this reach.

A swim on a summer day feels great. Photo © Al Braden

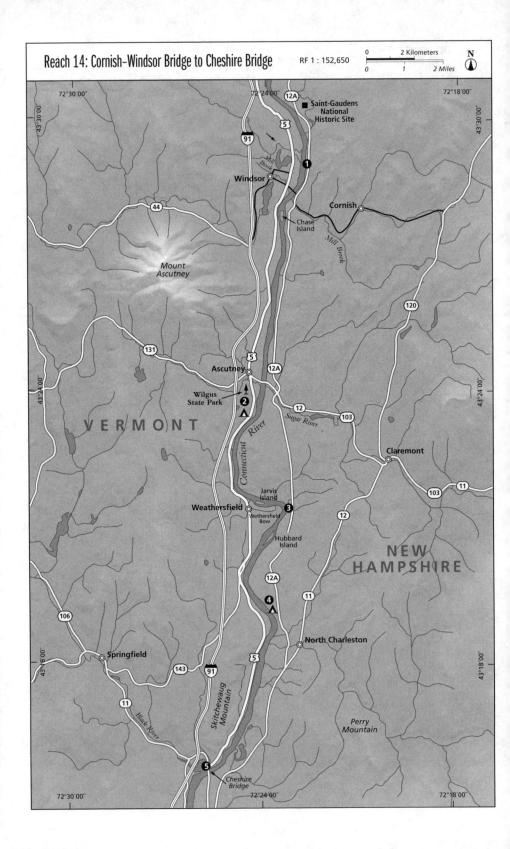

Reach 14: Cornish–Windsor Bridge to Cheshire Bridge

RF 1 : 152,650

Boating Facilities Table for Reach 14

Access Point, Directions	Boat Type	Fee	Parking	Picnic	Toilets	Camping	Rentals	Supplies
❶ Cornish Boat Landing NH 12A, Cornish, NH *Off NH Route 12A just north of covered bridge.*	Unimproved ramp for all boat types	N	Y	N	N	N	N	N
❷ Wilgus State Park Boat Ramp and Campground US 5, Ascutney, VT *South of Ascutney right after passing under power lines on right bank; by land, directly off US 5. Reservations: (802) 674-5422 or www.vtstateparks.com.*	Unimproved ramp for car-top boats	N	Y	Y	Y	Y	Y	N
❸ Ashley Ferry Boat Ramp NH 12A, Claremont, NH *At sign off NH 12A west of town of Claremont. Managed by New Hampshire Parks.*	Improved ramp for all boat types	N	Y	N	N	N	N	N
❹ SCA Campsite Charlestown, NH *River access only. Two miles below Hubbard Island on New Hampshire side. Managed by Student Conservation Association, Lew Shelley, P.O. Box 550, 689 River Road, Charlestown, NH 03603; (603) 543-1700.*	Unimproved access from river only	N	N	N	N	Y	N	N
❺ Hoyt's Landing, VT 11 and US 5, Springfield, VT *At junction of US 5 and VT 11 just west of Cheshire Bridge.*	Improved ramp for all boat types	N	Y	Y	Y	N	N	N

Mile 188: After turning south-southwest again, you will approach **Hubbard Island**, a splintered piece of the New Hampshire bank that has become an island. Keep it on the left as you pass by.

Mile 185.5: About 2 miles below Hubbard Island, as the river begins a slight bend southeast, you will find the small **SCA Campsite** on the New Hampshire side. The Student Conservation Association manages the site and uses it for part of the summer to house its crew, so check before you camp there.

Mile 181: The rest of the reach is a leisurely ride to **Cheshire Bridge** just upstream of Vermont's **Black River**, which enters the Connecticut at a small lagoon. Take out on the upstream side of the lagoon at **Hoyt's Landing** in Vermont. This is one of the few spots on the whole river that is wheelchair accessible and is also geared toward anglers.

Saint-Gaudens and the Cornish Art Colony

Cornish, New Hampshire, is home to the Saint-Gaudens National Historic Site, a lovely house and grounds where Augustus and Augusta Saint-Gaudens lived at the turn of the twentieth century, hosting a variety of artists who formed the Cornish Art Colony, one of the first art colonies in America. Saint-Gaudens, born in Ireland in 1848, the year of the great potato famine, came to the United States as a six-month-old baby and grew up in New York City, where he became a cameo maker as a teenager and a sculptor from the age of twenty. His best-known works are statues of Abraham Lincoln in Chicago and General Sherman in New York's Central Park, but his contemporaries knew him best for scores of bas-reliefs, coins, and medallions.

At the National Historic Site, you get a sense of the place of the arts in America's Gilded Age during the late nineteenth century, when wealthy people hired Saint-Gaudens literally to gild their mansions. When the Saint-Gaudenses arrived in Cornish in 1885, they set about turning an old inn into a summer home that would become the social center for dozens of artists—the Cornish Art Colony—and what for current time travelers is a chance to glimpse life a hundred years ago. Botanists will be thrilled with a wonderful collection of ferns, beautiful gardens, and a set of trails around the property.

Cornish provided a perfect setting for Victorian artists, who were looking to get away from urban areas. Here they found an affordable place to stay in an idyllic setting that looks west to Mount Ascutney and the rolling hills of a valley that reminded many artists of the Italian countryside.

Art colonies have since become established in a number of Connecticut River watershed communities. The Marlow Art Colony, established south of Cornish in 2001, models itself after the Cornish Colony. Large numbers of artists live in the hill towns of Massachusetts and the communities of Northampton and Easthampton. Cummington, Massachusetts, is home not only to artists, but famous poets as well. And both Old Saybrook and Old Lyme, Connecticut, boast art colonies at the mouth of the river.

Reach 15 Cheshire Bridge to Bellows Falls-North Walpole

Miles from mouth: 181–170 (11-mile span).
Navigable by: Kayaks, canoes, motor boats.
Difficulty: Class I, quick water.
Portage: *Mile 171:* About 1.5 miles after Bellows Falls Dam; call Bellows Falls Taxi, (800) 463–4600, for portage assist.

Camping: *Mile 173:* Lower Meadow Campground, South Charlestown, New Hampshire.
USGS maps: Claremont 15, Bellows Falls 15.

The Reach

This portion of the Connecticut River extends from the Cheshire Bridge to Bellows Falls, Vermont, and the neighboring town of North Walpole, New Hampshire. This wonderfully diverse reach begins in the wild wetlands at the Black River confluence, passes by a restored seventeenth-century wooden fort, and ends in the historic town of Bellows Falls, a Connecticut River Byway Waypoint Community. The river is wide, windy, and lazy for most of the reach because it backs up behind the Bellows Falls Dam, and its coves and wetlands make for great fishing and exceptional bird-watching. *Caution:* Be observant of fluctuating water levels above the dam.

Toward the end of the reach, the river narrows dramatically as it carves through a dramatic bedrock gorge before tumbling over Bellows Falls. Although much of the water is now channeled away from the main stream to garner hydropower, the falls truly roar during the spring freshet. Abenaki Indians once gathered at these ledges to harvest salmon and shad migrating upstream. Their petroglyphs are visible below the falls and the Vilas Bridge at very low water. The first bridge ever to cross the Connecticut River was installed across these narrow falls in 1785, linking New Hampshire and Vermont and providing a foundation for the roads and rails that came a century later with the industrial era. These falls require you to portage your boat along a rather long but well-marked trail on the New Hampshire side—a great excuse to explore the twin towns of Bellows Falls and North Walpole.

Bellows Falls has a Byway Waypoint Visitor Center adjacent to the Bellows Falls Canal near the train station. The power company's visitor center, now run by the Museum of Natural History at Grafton, Vermont, is open Friday through Sunday during the summer months. From late May through June, the viewing window to the fish ladder is open. You can see not only shad, lamprey, and the occasional salmon that have made it 170 miles upriver, but also resident fish, particularly bass and trout. Smallmouth bass have a peculiar habit of swimming up the ladder, only to turn around and take a fast ride down, almost as though they were sledding.

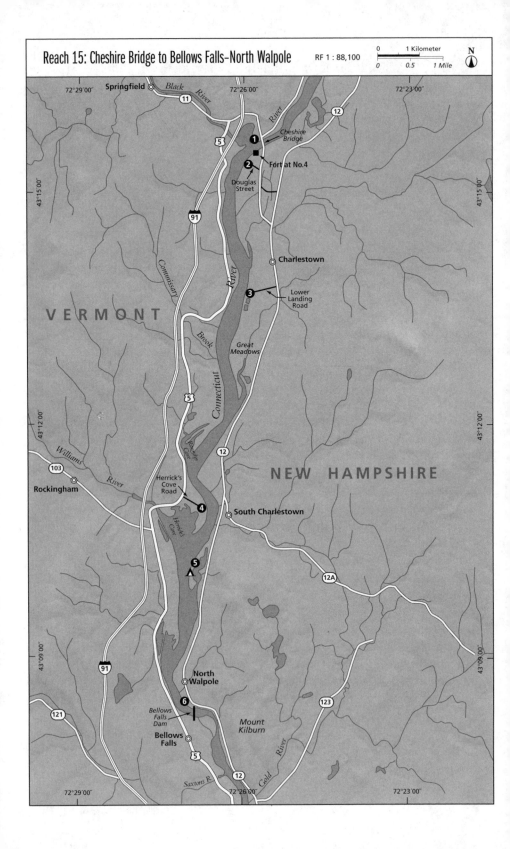

Reach 15: Cheshire Bridge to Bellows Falls–North Walpole

RF 1 : 88,100

0 ___ 1 Kilometer
0 ___ 0.5 ___ 1 Mile

N

72°29'00" Springfield *Black* *River* 72°26'00" 72°23'00"

11

River

12

❶ Cheshire Bridge

5

43°15'00"

❷ Fort at No.4

Douglas Street

91

Commissary

V E R M O N T

River

Charlestown

❸ Lower Landing Road

Brook

Great Meadows

43°12'00"

Connecticut

Roundy Cove

12

N E W   H A M P S H I R E

Williams

103

River

Rockingham

Herrick's Cove Road

❹

Hermit's Cove

South Charlestown

❺
⛺

12A

91

43°09'00"

North Walpole

121

❻

123

Bellows Falls Dam

Mount Kilburn

Bellows Falls

5

Cold

River

72°29'00" *Saxtons R.* 72°26'00" **12** 72°23'00"

Boating Facilities Table for Reach 15

Access Point, Directions	Boat Type	Fee	Parking	Picnic	Toilets	Camping	Rentals	Supplies
❶ **Hoyt's Landing** VT 11 and US 5, Springfield, VT *At junction of US 5 and VT 11 just west of Cheshire Bridge.*	Improved ramp for all boat types	N	Y	Y	Y	N	N	N
❷ **Patch Park** Douglas Street, Charlestown, NH *Turn west off Springfield Road onto NH 11.*	Unimproved ramp, car-top boats only	N	Y	Y	Y	N	N	N
❸ **Charlestown Lower Landing** Lower Landing Road, Charlestown, NH *Turn southwest off NH 12 (Main Street).*	Improved ramp for all boat types	N	Y	Y	Y	N	N	N
❹ **Herrick's Cove Picnic Area and Boat Launch** Herrick's Cove Road, Rockingham, VT *Turn east onto Herrick's Cove Road from US 5.*	Improved ramp for all boat types	N	Y	Y	Y	N	N	N
❺ **Lower Meadow Campground** South Charlestown, NH *River access only for nonmotorized boats.* *Primitive camping. Limit 1-night stay, no fires.* *Call power company for more information:* *(802) 291-8104.*	Unimproved access for canoes and kayaks	N	Y	N	Y	Y	N	N
❻ **Pine Street Boat Launch** Pine Street, North Walpole, NH *Turn west off NH 12 (Church Street) onto Pine Street.*	Unimproved ramp, car-top boats only	N	Y	N	N	N	N	Nearby

Miles and Directions

Mile 181: All types of boats can put in at **Hoyt's Landing**, a well-equipped launch on the right bank at the Cheshire Bridge (junction of U.S. Route 5 and New Hampshire Route 11). Just 0.2 mile below the Cheshire Bridge (NH 11), you will be able to glimpse the wooden turrets and tall fences of the **Fort at No. 4** on the Charlestown, New Hampshire, side. This living history museum is a reconstruction of a stockade, province houses, lean-tos, a great hall, barns, a blacksmith shop, and a watchtower, all originally located where downtown Charlestown is now. When constructed in 1745, this was the northernmost English settlement in the Connecticut River Valley and saw battle during the French and Indian Wars. There is a small dock at the fort where you can tie up and visit the site (there is an admission fee). Just downstream on the left bank is **Patch Park**, an expansive, grassy picnic area and playing field with a ramp that accommodates small boats.

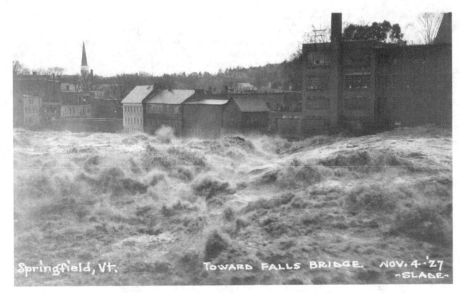

The river's power was unleashed in the 1927 flood on the Black River in Springfield, Vermont. Photo courtesy of Vermont Historical Society

Mile 178.5: Lush, grassy meadows lie on the left bank, while the steeper hills of Vermont rise above the right bank. The **Charlestown Lower Landing**, on the New Hampshire side, is maintained by the power company for all types of boats. The town of Charlestown is a National Historic Site with a wealth of interesting colonial architecture. There is also an historical marker commemorating John Stark's famous expedition to Bennington, Vermont, where, fresh from successful forays at the Battle of Bunker Hill, he led a ragtag New Hampshire militia of 1,500 men to defeat the British—a decisive victory in the Revolutionary War.

Mile 176.5: You will now pass the first of several coves and wetland complexes where the river backs up behind the Bellows Falls Dam. **Great Meadows** on the right bank and **Roundys Cove** on the left mark areas where the river once meandered more widely than it does now. Be aware of shallow areas near Great Meadows, where **Commissary Brook** flows in from Vermont.

Mile 174: After jogging left just beyond the mouth of Roundys Cove, you will see a large sign for the Green Mountain Marina (see Appendix C). Around the bend to the right is **Herrick's Cove Picnic Area and Boat Launch** on the right bank. Maintained by the power company, this is a large, peaceful park. More than 300 bird species have been identified in this large delta formed by the outflow of the **Williams River**; the National Audubon Society has designated Herrick's Cove an Important Bird Area. Anglers will find Herrick's Cove and the Williams River fine smallmouth bass fishing.

Miles 173–171: Just across the river from Herrick's Cove is the **Lower Meadow Campground**, designed for one-night stays by nonmotorized boaters. You will pass the mouth of Meany Cove on the left bank; another mile down, Albees Cove will beckon on the right. Here, the river will narrow considerably. *Caution:* Avoid creating a wake that impacts the unstable steep bank on the New Hampshire side; ice jams have dislodged submerged log booms left over from the log drive days, resulting in substantial erosion here. The rugged massif of New Hampshire's **Mount Kilburn** (locally known as Fall Mountain) looms over the river and the town of Walpole. Another 0.5 mile below Albees Cove is the **Pine Street Boat Launch** on the left bank, a small ramp next to an old brick building by the water's edge. This is the point at which to take out and portage Bellows Falls on the New Hampshire side. Follow signs for the 1.5-mile portage to the **North Walpole Portage Access** south of the dam off New Hampshire Route 12. Take some time to explore on foot the rock formations and Indian petroglyphs that lie beneath the Vilas Bridge (NH 12) below the dam, which are pockmarked with glacial potholes. These smooth hollows are carved out by boulders and cobbles that swirl around in raging floodwaters, creating bowls like a potter's hand in soft clay. Also, be sure to visit the Bellows Falls Waypoint Visitor Center as well as the fish ladder at the dam.

Spring runoff at the Vilas Bridge in Bellows Falls, Vermont, shows why no one paddles the river in flood season. Photo © Al Braden

Agriculture in the Connecticut Valley

It's probably no exaggeration to say that more than half of the Connecticut River courses through farmland. It's hard to boat more than a mile down the river without passing a cornfield, for example, even within a stone's throw of a city. For millennia the Connecticut River Valley has fostered the most intensive and lucrative agricultural activity in New England. Yearly flooding by the river replenishes the soils with a rich mixture of silt and loam—perfect for crops.

The Abenaki of southern New Hampshire and Vermont grew corn, beans, and squash for almost 1,000 years, crops that provided the foundation of their diet, supplemented with fish and venison. Colonial farms sprang up along the Connecticut within decades of the Pilgrims' landing at Plymouth; Europeans knew good soils when they saw them. Self-sufficient rural families maintained subsistence farms, gradually clearing the great floodplain forests that lined the river.

Abundant crops created excellent fodder for livestock. Merino sheep were introduced into Vermont in the early 1800s, and much additional land was cleared for pasturage. Within a few decades less than half of the Connecticut River Valley remained in forest, and the river cut a swath through open vistas of bucolic hills. More than one million sheep were being raised in Vermont by 1840, vastly outnumbering people. Wool provided an agricultural mainstay in New England until less expensive material produced on western farms flooded the market. Dairy cattle replaced sheep in the early 1900s as a source of farming income.

Tobacco has been a mainstay crop in the lower Connecticut River Valley since the late nineteenth century, although it was grown for local consumption much earlier. The colonial settlers first learned to enjoy tobacco from contact with Native Americans. By 1760 or so the first cigar made its way into New England, and by 1900 some of the finest cigar wrappers in the world were being cultivated in shade houses along the river. Chestnut boards were used to construct long, airy barns in which the harvested tobacco leaves could be hung to dry. These barns still stand from Deerfield, Massachusetts, to Windsor, Connecticut, and beyond. Every summer, acres of shadecloth tents become a familiar sight along the river, and migrant workers from the Caribbean and other areas arrive to harvest the crop.

Farmers' markets and agricultural fairs are flourishing in the towns that neighbor the river, with all sorts of innovative crops showing up: unusual gourds, arugula, heir-

Local farmers use raccoons as good advertising for their sweet corn. Photo by Wendy Sinton

loom varieties of carrots—just about anything edible can grow in deep floodplain soils. Farmers are rejuvenating their relationship with the nurturing floodwaters of the river, promoting lower-impact organic techniques, cultivating buffers that reduce runoff of manure, fertilizers, and pesticides, and utilizing rather than diverting the life-giving seasonal freshets. Likewise, the Farmland Trust and state and local programs throughout the Upper Valley have invested significant resources into farmland preservation.

Reach 16 Bellows Falls–North Walpole to Putney

Miles from mouth: 170–153.5 (16.5-mile span).
Navigable by: Kayaks, canoes, and small motor-boats only at high water.
Difficulty: Quick water, flat water.
Flow information: http://water.usgs.gov/water watch or www.h2oline.com; (800) 452-1737.

Portages: None
Camping: *Mile 159:* Windyhurst Campsite, Walpole, New Hampshire; access from river only.
USGS maps: Bellows Falls 15, Keene 15, Bratteboro 15.

The Reach

This reach begins just south of the bustling small towns of Bellows Falls, Vermont (a Connecticut River Byway Waypoint Community), and North Walpole, New Hampshire, then traverses rolling farmland overshadowed by high hills to end at the charming town of Putney, Vermont. Along the way bank swallows will accompany you, and a bald eagle may even make an appearance. Diverse wetland meadows, wonderful places for botanizing and bird-watching, are a recurring theme throughout the reach. A beautiful remnant floodplain forest of large silver maples is a shady spot for a rest. Although this is an easy, leisurely stretch, be aware of many shallow areas and shoals, especially in the first few miles south of the Bellows Falls Dam, which can make navigation tricky for motorboats. The river banks are steep and muddy for the most part, so there are few opportunities to take out along this stretch.

Miles and Directions

Mile 170: Put in below the **Bellows Falls Dam** at the access ramp on the New Hampshire side in North Walpole. *Caution:* The currents here are challenging, especially in high water; scout carefully before entering the water, and do not anchor just below the dam. About 0.5 mile downstream the **Saxtons River** meets the Connecticut River on the right bank; steer clear of the shallows around its mouth. Another half-mile downstream the **Cold River** empties into the Connecticut on the left bank. A gravel bar created by the confluence here extends much of the way across the main stem, so stay well to the right bank to avoid it. This segment of the reach parallels the old **Bellows Falls Canal**, one of America's earliest shipping canals, built in 1802 (see the "Connecticut River Canals" sidebar in Reach 18).

Miles 169–167: Farmland and wet meadows occupy both sides of the river. In July these fields are chest-high with corn, but when the vegetation is young or after harvest, you might spot the head of a turkey craning over the stalks. The river cuts deeply through the soft, rich sediments it has deposited, creating steep banks. Animal tracks abound in the mud; look for otter slides and the unmistakable, five-fingered prints of raccoons.

The Sacketts Brook Bridge at Putney, Vermont, frames paddlers on the Connecticut River.
Photo by Elizabeth Farnsworth

Mile 166.5: Blanchard Brook snakes its way to the Connecticut River on the left bank, and just downstream the silty terraces of the **Connecticut River Car-Top Access** in Walpole come into view. Shaded by enormous silver maples, this site is an excellent example of the floodplain forest that once lined much of the Connecticut River in this region. These majestic trees are adapted to flooding and help stabilize the silty banks against erosion. Another 0.3 mile downstream, the New Hampshire Route 123 bridge connecting Walpole, New Hampshire, and Westminster Station, Vermont, passes overhead. Anglers will find good bass fishing opportunities here as in many areas surrounding floodplain forests.

Miles 165–163.5: Dunshee Island, a state Wildlife Management Area, appears in midstream. Another 1.5 miles downstream, around a bend, New Hampshire's **Boggy Meadows** lies on the left bank. On the opposite bank is the town of Westminster, where the state of "New Connecticut"—later renamed Vermont—was declared in 1777.

Mile 161: Spencer Island marks the beginning of a swooping, 5-mile-long pair of meanders, doing a pas de deux with the railroad line on the Vermont side. The first meander encloses the **Putney Great Meadows** on the right bank. Birders may want

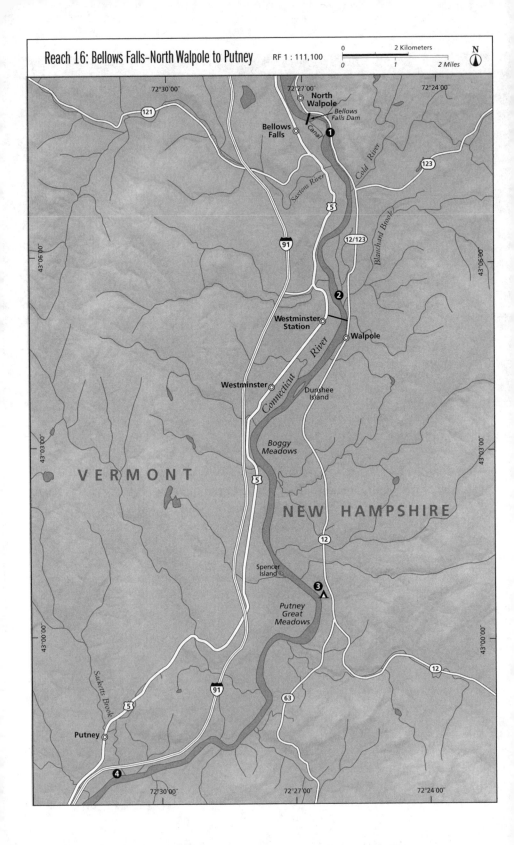

RF 1 : 111,100

0   2 Kilometers

0   1   2 Miles

N

72°30'00"

72°27'00"

72°24'00"

121

North
Walpole

Bellows
Falls Dam

Bellows
Falls

❶

Canal

Saxtons River

Cold River

123

5

91

12/123

Blanchard Brook

43°06'00"

43°06'00"

❷

Westminster
Station

Walpole

River

Westminster

Dunshee
Island

Connecticut

Boggy
Meadows

43°03'00"

43°03'00"

V E R M O N T

N E W   H A M P S H I R E

5

12

Spencer
Island

❸ ⛺

Putney
Great
Meadows

43°00'00"

43°00'00"

12

Sackets Brook

91

5

63

Putney

❹

72°30'00"

72°27'00"

72°24'00"

to take out their binoculars at this point, as great blue herons and other species frequent the area.

Mile 159: Windyhurst, a primitive campsite open to the public, lies on the river's left bank near the spot where red barns become visible at the river bend.

Miles 156–153.5: Although steep, rocky, forested hillsides still dominate the landscape and houses are few, distant sounds of Interstate 91 may accompany you on your last straightaway to the take-out point at **Putney Landing**. This is a popular stretch for motorboats, which congregate here on weekends. Just upstream of the landing is the confluence with **Sacketts Brook**, marked by a striking stone archway. This granite arch bridge was built in 1906 by a self-taught local engineer and mason, James Otis Follett, and has remained structurally sound during the past century even as it supports traffic loads Follett could never have imagined. The brook is fun to explore with a small boat (although tree trunks downed by beavers can bar the way). Putney Landing is about 0.5 mile from the Putney Inn (on U.S. Route 5), which maintains an informational kiosk on shops and sights in the area. Putney is home to the Green Mountain Head rowing regatta in the fall. Since the river here is wide and protected by a deep valley between the hills of Vermont and New Hampshire, it provides an ideal site for rowing. Putney is also famous for a summer music festival, and many local crafts studios are located here, including the Green Mountain Spinnery, a cooperative that raises sheep, prepares wool, spins yarn, and produces knitted garments.

Boating Facilities Table for Reach 16

Access Point, Directions	Boat Type	Fee	Parking	Picnic	Toilets	Camping	Rentals	Supplies
❶ North Walpole Portage Access NH 12, North Walpole, NH *Hairpin turn west off NH 12.*	Unimproved ramp for all boat types	N	Y	N	N	N	N	Nearby
❷ Connecticut River Car-Top Access NH 12, Walpole, NH *Turn west off NH 12 just north of NH 123 bridge.*	Unimproved ramp, car-top boats only	N	Y	Y	N	N	N	N
❸ Windyhurst Campsite Walpole, NH *River access only for nonmotorized boats. Primitive camping. Limit 1-night stay; no fires. Do not disturb farming operations. Call power company for more information: (802) 291-8014.*	Unimproved access for canoes and kayaks	N	Y	N	Y	Y limit 1-night stay; no fires	N	N
❹ Putney Landing, Town Landing Road, Putney, VT *Turn south off US 5 at the junction with I-91 and take Town Landing Road down hill behind Putney Inn.*	Improved ramp for car-top and small motorboats	N	Y	N	N	N	N	Nearby

Invaders of the Connecticut River

The Connecticut River is wondrously full of life: Dozens of species of fish, mussels, insects, and plants spend all or part of their lives beneath the water's surface. Non-native plants and animals, however, are threatening the habitat of native species. These invasive species lurk in the depths and shallows, causing concern for biologists who monitor the biodiversity of the river and for boaters who have to untangle unwanted vegetation from a paddle or a propeller. Shallow backwaters and bays can be thick with submerged aquatic plants in the height of summer, making travel difficult. Some of these plants are relatively new arrivals: introduced, exotic species that are spreading aggressively throughout the watershed.

One such invader is Eurasian water-milfoil. First introduced into the United States from Europe and Asia in the 1940s, the species has spread to forty-five states and inhabits parts of the Connecticut River from central Vermont and New Hampshire to

Eurasian milfoil is an invasive species that chokes out native river plants. Photo by Holly Crosson, courtesy of New England Wildflower Society

southern Connecticut. It was first spotted on the upper Connecticut River at Hoyt's Landing in Spring-field, Vermont. It roots in the river bottom and quickly sends highly branched stems upward, clogging waterways. Each stem bears dense whorls of feathery leaves, and red-dish flower stalks often poke above the water's surface. Broken frag-ments of stems float long distances and can give rise to new plants; thus, it readily colonizes new areas. Tolerant of cold temperatures, it begins its spring growth earlier than other aquatic plants and its dense canopy shades out native plant species. This competition leads to reduced diversity of the native

aquatic plant community, which in turn supports fewer species of invertebrates—the main source of food for young fish. Larger fish find it hard to locate prey in thick stands of Eurasian milfoil. It is also less nutritious for waterfowl than the other aquatic species it replaces. When milfoil dies back in the fall, its breakdown by bacteria con-sumes oxygen, and water quality deteriorates. Dense growth of Eurasian water-milfoil impedes boating and swimming, and decaying mats can foul beaches.

Researchers throughout North America are working hard to identify native fish and insects that eat Eurasian water-milfoil and can help control infestations. But no control agent can work effectively unless the transport of the plant is stopped.

Humans provide milfoil with its main means of transport from place to place. Plant pieces cling to motors, paddles, and trailer wheels and accompany unsuspecting boaters from one water body to another. To prevent the spread of this and other invasive plants, it is extremely important to clean vegetation from all parts of your boat when you exit the water. This simple act is smart boat hygiene as well as critical for stopping invasions and maintaining a healthy river ecosystem.

Reach 17 Putney to Vernon Dam

Miles from mouth: 153.5–138.5 (15-mile span). **Camping:** *Mile 142:* Wantastiquet Primitive
Navigable by: Kayaks, canoes, and motorboats. Campsite, Brattleboro, Vermont.
Difficulty: Quick water, flat water. **USGS maps:** Brattleboro 15.
Portage: *Mile 138.5:* Vernon Dam (0.5 mile).

The Reach

This reach transports you from the southernmost foothills of the Green Mountains in Vermont to rugged Wantastiquet Mountain near the New Hampshire–Vermont–Massachusetts border. The dark conifer forests of the north and high elevations give way completely to maples, sycamores, oaks, and ashes—tree species with a more southerly affinity. The Retreat Meadows wetlands at the mouth of the West River are fascinating to explore; bring your favorite birding guide. Houses will be more frequent along this route, interspersed with some large buildings, railroad lines, and the skyline of Brattleboro, Vermont, with its dense jumble of brick buildings dating to the Industrial Revolution. The Vermont Yankee Nuclear Power Plant occupies the Vermont shore at the end of this route. As the river backs up behind Vernon Dam, it enters a maze of berms, islands, and stillwater wetlands full of water lilies. *Caution:* Keep to the main channel (right bank) of the river between Brattleboro and Hinsdale, New Hampshire, to avoid beaching your boat in the shallows and backwaters. Take out at the boat ramp on Prospect Street in Hinsdale or at the Vernon Dam portage.

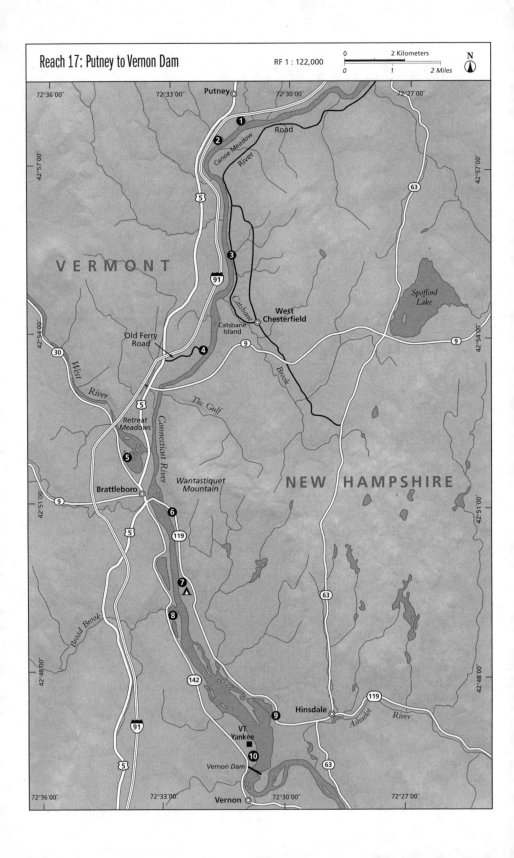

RF 1 : 122,000

0   2 Kilometers

0   1   2 Miles

N

72°36'00"   72°33'00"   **Putney**   72°30'00"   72°27'00"

①

②

Canoe Meadow   Road

River

42°57'00"

63

5

42°54'00"

③

91

Catsbane

West
Chesterfield

42°54'00"

V E R M O N T

*Catsbane
Island*

Old Ferry
Road

④

9

*Spofford
Lake*

30

9

West

River

5

The Gulf

Brook

*Retreat
Meadows*

Connecticut River

⑤

N E W   H A M P S H I R E

*Wantastiquet
Mountain*

Brattleboro

42°51'00"

⑥

9

119

5

⑦
△

63

⑧

Broad Brook

42°48'00"

142

119

Hinsdale

⑨   *Ashuelot*   *River*

91

VT
Yankee
■

5

⑩

63

Vernon Dam

Vernon

72°36'00"   72°33'00"   72°30'00"   72°27'00"

Boating Facilities Table for Reach 17

Access Point, Directions	Boat Type	Fee	Parking	Picnic	Toilets	Camping	Rentals	Supplies
❶ Putney Landing Town Landing Road, Putney, VT *Turn south off US 5 at junction with I-91;* *follow Putney Landing Road down hill behind* *Putney Inn.*	Improved ramp for car-top and small motorboats	N	Y	N	N	N	N	Nearby
❷ Dummerston Landing Dummerston, VT *Turn east onto small lane south of Putney Inn.* *As road splits, right fork goes to Dummerston* *Landing while left fork goes to Putney Landing.*	Improved ramp for car-top and small motorboats	N	Y	N	N	N	N	N
❸ Chesterfield River Road Boat Access River Road, Chesterfield, NH *Turn west off River Road, 0.8 mile south of* *junction with Stoneleigh Heights Road.*	Improved ramp for all boat types	N	Y	N	N	N	N	N
❹ Old Ferry Road Boat Access Old Ferry Road, Brattleboro, VT *Turn east off US 5 where it crosses I-91 in* *northern Brattleboro. Proceed past industrial* *parks and take hard right just after passing* *under train trestle. Access point is at end* *of road.*	Improved ramp for all boat types	N	Y	N	N	N	N	N
❺ Retreat Meadows Access VT Route 30, Brattleboro, VT *Opposite Retreat Farm on VT 30 in* *Brattleboro. Limited parking along road.*	Improved ramp for car-top boats	N	Y	N	N	N	N	N
❻ Hinsdale Access NH 119, Hinsdale, NH *Turn west into small gravel parking area off* *NH 119 just south of Brattleboro–Hinsdale* *Bridge in Hinsdale.*	Unimproved access, car-top boats only	N	Y	N	N	N	N	N
❼ Wantastiquet Campsite Brattleboro, VT *River access only for nonmotorized boats.* *Primitive camping. Limit 1-night stay; no fires.* *Call power company at (802) 291-8014 for* *more information.*	Unimproved access for canoes and kayaks	N	Y	N	Y	Y	N	N
❽ Broad Brook Access VT 142, Brattleboro, VT *On VT 142 inside arch of railroad bridge.*	Unimproved access, car-top boats only	N	Y	N	N	N	N	N

Boating Facilities Table for Reach 17 continued

Access Point, Directions	Boat Type	Fee	Parking	Picnic	Toilets	Camping	Rentals	Supplies
❾ Prospect Street Boat Launch Prospect Street, Hinsdale, NH *Turn sharply west onto Prospect Street from NH 119 in Hinsdale. Bear right into gravel parking area. Note: Access to river requires passing under low-lying railroad trestle.*	Unimproved access, car-top and small motorboats only	N	Y	N	N	N	N	N
❿ Vernon Dam Portage Trail Vernon, VT *Take out below Vermont Yankee Plant on right bank of river, following signs for trail. Cable across path prevents cars from entering trail. Portage ends at Governor Hunt Recreation Area downstream of dam.*	Improved ramp for car-top boats	N	N	N	N	N	N	N

Miles and Directions

Mile 153.5: Put in at **Putney Landing**, a small ramp on the river's right bank near the Putney Inn. The inn provides information on the shops and facilities in the lovely town of Putney, Vermont. The fertile, green fields of **Canoe Meadow** lie on the New Hampshire shore just opposite this access point. Five hundred yards downstream of Putney Landing, on the right bank, is **Dummerston Landing**, a small access point maintained by Vermont Fish and Game.

Mile 150: After rounding Canoe Meadows, the river enters a straight, southerly course. Another 2 miles south, you will find the **Chesterfield River Road Boat Access** on the left bank.

Mile 148.5: **Catsbane Brook** enters as the river makes a bend to the right; **Catsbane Island** is another 0.5 mile downstream of the confluence. Despite the presence of many houses on this stretch, gnawed tree trunks and an abundance of mussel shells along the shore are evidence that wildlife, including beavers, mink, and raccoons, abounds here.

Miles 147–146: The **Old Ferry Road Boat Access** lies on the right bank as the river makes another right turn. Another mile south, the Vermont Route 9 bridge will cross the river at the confluence with **The Gulf**, a stream flowing in from New Hampshire.

Mile 144.5: The **West River** joins the Connecticut River here on the right bank, and it is well worth it to explore the area. This confluence forms a wide bay surrounded by the **Retreat Meadows** wetlands. This area is a major stopover point for migratory birds, which pause here in early spring before heading farther north. Bald

You never know what biodiversity lurks in the river. The Loch Ness Monster has taken up residence at the West River confluence. Photo by Elizabeth Farnsworth

eagles and ospreys frequent the area. Small boats can pass quite a way up the West River, depending on the water flow, and anglers should drop a line in this section. Let the *Belle of Brattleboro,* a beautifully restored motor launch, take you on a leisurely cruise around the waters of the Connecticut River; it leaves from a marina 150 yards upstream of the confluence of the West and Connecticut Rivers. Small boats can also proceed to the southwest shore of the West River embayment and take out at the **Retreat Meadows Access** ramp on Vermont Route 30.

Mile 144: Majestic, 1,300-foot **Wantastiquet Mountain** looms over the river on the New Hampshire side, while the buildings of Brattleboro, Vermont, claim the right bank south of the West River. Founded as a military outpost in 1724, Brattleboro is now a charming town filled with shops and restaurants, and is a Connecticut River Byway Community. Rudyard Kipling was inspired to build a home, Naulakha, and write his *Jungle Books* here in the early 1890s. The ornate brick facades lining Brattleboro's streets hark back to the Industrial Revolution, when waterpower from Whetstone Brook and the West and Connecticut Rivers fueled its factories. The first Saturday in June, Brattleboro hosts the annual "Strolling of the Heifers," a lighthearted and educational celebration of Vermont's dairy industry.

Mile 143.5: The New Hampshire Route 119 bridge passes overhead, spanning a small island in midstream. This island was once much larger, the former home of a very popular fairground. Immediately downstream of the bridge, Norm's Marina is visible on the left bank. A muddy beach in the adjacent cove serves as an informal access point, known as **Hinsdale Access**, for small boats; ice fishermen congregate here in large numbers during the winter. The slow waters behind the Vernon Dam provide excellent habitat for warm-water fish such as walleye, bass, and perch. Dragonflies and damselflies, good sources of food for fish, are also abundant here. Dozens of them may dart acrobatically around your boat.

Miles 143–142: A railroad bridge passes over the river, and another mile downstream on the left bank, the primitive **Wantastiquet Campsite** accommodates small groups of canoeists and kayakers.

Mile 142: From the confluence with **Broad Brook** on the right bank to the end of the reach, it's advisable to stay in the main channel of the river, which skirts the right bank. Broad Brook looks less like a brook than a flow as it enters the main river under a railroad arch bridge, where there is a car-top launch known as the **Broad Brook Access**.

Miles 141–139.5: A confusing welter of wetlands and shoals, locally known as the Hinsdale setbacks, lie on the river's New Hampshire shore. While these are fun to explore, thick water lilies and shallow mud can make boating a challenge. About 4 miles south of the railroad bridge and just downstream of two islands on the left bank, you will see a railroad trestle on the left bank. This bridge marks the entrance to the **Prospect Street Boat Launch** in Hinsdale. *Caution:* Clearance under this bridge can be very low, depending on water level.

Mile 138.5: The smokestack, reactor building, and cooling towers of **Vermont Yankee Nuclear Power Plant** lie on the right bank as you near the **Vernon Dam**. The dam's fish ladder allows migrating fish to reach their spawning waters. Just below the plant, a sign will direct you to a 0.5-mile portage trail around the dam.

Floods

Great floods mark the lives of people who live on the river: Lives and landscapes are turned upside down, and the memories of grandparents and great-grandparents are mined for stories of these events. The floods of 1927 and 1936 are the most memorable on the Connecticut River.

On the evening of November 2, 1927, the remnants of a severe hurricane struck northwestern New England. It began to rain on ground already saturated by a wet autumn and continued to rain heavily for the next two days. By the morning of November 4, the Connecticut River had risen 30 feet at Hanover, New Hampshire; downstream, the streets of Claremont, New Hampshire, were 20 feet underwater, and Brattleboro, Vermont, was witnessing the worst natural disaster in its history.

Eight and a half years later, another calamity struck. After a snowy winter, starting on March 12, 1936, it began to rain heavily, pouring down rain for the next nine days, melting snows and breaking the river's ice into huge chunks that piled up behind bridges, tearing out roads and sending floodwaters into river towns all along the river. Many of the covered bridges of Vermont and New Hampshire were swept away. These two historic floods set in motion major dam and dike construction for the next fifteen years; a number of large dams were built on the main stem and major tributaries of the river during this period.

As if to remind residents that the river will flood regardless of how many dikes and dams are built, the river flooded once again in October 2005, another memorable event that sent boats and docks, as well as a huge fleet of pumpkins, downstream, tumbling over dams from Vermont to Connecticut. These so-called pumpkin floods occur during hurricane season. Tropical storms, with their quirky rainfall patterns, will dump 15 inches of rain in some spots and only a few inches in others, sending torrents of warm, muddy water that nourish floodplains but destroy buildings, roads, and bridges. Spring floods, on the other hand, that result from rapid snowmelt and ice jams can be particularly destructive because of their sudden discharges of cold water and ice.

Boaters have been killed in Connecticut River floods, chiefly in late summer and early fall. The river reveals its power on its own time schedule, not waiting until we are prepared. In a phrase, respect the river.

Massachusetts

The Connecticut River from the top of Mount Sugarloaf looks much as it did in colonial times.
Photo by John S. Burk

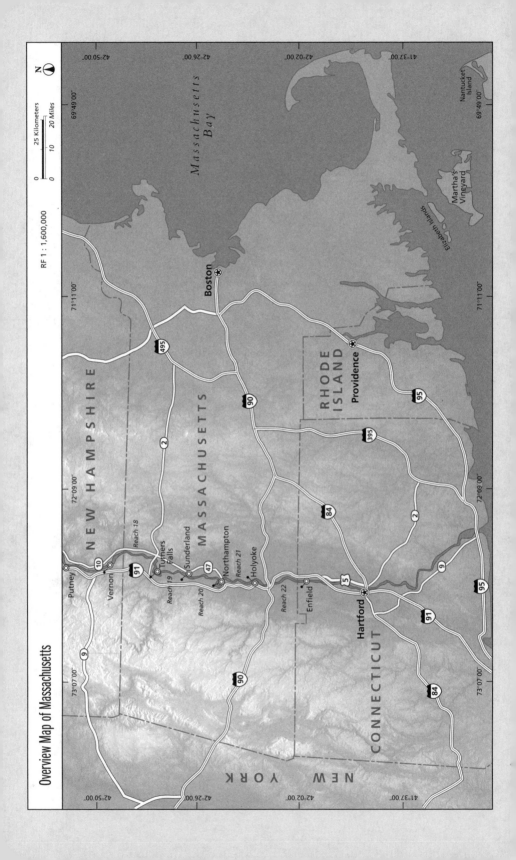

Reach 18 Vernon Dam to Turners Falls Dam

Miles from mouth: 139–117 (22-mile span).
Navigable by: Kayaks, canoes, small powerboats.
Difficulty: Flat water to Class I.
Flow information: http://water.usgs.gov/water watch or www.h2oline.com; (800) 452-1737.
Portage: *Mile 117:* Turners Falls, 2 miles; portage service: (413) 659-3761.
Fishing regulations: Limit of two shad per day in New Hampshire; limit of six shad per day in Massachusetts; no fishing within 150 feet of the base of the Vernon Dam.

Camping: *Mile 138:* Stebbins Island, Hinsdale, New Hampshire; river access only. *Mile 128:* Munn's Ferry, Northfield, Massachusetts; river access only. *Mile 118:* Barton Cove, Turners Falls, Massachusetts.
USGS maps: Brattleboro 15, Keene 15, Northfield 7.5, Millers Falls 7.5, Greenfield 7.5.

The Reach

This reach begins near Vernon Dam in Vermont, just 5.5 miles north of the Massachusetts border, and ends at Turners Falls Dam in Massachusetts. This extraordinary reach not only crosses a tristate border but also passes through unique geology and famous Native American and historical sites. On your way you will leave the Upper Valley of New Hampshire and Vermont and enter the Pioneer Valley of Massachusetts. The river's path follows the French King Gorge, straight along the great geological fault that witnessed the separation of the American and African continents more than 200 million years ago, then into a large cove with an abundance of bird life, including an eagle nest, and one of the most historic spots on the river at Turners Falls where migrating fish gather each spring.

The upper half of the reach, generally over quick water with some shallow spots, includes a campsite and the scenic Riverview Picnic and Recreation Area at the Northfield pumped-storage facility, which pumps river water up a mountain, then releases it to generate electricity. The power company provides not only hiking trails within walking distance of the river, but also a portage service between Barton Cove and access sites up to the Vernon Dam.

The lower end of this reach, the Barton Cove–Turners Falls area, is a paradise for geologists, archaeologists, bird-watchers, anglers, and historians. Anglers fish for trout and bass and plumb the depths for walleye; birders await the fall migration for sightings of exotic waterfowl, shorebirds, and gulls. There are dinosaur footprints, fish fossils, and peculiar round rock objects called armored mudballs. Because the area had rich farmland upstream, and great gatherings of shad and other anadromous fish at the base of Turners Falls, it served for centuries as a gathering place for Native Americans and a trading center for various tribes. After driving out the Native Americans, colonial Americans left their own historical remains, most of them now underwater along with the Indian sites.

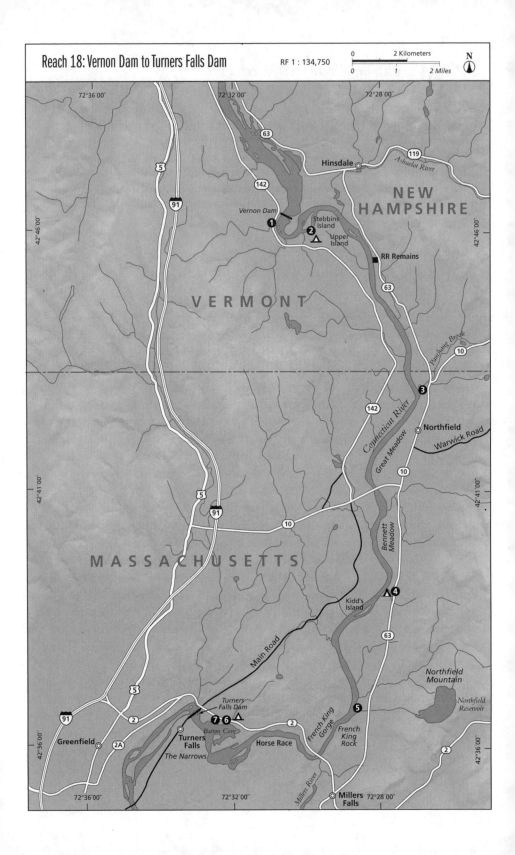

Reach 18: Vernon Dam to Turners Falls Dam

RF 1 : 134,750

0 — 2 Kilometers
0 — 1 — 2 Miles

N

NEW HAMPSHIRE

VERMONT

MASSACHUSETTS

Hinsdale
Ashuelot River

Vernon Dam
Stebbins Island
Upper Island
RR Remains
Paulieg Brook
Connecticut River
Northfield
Warwick Road
Great Meadow
Bennett Meadow
Kidd's Island
Northfield Mountain
Northfield Reservoir
Turners Falls Dam
Barton Cove
Turners Falls
The Narrows
Greenfield
Horse Race
French King Gorge
French King Rock
Millers River
Millers Falls

Main Road

Boating Facilities Table for Reach 18

Access Point, Directions	Boat Type	Fee	Parking	Picnic	Toilets	Camping	Rentals	Supplies
❶ Governor Hunt Recreation Area Governor Hunt Road, Vernon, VT *From VT 142, turn east onto Governor Hunt Road; turn right after 200 yards down steep paved road to parking area. Managed by power company.*	Unimproved ramp for all boat types	N	Y	Y	Y	N	N	N
❷ Stebbins Island Campsite *Located 0.8 mile downstream of Vernon Dam at northeast bend in the river toward Vermont side.*	River access only	N	N	N	N	Y	N	N
❸ Pauchaug Brook Launch MA 63, Northfield, MA *From MA 63, turn west at Pauchaug Brook sign and drive 0.75 mile to site. Managed by Massachusetts Fish and Wildlife.*	Unimproved ramp for all boat types	N	Y	Y	Y	N	N	N
❹ Munn's Ferry Campsite Northfield, MA *On left bank as river bends southwest, 500 yards upstream from Kidd's Island. Open Memorial Day to Columbus Day. Reservations and advance payment required: (413) 863-9300.*	River access only	Y	N	N	N	Y	N	N
❺ Riverview Picnic and Recreation Area MA 63, Northfield, MA *Turn west off MA 63, across from Northfield Mountain Recreation Area. Managed by power company.*	Car-top only	N	Y	Y	Y	N	N	N
❻ Barton Cove Campground MA 2, Gill, MA *Found 1.7 miles east of Turners Falls on south side of MA 2. Boaters should check with campground office for best launch location. Open Memorial Day to Labor Day. Reservations recommended: (413) 863-9300. Managed by power company.*	Car-top only	Y	Y	Y	Y	Y	Y	Nearby
❼ State Boat Ramp at Barton Cove MA 2, Gill, MA *Located 1.5 miles east of Turners Falls on south side of MA 2. Managed by Commonwealth of Massachusetts.*	Improved ramp for all boat types	N	Y	N	Y	N	N	Nearby

In 1676 Turners Falls was the site of one of the more infamous events in the century-long war between Native Americans and English settlers. The Indians had gathered that May for the fish run at the 40-foot-high falls at Peskeompscut, the Abenaki name for Turners Falls. Earlier that spring, a small group of Indians had raided the English settlement of Hatfield, Massachusetts, for cattle. In revenge, 150 English surprised and killed a large number of Indians, including women and children. In a panicky retreat, forty of the settlers were killed.

The long portage at the end of this reach is negotiated by car or by the portage service provided by the power company (call 413–659–3761) that takes boaters to the Montague, Massachusetts, access; there is also an access on the Deerfield River. Motorboats must go to Sunderland, Massachusetts.

Miles and Directions

Mile 139: Put in below **Vernon Dam** at the **Governor Hunt Recreation Area** in Vernon, Vermont, at a shady, sandy picnic area. *Caution:* Beware of the turbulence from the dam, especially at high water. Avoid the middle of the river and do not try to cross from the launch site to the left bank. To miss the whitewater, keep hard right after you put in and head south, keeping a small island to your left. *Caution:* During high water, strainers may block this channel. Inexperienced paddlers should avoid putting in at high water.

Mile 138: Stebbins Island, with its campsite managed by the power company, appears 0.8 mile downstream from the Vernon Dam as the river bends sharply northeast. *Caution:* There is a bald eagle nest on the island. Do not disturb the nesting birds.

Mile 137: Just north of **Upper Island**, the **Ashuelot River** enters from New Hampshire, a fine tributary to explore in a kayak or canoe. A railroad bridge crosses the Ashuelot at its confluence with the Connecticut.

Mile 136: A **dismantled railroad bridge** is visible south of Upper Island, marked by the remaining big pylons in the river. Watch for some turbulence around the pylons; stay to the middle of the river.

Mile 133.5: At 3.5 miles south of the Ashuelot confluence, your boat will cross into Massachusetts, passing over the "Mud Turtle" monument, marking the tristate borders among Vermont, New Hampshire, and Massachusetts. Built in 1897, it has been underwater since the 1915 construction of the Turners Falls Dam.

Mile 132.5: Pauchaug Brook State Ramp and Wildlife Area is the northernmost access in Massachusetts. This area can be muddy when the river has recently been in flood, but it's an easy-to-use entry and exit point.

French King Bridge spans the beautiful French King Gorge. Photo by Wendy Sinton

Miles 132.3–131.8: Just downstream from Pauchaug Brook is the Schell Bridge, now in disrepair, although local citizens are trying to preserve it as a historic site. Another 0.5 mile downstream you will pass under the active NECR Railroad Bridge.

Miles 131–130: The rich agricultural soil of **Great Meadow** appears on the left bank as you paddle past the center of Northfield, Massachusetts, hidden from sight above the left bank. Bennett Meadow Bridge (Massachusetts Route 10) crosses the river here, and **Bennett Meadow Wildlife Management Area** is on the right bank just below this bridge. You can see the boathouse for the Northfield Mount Hermon School's perennially ranked crew team adjacent to Bennett Meadow.

Mile 128: After some pleasant quick water, you will approach **Munn's Ferry** on the left bank, a pretty camping and picnicking site operated by the power company, accessible only by boat. The steep west-facing slopes provide good botanizing.

Mile 127.5: Kidd's Island appears shortly downstream from the campsite; note the steep, eroded sand banks on the river's left side, which provide nest holes for bank and cliff swallows. *Note:* The Franklin County Boat Club has exclusive use of this island.

Mile 124.5: You have now arrived at the **Riverview Picnic and Recreation Area** at **Northfield Mountain** on the left bank, which has a dock to accommodate the *Quinnetukut II* riverboat, offering river cruises for the general public (phone 800–859–2960). The Northfield Mountain pumped-storage generating plant is sheltered in the mountain behind this site. The main dock area must be kept clear for the *Quinnetukut II*, but boaters and paddlers may use the dock for brief stops to load and unload. The dock is inaccessible directly by car and can only be reached on foot from a parking area 100 yards away. Access is difficult, and the dock is unavailable from mid-April to mid-June. The power company stretches a fish net across the intake of Northfield Mountain during this time to prevent salmon smolt, which are heading downriver, from getting caught in the pumped-storage station. *Caution:* Avoid the discharge area marked by orange floats on the left bank, which can release enough water to swamp a small boat.

Mile 123: Riverview Picnic Area lies at the head of the **French King Gorge**. *Caution:* **French King Rock**, a boulder that lies north–south at the north end of the gorge, creates turbulence; run the river close to the bank on either side of the rock. French King Rock was named by a French raiding party that came down from Quebec in the early eighteenth century. When they saw the enormous rock in the middle of what was then whitewater, they claimed the territory in the name of the king of France, Louis XV. On the right bank, opposite French King Rock, is The Nature Conservancy's 169-acre Stacy Mountain Preserve (accessible off Massachusetts Route 2), with many rare and threatened species, vernal pools, and ravens.

Mile 122.5: You will shortly reach the French King Bridge, which carries MA 2 across the river at the south end of the French King Gorge; it is a particularly graceful three-span arch built in 1932, the recipient of many engineering and historic preservation awards. You are now at the 250-million-year-old geological fault that created the original Connecticut River; the rock wall on the right bank is tens of millions of years younger than the ancient bedrock on the left wall.

Mile 122.5: Right below the bridge, the **Millers River** comes in on the left bank. It doesn't look large, but it carries a lot of water. *Caution:* Beware of the sometimes treacherous currents and eddies here. The mouth of the Millers is the site of historic Cabot Camp, with its sawmill and dam dating back to 1799.

Mile 122.2: The remains of an 1806 dam, two locks, and the foundations of a hotel can be found 200 yards downstream from the bridge; the hotel was on the right bank and the locks on the left. To find the hotel that housed dam and lock workers, land at the first small sandy area on the right bank below the bridge and take the trail into the woods; the foundations are 100 yards in and to the right. The remains of a lock are opposite the hotel on the left bank; if water levels are low enough, you can run your boat through the lock between the lock's rock wall and the river's left bank. *Caution:* This area acts as a repository for river debris, so stay to the right bank during high water to avoid being swept into the strainers that form on the left bank.

Connecticut River Canals

Canals and dams were at the heart of the Transportation and Industrial Revolutions at the turn of the nineteenth century, and the Connecticut River was America's first major river on which transportation improvements were built. In this reach you pass by the remains of one of the smaller, older locks at the end of French King Gorge and finish at the Turners Falls Dam and canal system, originally built in 1798 and the second oldest on the river. Bellows Falls, 50 miles upstream, was the site of America's first effort at an industrial canal in 1791, but it was washed out and only completed in 1802. It remains possibly the oldest industrial canal still in use in America. Other small canals in the Upper Valley were completed by 1812 at Sumner Falls, Cornish–Windsor, and Wilder–Lebanon.

Pride of place for America's first successful canal, however, goes to the South Hadley Canal, completed in 1794 as a route around South Hadley Falls where the city of Holyoke, Massachusetts, was built half a century later. What a wondrous canal it was, without locks, but with two large waterwheels that provided the power to pull a strange-looking cart, hauling a ten-ton flatboat with its thirty-ton cargo up a 275-foot stone ramp past the falls.

Some early canals, like that in South Hadley, were a great economic success, not only providing handsome profits but creating regional business opportunities as well. That success spawned the "Canal Craze" of the 1820s, especially after the 1825 opening of the Erie Canal. In the 1830s venture capital funded the construction of the Connecticut River's longest and largest system from New Haven, Connecticut, to Northampton, Massachusetts, which officially opened in 1835 to accommodate 75-foot barges and pleasure boats for up to 250 people, who would pay the $3.75 fare, including meals, for the thirty-six-hour ride. Boats passed through sixty locks on their 80-mile journey. Twelve years after it opened, the New Haven & Northampton Canal Company declared bankruptcy, the victim of grandiose planning and especially of railroads, which quickly obviated the need for canal transportation.

The most beautiful remains of the Connecticut River canal systems can be found at Windsor Locks (Reach 23). The canal, opened in 1829, went out of business in the 1840s, leaving paddlers a small piece of history to explore.

Mile 122: The river narrows into what is called the **Horse Race**, although the fast water is by no means dangerous. As the river turns due west, you will be passing over one of its deepest parts, with sheer walls descending more than 100 feet. Exploring these rocks, divers have discovered sponges and other previously unrecorded aquatic life. The Horse Race leads to a big wide pool with mudflats and wetlands famous for their concentrations of migrating shorebirds and waterfowl.

Mile 119.5: The river turns north through **The Narrows** to **Barton Cove**. The island on the east side, immediately after The Narrows, hosts perhaps the most famous pair of nesting bald eagles in Massachusetts: They have a Web cam trained on them throughout the nesting season. *Caution:* Please respect the barriers around the nest and stay at least 100 yards from the island. Barton Cove is also one of New England's premier birding spots for fall, winter, and spring waterfowl. In the nineteenth century logging companies built a barrier to retain logs upstream, and you can see evidence of it on the western shore of The Narrows where a large metal hoop was driven into the rock. *Caution:* It's easy to run aground in the shallows between the island and the peninsula on the right bank.

Mile 118: Once in Barton Cove, you will find the **Barton Cove Campground** and the state boat ramp at Barton Cove. *Caution:* You must take out at one of these two access points; do *not* approach the barrier of orange buoys that crosses the river. The **Turners Falls Dam** is just downstream of the barrier. On busy summer days paddlers are advised to use the state boat ramp. The campground office and kayak/canoe rental is on the north shore of the cove. Barton Cove Campground is on the peninsula on the southeast border of the cove. After getting ashore, through-paddlers may contact the power company's portage service.

Mile 117: Turners Falls Dam is the end of this reach. "Turners," as the locals call the area, was a central location year-round for Abenaki and a huge gathering place for all local Indians during the shad and salmon run. The original 1796 dam at Turners Falls was one of the first dams on the main stem of the Connecticut River and one of America's first large-scale dams. Successive dams in 1915 and 1970 have put the original landscape of wetlands and plowed fields some 30 feet underwater.

Reach 19 Turners Falls Dam to Sunderland

Miles from mouth: 117–106 (11-mile span).
Navigable by: Kayaks, canoes, small powerboats.
Difficulty: Flat water.
Flow information: http://water.usgs.gov/water watch (Montague gauge); (413) 659-3761.
Portages: None.

Boating regulations: *Between Turners Falls and Hatfield Boat Ramp:* 15 miles per hour maximum speed; Jet Skis prohibited.
Camping: No established sites.
USGS maps: Greenfield 7.5, Mt. Toby 7.5.

The Reach

Firmly in Massachusetts, you are now entering the heart of the Pioneer Valley, with its rich farmlands, former home to large Native American populations. The lower part of the Pioneer Valley was settled by English colonists only fifteen years after they landed in Boston, and the stretch from Deerfield north to Northfield formed a floating boundary between colonists and Native Americans until the mid–eighteenth century. Between the Deerfield and Connecticut Rivers lies Old Deerfield, site of one of New England's most famous battles between colonial settlers and Native Americans —the 1704 Deerfield Raid. Take some time to visit Turners Falls, an interesting old mill village within the town of Montague that houses the Great Falls Discovery Center with exhibits on Connecticut River ecosystems. It's situated at the Turners Falls end of the Turners Falls Dam Bridge, and is part of the Silvio O. Conte National Fish and Wildlife Refuge. Just to the west, Greenfield is an excellent town in which to find plenty of supplies and good food.

The Massachusetts Department of Conservation and Recreation is actively working with the Conte Refuge, local towns, land trusts, and other nonprofits to preserve river habitat and develop recreational resources, such as campsites, since no public sites exist in the Massachusetts river reaches. The state has created a Connecticut River Greenway State Park out of the pieces of land and islands it owns on the river. Within that park is the Connecticut River Water Trail from Turners Falls to the Hatfield Access Site, where state and local land trusts are working to conserve farmland and shoreline for recreational use, yet keep it in private hands. Almost all the shoreline on the Water Trail is privately owned. Please respect the rights of landowners so that future boaters can benefit from the amenities of the Water Trail. *Caution:* Special boating regulations apply here, with a 15-mile-per-hour speed limit and no Jet Skis.

Most of this reach is quiet, bordered by farm fields and low-lying woodlands. The shallow, quick water is unsuitable for all but the smallest motorboats. Enjoy the birdwatching, do some fishing, and check out the floodplain forests of cottonwoods, willows, silver maples, box elders, pin oaks, and sycamores, all adapted to occasional, sometimes violent flooding. Look for evidence of haystacks and cornstalks in the branches to gauge the height of the last flood, and see if you can find dents and slash scars on tree trunks from the ice floes that smash them each spring. These forests are

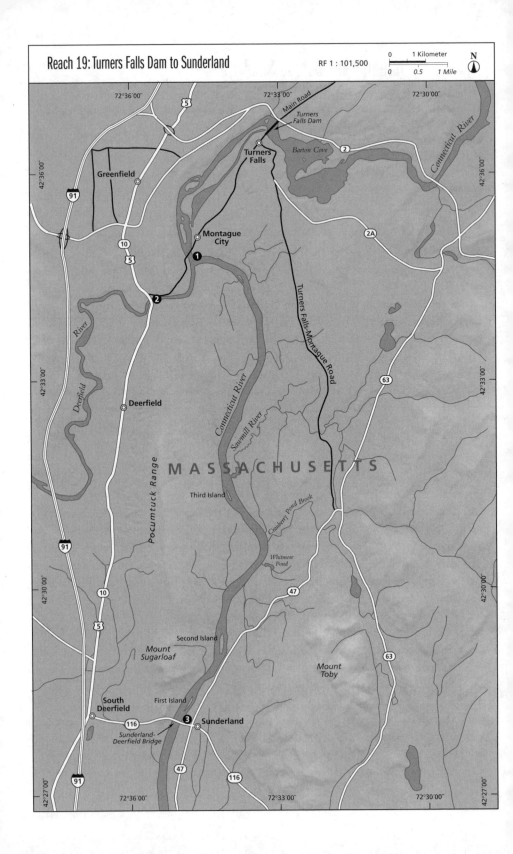

Reach 19: Turners Falls Dam to Sunderland

RF 1 : 101,500

0   1 Kilometer

0   0.5   1 Mile

N

vital habitat for reptiles, frogs, salamanders, insects, and bird life, especially water-loving songbirds.

Caution: You cannot put in directly below Turners Falls Dam; the river is exceedingly dangerous, and water releases can occur when you least expect them. Motorboats must access this reach from Sunderland.

Miles and Directions

Mile 117: Kayaks and canoes can access the river either at Montague City or on the **Deerfield River**; both access points are primitive, with steep slopes down to the water. The Deerfield River Access, while easier to find, is on a part of the river with traffic and gravel quarry noise in the background. *Caution:* The Deerfield River enters the Connecticut River at the Montague Access, and you can encounter dangerous crosscurrents, especially during high water. Stay near the left bank. The 70-mile-long Deerfield River has a 665-square-mile watershed with good fly-fishing and whitewater opportunities. The Deerfield Watershed Association serves as the river's watchdog.

Miles 115.5–112.5: The river turns due south after Montague City, and 3 miles downstream the **Sawmill River** enters from the left bank. This is good bald eagle

Boating Facilities Table for Reach 19

Access Point, Directions	Boat Type	Fee	Parking	Picnic	Toilets	Camping	Rentals	Supplies
❶ Poplar Street Access Poplar Street, Montague, MA *Cross Turners Falls Bridge from MA 2; go straight on Avenue A, which becomes Montague City Road; turn left onto Greenfield Road, and take first right onto Poplar Street; park at end of street and put in near railroad bridge. Be sure to stay on power company property—trail to river on right is private property, and access is not allowed.*	Unimproved ramp, car-top boats only	N	Y	N	N	N	N	N
❷ Deerfield River Access US 5, Deerfield, MA *On south side of the US 5 bridge over Deerfield River; park on east side of road and put in directly under the US 5 bridge.*	Unimproved ramp, car-top boats only	N	Y	N	N	N	N	N
❸ Sunderland Ramp School Street, Sunderland, MA *Turn north off MA 116 onto North Main Street (MA 47); immediately turn left onto School Street. Go to end, unload boat, and carry down marked path to river. Park on School Street at town library parking lot.*	Unimproved ramp, car-top and small motorboats only	N	Nearby	N	N	N	N	N

territory, and if you are on the river toward the end of the shad run, you cannot help but see eagles feasting on fish carcasses. In addition to the Barton Cove eagle nest upriver, you may see a nest on the left bank that was discovered in winter 2006 and another on **Third Island**, which is the property of the U.S. Fish and Wildlife Service. *Caution:* You are not allowed to land on Third Island during eagle nesting season from early March to mid-July. At other times Third Island is for day use only; no camping is allowed.

Mile 110: At the next bend in the river on the left bank, just north of the Montague–Sunderland town line, you may hear the sound of a small waterfall on the left bank; this is the **Cranberry Pond Brook Falls**, but be aware that it's on private land. Just downstream, **Whitmore Pond** drains into the river from the left bank at a former ferry crossing. During low water, look for fish fossils in the rocks here.

Miles 108–106: As you approach **Second Island**, the quiet of the river will be broken by increasing sounds of traffic from the busy crossroads at the **Sunderland–Deerfield Bridge**. Both Second Island and **First Island**, just up from the bridge, are property of the Massachusetts Department of Fish and Wildlife; no camping is permitted on these islands. The takeout, which can accommodate small motorboats, is on the left bank (Sunderland side) of the Sunderland–Deerfield Bridge (Massachusetts Route 116). **Mount Sugarloaf** is Sunderland's most obvious landmark, easily recognized by the building on the mountaintop. Abenaki tradition has it that, after a giant beaver flooded the river valley, he was turned to stone, and Sugarloaf is his head. Clearly marked hiking trails will take you to the summit with its excellent view up and down the valley.

The 1704 Deerfield Raid

The facts of the 1704 Deerfield Raid seem simple enough: On February 29 allied troops, composed of 48 French and Quebecois soldiers and more than 200 Abenaki (Wôbanakiak), Mohawk (Kanienkehaka), and Huron (Wendat), attacked the small English settlement at Deerfield before dawn, capturing 112 men, women, and children and taking them on a 300-mile march to Canada in the dead of winter, killing several, ransoming and releasing most of rest, and allowing some 30 others to remain living with them. By the end, forty-one English were dead either in the raid or on the march, along with six of the allied forces.

The causes and results of the Deerfield Raid, however, are complicated, depending on who is telling the history.

The English: Deerfield was a frontier village on the edge of dangerous territory where English and Wôbanakiak had already clashed and part of the larger region contested by the French. Although two Deerfield settlers had been captured while working their fields in September 1703, the Deerfield settlers had let down their guard, so the attack came as a surprise, and the attackers met with little resistance. The raid made a huge impact on the next two generations of English settlers in the Connecticut River Valley, striking fear in the hearts of children and giving rise to an immensely popular memoir, *The Redeemed Captive,* by the Reverend John Williams. The raid became a lesson in the perfidious Indian and righteous Englishman for future generations.

The French: In 1701 the French and forty Native American groups from all over the Great Lakes and Northeast had concluded the Great Peace Treaty by which France tried to ally herself with all the neighboring Native American groups, especially the Iroquois, who tended to work closely with British interests. The French hoped to gain control of the fur trade while thwarting the English; the Native Americans had various goals, one of which was to unite against the English. The Great Peace set the stage for the 1704 Deerfield Raid, which, for the French, was part of a game to gain Native American allies and prevent British incursions throughout the region.

The Wôbanakiak: With the 1676 English raid on Turners Falls still in their memory (see Reach 18) and hoping to regain territory in their homeland, the Wôbanakiak had all the reasons they needed to participate in the raid. It was Wôbanakiak warriors who captured the Reverend John Williams, knowing he would bring the greatest ransom money.

The Kanienkehaka: Among the largest contingents, the Mohawk had several reasons to participate in the raid. They wanted to retrieve a church bell they thought the English had stolen; they hoped for plunder and ransom money; they had an abiding interest in expanding into the Connecticut River Valley; and, furthermore, the warriors hoped to bring prisoners back to their families to replace loved ones who had died or been killed in war.

The Wendat: While the twenty Huron warriors also hoped to take some captives and booty, their chief aim was to cement the strong alliances they already had with the Kanienkahaka and Wôbanakiak.

In its larger context the Deerfield Raid was just one of many battles in the 200-year struggle to dominate the Connecticut River Valley. For more information, go to the wonderfully rich Web site of the Pocumtuck Valley Memorial Association and Memorial Hall Museum at Deerfield (http://deerfield-ma.org).

Reach 20 Sunderland to Northampton

Miles from mouth: 106-92.5(13.5-mile span).
Navigable by: Kayaks, canoes, small powerboats. only above Hatfield Town Ramp at Cow Bridge Brook; all boats permitted downstream of that.
Difficulty: Flat water.
Portages: None.

Boating regulations: *Between Sunderland and Hatfield Town Ramp:* 15 miles per hour maximum speed; Jet Skis prohibited.
Camping: No established sites.
USGS maps: Mt. Toby 7.5, Mt. Holyoke 7.5, Easthampton 7.5.

The Reach

The first part of this reach is the last quiet stretch for the next 20 miles, and by the time you end at the busy communities of Northampton and Hadley, Massachusetts, you will have encountered all kinds of motorized craft from houseboats to Jet Skis and racing boats. Regardless of the traffic, you can expect to see plenty of birds and wildlife, including eagles, various species of hawks, waterfowl, raccoons in the evening, and, perhaps, an otter.

This reach runs through some of New England's most historic areas, which English colonists settled in the mid–seventeenth century on some of the nation's most productive farmland. Farms here have produced anything that markets have demanded. Once it was broom corn for brooms, then it was tobacco, and always there have been dairy cattle and produce from family farms.

On the right side of the river lies the city of Northampton, a regional cultural magnet that draws visitors from all over the Connecticut Valley for entertainment and dining. In the mid–eighteenth century Jonathan Edwards's church here was a central focus of the Great Awakening, a religious phenomenon that swept the colonies. Sojourner Truth lived here in the nineteenth century, and Calvin Coolidge was mayor in the twentieth. Motorboats end this reach on the left bank in Hadley, and paddlers on the right bank at the Elwell Recreation Area in Northampton, which has one of the nation's few rowing programs for people with disabilities.

If you stop to visit Northampton, you will likely find it filled with young people, since there are five colleges within a 10-mile radius—Mount Holyoke, Smith, Hampshire, and Amherst Colleges and the University of Massachusetts.

Miles and Directions

Mile 106: There is a put-in on the left bank at the **Sunderland–Deerfield Bridge** (Massachusetts Route 116). The river is a straight shot south for about 5 miles on a wide, often shallow river with high mud banks on both sides. About 3 miles downstream of the bridge, **Mohawk Brook** will enter from the left bank near the Sunderland–Hadley town line, and the outline of **Mount Warner** will appear in front of you. Since special boating regulations apply here and the river is often shallow, you will generally see very few other craft, even on a lovely summer weekend.

Canoeists are enjoying a hot and hazy summer day paddling the river. Photo by Wendy Sinton

Mile 101: At the end of the straight stretch, in low water, you cannot help but scrape bottom on the shallow section that leads into a hairpin turn to the right. In summer you will see three small, sparsely vegetated cobble islands that make good picnic spots, but are important sites for such endangered species as the cobblestone tiger beetle. *Caution:* Please tread carefully on all small islands; respect the habitat, and pick no plants. As you head west at the hairpin turn, you will find a long sandy shore on the right bank called **The Bashan**, a fine picnic and swimming spot owned by the Commonwealth of Massachusetts and maintained by the Department of Conservation and Recreation; there are no facilities here.

Mile 100: The **Hatfield Town Ramp (Cow Bridge Brook Ramp)** is located on the right bank as you head south from the hairpin bend. This is the end of the special boating regulations area. *Caution:* Heavy boat traffic! Expect racing boats, Jet Skis, and water-skiers from here to the end of the reach. **Cow Bridge Brook** is, in fact, a former oxbow that is currently good habitat for waterbirds. Opposite the access is a small beach owned by the Department of Conservation and Recreation, which offers fine swimming, but is typically crowded and has no facilities.

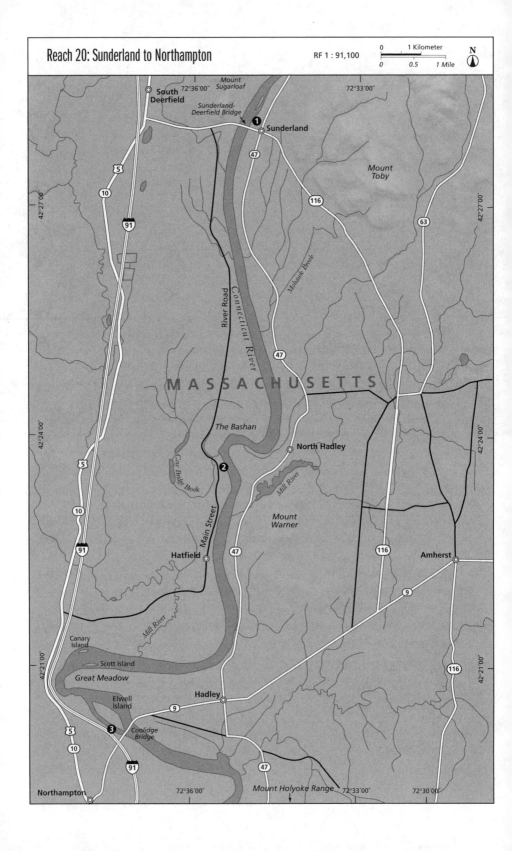

RF 1 : 91,100

0   1 Kilometer

0   0.5   1 Mile

N

South
Deerfield

Mount
Sugarloaf

72°36'00"

72°33'00"

Sunderland-
Deerfield Bridge

❶ Sunderland

47

Mount
Toby

5

10

116

63

91

42°27'00"

42°27'00"

River Road

Connecticut River

Mohawk Brook

47

M A S S A C H U S E T T S

The Bashan

North Hadley

42°24'00"

42°24'00"

Cow Bridge Brook

❷

Mill River

47

Mount
Warner

5

10

Main Street

116

Amherst

91

Hatfield

47

9

Mill River

Canary
Island

42°21'00"

42°21'00"

Scott Island

Great Meadow

Hadley

9

Elwell
Island

116

5

10

❸

Coolidge
Bridge

91

47

Northampton

72°36'00"

Mount Holyoke Range

72°33'00"

72°30'00"

Fishing is fine on the Northampton Oxbow. Photo by Wendy Sinton

Boating Facilities Table for Reach 20

Access Point, Directions	Boat Type	Fee	Parking	Picnic	Toilets	Camping	Rentals	Supplies
❶ Sunderland Ramp School Street, Sunderland, MA *Turn north off MA 116 onto North Main Street (MA 47); immediately turn left onto School Street. Go to end, unload boat, and carry down marked path to river. Park on School Street at town library parking lot.*	Unimproved ramp, car-top and small motorboats only	N	Nearby	N	N	N	N	N
❷ Cow Bridge Brook Ramp (Hatfield Town Ramp) Kellogg Hill Road, Hatfield, MA *At 1.5 miles north of center of Hatfield (Main Street), turn right at wastewater treatment plant onto unmarked dirt road (Kellogg Hill); parking lot and ramp are 500 yards from the turnoff.*	Unimproved ramp for all boat types	N	Y	N	Y (seasonal)	N	N	N
❸ Elwell Recreation Area Damon Road, Northampton, MA *On the northeast corner of Damon Road, exit 19 off I–91 and MA 9 in Northampton, adjacent to rail-trail parking; bear right down hill to dock parking. Accessible to disabled.*	Improved ramp for car-top boats	N	Y	Y	Y (seasonal)	N	N	N

Mount Holyoke and Mount Tom

Mount Tom and Mount Holyoke are the Pioneer Valley's signature landmarks, sacred to the Native Americans, a signpost in the history of American landscape painting, and a rallying cry for land preservation in the region. These are more like hills, really, than mountains, but their size belies their significance. Thomas Cole made them famous in the nineteenth century when he painted a landscape of the Northampton Oxbow from the summit of Mount Holyoke in 1836; the painting now holds a prominent place in the Metropolitan Museum of Art. Other painters followed, presenting an ideal arcadian picture of America at that period.

Both Mount Tom and Mount Holyoke became major tourist destinations in the nineteenth and early twentieth centuries, complete with mountain houses, mountain paths, fancy restaurants, and cog railways. Today thousands of locals and tourists hike up the mountains annually; college students have special "mountain days," and residents have recently enlisted the support of local, state, and federal agencies to preserve the mountainscapes from development.

The two mountains are also of considerable scientific interest. Created by major volcanic episodes more than 200 million years ago as Pangea broke apart, the Metacomet Range, which includes Mounts Tom and Holyoke, erupted into the valley, pouring lava and ash onto the valley floor. The cores of those eruptions remain as columns of very hard basalt that resist weathering and erosion. For millions of years geological pressures have warped the Mount Holyoke Range, at the northern end of the Meta-

The group Rocking the Boat built their own boats and rowed them down the river. Mount Tom appears behind them. Photo by Joaquin Cotten, courtesy of Rocking the Boat

comet Range, into an east-west orientation, an anomaly in North America where mountains generally run north-south. The river found the softest part of the Mount Holyoke Range and cut through it, leaving Mount Tom on the right bank and Mount Holyoke on the left. Because the topography and soils of the peaks differ from the rest of the Pioneer Valley landscape, they harbor rare and endangered species, such as copperheads.

Mile 99.5: As you begin the next wide, straight section of river, the **Mill River** will enter on the left bank from Lake Warner in Hadley. At this spot, a former ferry landing, you can see clearly the **Mount Holyoke Range** straight ahead (see the sidebar).

Mile 97: At the end of this stretch, the river heads west, passing Hadley's historic **Great Meadow** agricultural area along the left bank. In the 1660s the original English settlers divided the Great Meadow into long, narrow strips, which they allotted to each family in town, and the pattern remains to this day. This is one of the last surviving examples of the "open field system," once common in medieval Europe, but long since abandoned in the Western world. The combined efforts of Hadley citizens, the Kestrel Land Trust, and state and federal agencies may succeed in preserving the Great Meadow from development while allowing farming to continue.

Mile 94.5: Before the next bend in the river, you pass between **Canary Island** near the right bank and **Scott Island** near the left bank. Don't be surprised to find crowded boat parties in this section on weekends. The islands are actually extensions of private property on the shoreline; they have multiple owners and are not open to the public.

Mile 93: The river makes another hairpin turn to the east-southeast, where you immediately arrive at **Elwell Island**, close to the city of Northampton on the river's right bank; this sixty-acre island is one of the largest in the Connecticut River. It belongs to the City of Northampton, which allows swimming, walking, and fishing, but not camping. *Caution:* Canoes and kayaks should run down the right side of Elwell Island to miss motorboat traffic, but keep an eye out for shallows. Also stay clear of the University of Massachusetts rowing sculls and shells that are often on the river; their crew facilities are on the right bank, across from Elwell Island.

Mile 92.5: Canoes and kayaks can take out on the right bank at the **Elwell Recreation Area** in Northampton opposite the southern end of Elwell Island. The old railroad bridge that's now part of the **Norwottuck Rail Trail**, as well as the **Coolidge Memorial Bridge** (Massachusetts Route 9), cross the river here. Powerboats can take out at the Oxbow State Ramp about five miles downstream of the bridges.

Reach 21 Northampton to Holyoke Dam

Miles from mouth: 92.5–81.5 (11-mile span).
Navigable by: Kayaks, canoes, small powerboats.
Difficulty: Flat water.
Flow information: http://water.usgs.gov/water watch; (413) 536-9472.

Portage: *Mile 85.5:* Holyoke Dam, 1 mile: call Holyoke Gas and Electric for portage shuttle: (413) 536-9461.
Camping: No established sites.
USGS maps: Mt. Holyoke 7.5, Easthampton 7.5, Mt. Tom 7.5, Springfield North 7.5.

The Reach

This section of the river stretches from Northampton, Massachusetts, to the Holyoke Dam. With four boat marinas and a growing urban population, this reach has the busiest river traffic north of Essex, Connecticut. *Caution:* There have been several accidents in this reach because of the large number of craft and careless boat handling, especially when boaters are under the influence of alcohol.

The reach is also one of the river's most historically and culturally significant, containing both the Mount Tom and Mount Holyoke Ranges and the city of Holyoke, a touchstone in American industrial history. In the space of about 10 miles, you will pass the hills of Mounts Tom and Holyoke, bucolic fields along the river, a classic floodplain forest, and dinosaur tracks—all this next to a historic industrial city.

You can find plenty of natural areas along the first few miles of the reach. The Massachusetts Audubon Arcadia Wildlife Sanctuary and Headquarters is located in Easthampton at one of the river's most significant birding spots, and you can enjoy the sight of eagles, ospreys, and migrating songbirds of all sorts, along with beavers, otters, fishers, muskrats, raccoons, and mink. You will see many anglers on the river, and Northampton's Oxbow is a popular ice-fishing location. You end above the Holyoke Dam at South Hadley Falls, the most important staging point for anadromous fish runs in springtime with the largest fish elevator on the river.

Miles and Directions

Mile 92.5: Canoes and kayaks can put in at **Elwell Island Recreation Area** on the right bank at Northampton opposite the downstream end of Elwell Island. Powerboats can use the **Oxbow State Ramp** 5 miles downriver.

Miles 92.5–90.5: You will set out from the Coolidge Bridge area in the shadow of the **Mount Holyoke Range** with a fine view looking east up to the white Summit House on top of Mount Holyoke (see Reach 20). Just before the river turns south, you'll see **Hadley Cove** on the left bank; this is a good place to explore for waterbirds, although motorboats will get their propellers caught in vegetation during low water. The **Fort River** enters the Connecticut just downstream of Hadley Cove, opposite which is the extremely popular **Rainbow Beach**, so named either for the

You will see every kind of craft on the river, including houseboats. Photo by Wendy Sinton

colorful beach umbrellas in the summer or for the rainbow-shaped vegetative pattern as seen from atop Mount Holyoke. Co-owned by the City of Northampton and the Massachusetts Department of Fish and Wildlife, which manages it, this day-use area offers great picnicking and swimming, but no facilities or campsites. Use of Rainbow Beach is strictly regulated to protect the globally rare Puritan tiger beetle. *Caution:* All fires are prohibited here because they disturb the beetles. You will often see researchers on the beach during weekends, along with biologist-interpreters available to explain the life history of these interesting creatures.

Miles 90.5–89: The river turns southwest, passing the Northampton Meadows on the right bank, part of the river's floodplain that has been farmed since Native Americans first planted fields 1,000 years ago; it has been placed under strict agricultural zoning to protect the floodplain. Just south of Rainbow Beach, the river's action has turned **Shepherd's Island** into a peninsula, although you may still see it as an island on older maps. At mile 89 **Mitch's Island** will appear, opposite Mitch's Marina on the left bank. You may want to take a hike on a trail with blue blazes that leads from the marina

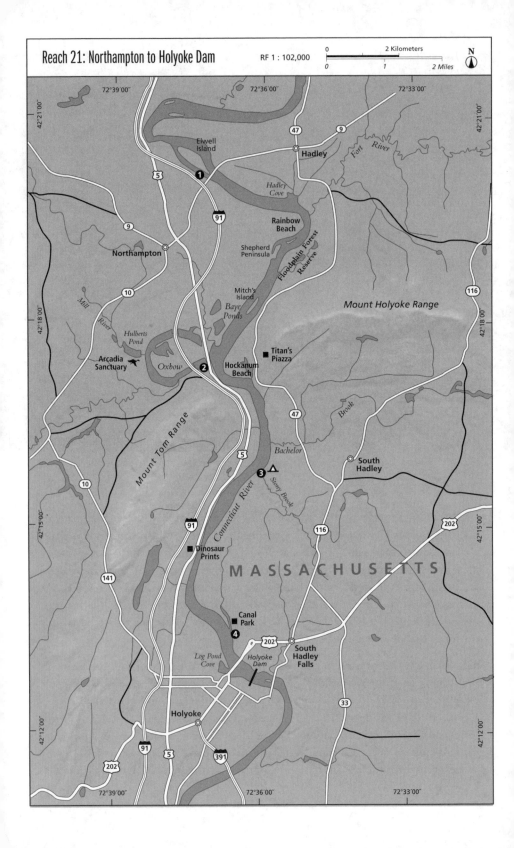

Reach 21: Northampton to Holyoke Dam

RF 1 : 102,000

0   2 Kilometers
0   1   2 Miles

N

72°39'00"   72°36'00"   72°33'00"

42°21'00"

Elwell Island

47
9

Hadley

Fort River

5

91

9

Hadley Cove

Rainbow Beach

Northampton

Shepherd Peninsula

Floodplain Forest Reserve

10

Mill River

Mitch's Island

Baye Ponds

Mount Holyoke Range

116

42°18'00"

Hulberts Pond

Arcadia Sanctuary

Oxbow

Titan's Piazza

Hockanum Beach

47

Brook

5

Bachelor

South Hadley

3 △

Stony Brook

42°15'00"

91

116

202

Dinosaur Prints

M A S S A C H U S E T T S

141

10

Canal Park

4

202

South Hadley Falls

Log Pond Cove

Holyoke Dam

33

Holyoke

42°12'00"

91
5

391

202

72°39'00"   72°36'00"   72°33'00"

north through the DCR-owned and -managed **Floodplain Forest Reserve**, containing one of the largest protected floodplain forests in Massachusetts with silver maples and enormous cottonwoods, some 3 feet in diameter. It is outstanding habitat for waterfowl, wading birds, and warblers. A local land trust owns Mitch's Island, which has a popular picnic and swimming spot on the north end. *Caution:* Powerboats should be aware that the water is deceptively shallow at the south end of Mitch's Island.

Mile 88.5: Just downstream from Mitch's Island on the right bank, paddlers will be able to scoot through a narrow channel into the two **Baye Ponds**. Formerly borrow pits used for gravel in constructing Interstate 91, they are fine fishing and birding spots. Adjacent to the Baye Ponds, but blocked from the river, is the northern arm of the **Oxbow**; Thomas Cole's 1836 painting shows the Connecticut River running straight into the Oxbow at this point and out the south end. At that time the **Mill River** entered the Connecticut just upstream from the Oxbow. The Mill River, which used

Boating Facilities Table for Reach 21

Access Point, Directions	Boat Type	Fee	Parking	Picnic	Toilets	Camping	Rentals	Supplies
❶ **Elwell Island Recreation Area** Damon Road, Northampton, MA *On northeast corner of Damon Road, exit 19 off I-91 and MA 9 in Northampton, adjacent to rail-trail parking; bear right down hill to dock parking. Accessible to disabled.*	Improved ramp for car-top boats	N	Y	Y	Y (seasonal)	N	N	N
❷ **Oxbow State Ramp** US 5, Easthampton, MA *At southern tip of Oxbow. On west side of US 5, 1.5 miles south of exit 18 off I-91.*	Improved ramp for all boat types	N	Y	N	Y	N	N	N
❸ **Brunelle's Marina** Ferry Road, South Hadley, MA *From MA 47 (Hadley Road) in South Hadley, turn west onto Ferry Road; Brunelle's is at end of road at riverbank. Call (413) 536-3132. For free shuttle between access points above and below Holyoke Dam, phone Holyoke Gas and Electric one day in advance: (413) 536-9461.*	Improved ramp for all boat types	Y	Y	Y	Y	Y	N	Y
❹ **South Hadley Canoe Ramp** West Summit Road, South Hadley, MA *At US 202 traffic circle in South Hadley, turn north onto North Main Street, then take first left turn onto West Summit Street to end; path to put-in is straight ahead; parking is on dirt road to right.*	Unimproved ramp, car-top boats only	N	Y	N	N	N	N	N

to have a score of factories on its banks, ran through Northampton, but after the devastating 1936 flood, it was diverted south of the city and now runs through a water treatment plant and into the Oxbow. As for the Oxbow itself, natural changes in the riverbed blocked off both ends of it, creating a classic oxbow pond; the south end was opened in the late twentieth century to allow for recreational boat traffic.

Mile 88: The Oxbow inlet, marked by safety buoys on the right bank, leads under the railroad bridge and U.S. Route 5 bridge. The Oxbow can be exceedingly busy on weekends and weeknights, and is particularly popular with anglers and birders. A state boat ramp is located a short distance from the Oxbow's confluence with the Connecticut River. The **Arcadia Sanctuary**, situated at the western end of the Oxbow, offers nature programs and several birding trails. Arcadia Sanctuary is, in fact, on a second former oxbow, now filled in and providing excellent wetland habitat for birds, animals, and plants; paddlers can get to this wetland under a bridge at the east end of the Oxbow that leads to **Hulberts Pond** at the south end of the former oxbow. *Caution:* The Oxbow is full of invasive plant species. Water chestnut and Eurasian milfoil are particularly plentiful and injurious to native plants. Motorboaters who have visited the Oxbow's quiet backwaters should be sure to clean off their propellers before reentering the river.

Mile 87.5: Just downstream of the Oxbow on the left bank is a steep sandy area called **Hockanum Beach**, formerly known as "Tent City." The beach, owned by the Massachusetts Department of Conservation and Recreation, is part of the Connecticut River Greenway State Park. Camping is prohibited.

Mile 87: As you pass the Oxbow, you enter a narrows that the Connecticut River cut through the ancient volcanic hills between Mount Holyoke and Mount Tom (see the sidebar in Reach 20). The coal-fired Mount Tom Power Plant will be on the right bank and the 200-foot-high cliffs of **Titan's Piazza** (also known as Titan's Pier) will be on the left bank. Part of the Mount Holyoke Range, this feature is composed of columnar basalt, a black volcanic rock that breaks into columns as it cools. On the right bank you will see Mount Tom, sibling to Mount Holyoke, and just as important a historic recreation area. Most of Mount Tom is now a state park and recreation area thanks to federal, state, and local cooperation.

Mile 86: Bachelor Brook enters from the left bank and for paddlers is worth a detour with its interesting twists and turns, floodplain forest, and open wetlands with pickerelweed sporting lovely purple flowers in midsummer; you might also see nesting ducks and even a red-headed woodpecker. In 2005 the Town of South Hadley bought and preserved the floodplain area of Bachelor Brook and adjacent land along the Connecticut River. *Caution:* Beware of water chestnut; do not allow your boat to carry it out to the main stem of the Connecticut River.

Mile 85.5: Another 0.5 mile downstream, on the left bank at the mouth of **Stony Brook**, is **Brunelle's Marina**, where you pick up the portage shuttle around **Holyoke Dam**. If you are paddling, you can take a trip up Stony Brook where you will find wonderful botanizing in a floodplain forest, but beware of the poison ivy. Opposite Brunelle's you will see the docks of the membership-only Holyoke Canoe Club, founded in 1888.

Mile 84.5: Dinosaur footprints are fossilized in the bedrock high up beyond the railroad tracks on the right bank, less than a mile south of Stony Brook (see the sidebar). The 190-million-year-old prints belong to three species of dinosaurs, the largest of which was probably 20 feet in length, standing 10 to 15 feet tall. Property of The Trustees of Reservations, this is a wonderful site, especially for children, but don't access it from the river—it's on the other side of the railroad tracks. There is a well-marked parking area off US 5 in Holyoke. *Caution:* The swift current here runs over slippery ledge rock, so boaters must take care. In high water a famous standing wave, called Wave-O-Saurus, occurs here and draws whitewater kayakers from around the region. *Motorboats must avoid the right shore* and run between the buoys along the left bank.

The endangered Puritan tiger beetle is found in a few locations on the river.
Photo by Chris Joyell

Miles 83–81.5: The river bends southeastward as you come into the built-up section of the city of Holyoke, and you will catch sight of the **Mueller Bridge (U.S. Route 202)** between Holyoke and South Hadley Falls. There is an inlet on the right bank, called **Log Pond Cove**, where logs for Holyoke's factories were collected. Boating here is not recommended because the cove is full of invasive plants, which your boat can spread to other parts of the river; furthermore, there may be unsanitary water during and after heavy rainfall due to Holyoke's antiquated combined sewage overflow system (the city is planning to upgrade this in the near future). *Caution:* All kayaks and canoes must take out on the left bank before the orange buoys marking the Holyoke Dam, and motorboats must take out at one of the upstream ramps. The **South Hadley Canoe Ramp** is upstream of the US 202 bridge, on the left bank at the edge of a small cove (called Cove Island locally, but it is a peninsula) just before the private Redcliffe Canoe Club.

After landing, you may want to take a pleasant walk along the river at **Canal Park**, site of America's first canal (1795). On the right bank is Holyoke, one of America's most interesting historic industrial cities (see the "America's First Planned City" sidebar in Reach 22). You can portage your boat a mile down Canal Street in South Hadley Falls to the put-in below the dam, or phone Holyoke Gas & Electric for free shuttle service: (413) 536–9461.

Dinosaur Footprints

More than 200 million years ago, when the Connecticut Valley region was closer to the equator, the valley's warm, humid climate created perfect conditions for dinosaurs to thrive. You can see their traces as huge footprints in ancient, rippled muds that fossilized in Holyoke and in Rocky Hill, Connecticut.

These rocks originated in the Triassic and Jurassic periods—times of violent geological upheaval. As the supercontinent of Pangea began to separate into the African and North American plates we recognize today, the land was torn gradually into a rift valley more than 100 miles long. Lava burbled up through cracks in the valley during three major eruption episodes and hardened into rock. During quieter intervals water wore down these basalts and deposited sand, mud, and tuff from the uplands into stagnant lakebeds. These soft sediments—stagnant, low in oxygen, and thus not conducive to decay—were perfect for preserving the most delicate details of life and death. Raindrop impressions, mud cracks, ripples, insect larvae, fern fragments, and fish scales are still retained in the rock. Dinosaurs crisscrossed these beds, often in groups; some of these footprint clusters look as if a flock of enormous wild turkeys has just passed through.

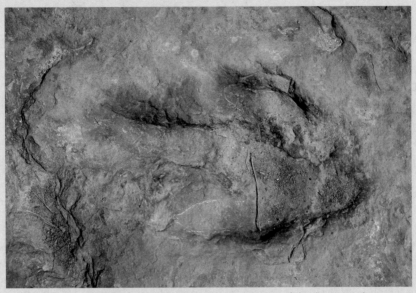

These footprints in Holyoke, Massachusetts, are a reminder of the dinosaurs that once wandered the river valley. Photo by Wendy Sinton

The dinosaur species responsible for Connecticut Valley tracks ranged in size from 1-foot-long crocodilians to the 20-foot-long, carnivorous *Grallator* species. The dinosaurs at Holyoke generally ranged in size from 3 to 13 feet long, but the largest were 15 feet tall and 20 feet long.

Rocky Hill, 50 miles downstream, has the largest dinosaur-track site in North America. The dinosaurs, which Amherst College professor Edward Hitchcock and a local doctor, James Deane, first described in the 1850s, are similar to those at Holyoke, but the site is more extensive, with thousands of tracks visible. Most tracks were made by a dinosaur named *Eubrontes,* which has become Connecticut's official state fossil. Today the colorful birds you observe as you boat down the river are the only direct descendants of the impressive reptiles that once roamed this valley.

Reach 22 · Holyoke Dam to Enfield

Miles from mouth: 81.5–63 (18.5-mile span).
Navigable by: Kayaks, canoes, small powerboats and sailboats.
Difficulty: Flat water.
Flow information: http://water.usgs.gov/water watch; (413) 536-9472.

Portage: *Mile 63:* Take out at Thompsonville Ramp, put in at Enfield Public Ramp below dam; 2 miles.
Camping: No established sites.
USGS maps: Springfield North 7.5, Mt. Tom 7.5, Springfield South 7.5, Broad Brook 7.5.

The Reach

This reach starts in Holyoke, Massachusetts, and ends just 2.5 miles over the Connecticut state line in Enfield, Connecticut. This stretch exemplifies the industrial history of the Connecticut River, and also the river's resilience.

The route begins in Holyoke, America's first planned industrial city; here, against the backdrop of enormous dikes and the brick facades of factories, you will see an incongruous collection of forests, smokestacks, and anglers. At Holyoke's annual Shad Derby in May, you can hear English, Spanish, Korean, and Russian spoken. Holyoke has attracted immigrants since its founding in the mid–nineteenth century (see the sidebar).

Heading south to Springfield, you will enjoy sweeping views of Mount Tom, and a bald eagle may fly overhead as you near the Chicopee River confluence. You will know Springfield mainly by its bridges and the otherworldly, spherical building that houses the Basketball Hall of Fame. Aside from the pretty Riverwalk Park and

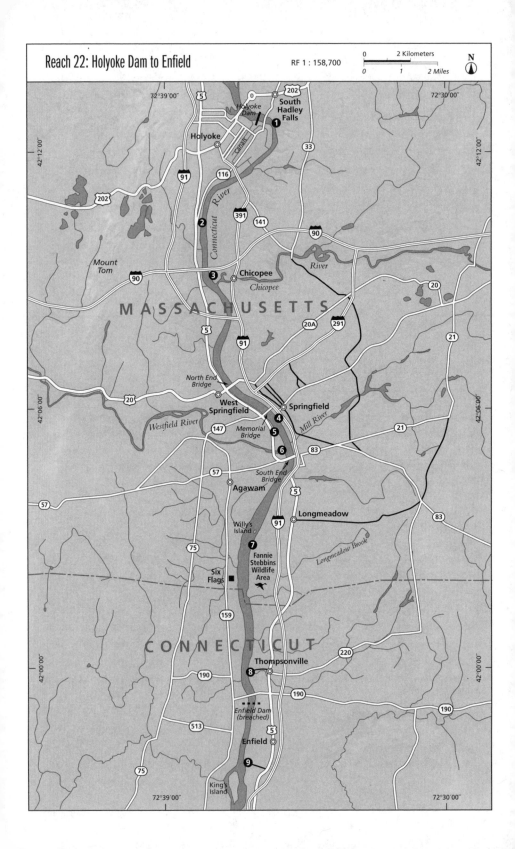

Reach 22: Holyoke Dam to Enfield

RF 1 : 158,700

0 ___ 2 Kilometers
0 ___ 1 ___ 2 Miles

N

42°12'00"

72°39'00"

5

Holyoke Dam

202

South Hadley Falls

1

Holyoke

Canal

33

91

202

116

391

141

Connecticut River

2

90

Mount Tom

90

3

Chicopee

Chicopee

River

20

M A S S A C H U S E T T S

5

91

20A

291

21

North End Bridge

West Springfield

20

Westfield River

4

Springfield

Mill River

21

147

Memorial Bridge

5

6

83

57

South End Bridge

Agawam

5

83

57

Willy's Island

91

Longmeadow

7

Longmeadow Brook

Six Flags

Fannie Stebbins Wildlife Area

75

159

C O N N E C T I C U T

Thompsonville

220

190

8

190

190

513

Enfield Dam (breached)

5

Enfield

9

75

King's Island

42°06'00"

42°00'00"

72°39'00"

72°30'00"

Boating Facilities Table for Reach 22

Access Point, Directions	Boat Type	Fee	Parking	Picnic	Toilets	Camping	Rentals	Supplies
❶ Perjovski State Ramp South Main Street, South Hadley Falls, MA *Take very sharp, westerly turn off South Main Street in South Hadley Falls (see sign for fishing access). Driveway is steep.*	Unimproved ramp for car-top and small motorboats	N	Y	N	Y Seasonal	N	N	N
❷ Jones Ferry Jones Ferry Road, Holyoke, MA *Turn east onto Jones Ferry Road from US 5 in Holyoke.*	Improved ramp for all boat types	N	Y	Y	Y	N	N	N
❸ Medina Street Ramp Medina Street, Chicopee, MA *From MA 116, turn west onto Wilson Road, then immediately south onto Chester Street. Right turn onto Whitin Avenue, left onto Oldfield Road, right onto Paderewski Street, left onto Granger, which becomes Medina Street (see water treatment plant sign). Ramp is at terminus of Medina Street.*	Improved ramp for all boat types	N	Y	N	Y	N	N	N
❹ Springfield Riverwalk and Bikeway Columbus Street, Springfield, MA *Parking at Riverfront Park near railroad tracks at State Street and West Columbus Avenue.*	Unimproved steps, lightweight car-top boats only	Y	Y	Y	Y	N	N	N
❺ Bondi's Island Launch Ramp M Street, West Springfield, MA *Exit US 5 at sign for Pioneer Valley Resource Recovery. Turn east onto M Street, then north into dirt parking area.*	Improved ramp for car-top and small motorboats	N	Y	N	N	N	N	N
❻ Pynchon Point Meadow Street, Agawam, MA *From US 5, take MA 57. At rotary, turn onto Meadow Street (also called River Road). Park on left just past Century Street.*	Unimproved ramp for car-top boats only	N	Y	N	N	N	N	N
❼ Riverfront Park Anthony Road, Longmeadow, MA *From US 5 in Longmeadow, turn west onto Emerson Road and right onto Anthony Road. Take westerly turn to river, south of Pioneer Valley Yacht Club.*	Unimproved ramp for car-top boats only	N	Y	N	N	N	N	N

Boating Facilities Table for Reach 22 continued

Access Point, Directions	Boat Type	Fee	Parking	Picnic	Toilets	Camping	Rentals	Supplies
❽ Thompsonville Town Ramp North River Street, Thompsonville, CT *Turn west onto North Main Street where US 5 junctions with CT 220. Drive through center of Thompsonville, bear right to stay on Main Street heading west, then bear left/ south onto North River Street after passing under train trestle. Turn right into parking lot.*	Improved ramp for all boat types	N	Y	Y	Y	N	N	N
❾ Enfield Public Ramp Parson's Road, Enfield, CT *Just south of junction of Bridge Street and Parson's Road (north of junction with Old King Road), west of railroad tracks in Enfield.*	Improved ramp for all boat types	N	Y	N	N	N	N	N

Bikeway, the city enjoys surprisingly little aesthetic or physical connection with its river. Plans to reattach Springfield to the river have languished for years because Interstate 91 and the railroad cut the city off from the riverfront. New attempts, however, may yet link the city to the river over the next decade.

Once out of earshot of the screaming roller-coaster riders at Six Flags amusement park, you will be enclosed by the tranquil floodplain, interspersed with few buildings, that straddles the Massachusetts–Connecticut border.

This reach is exceptionally easy for all boaters, with barely a breath of current most of the way. As such, it can make for a long day if you are paddling; be sure to bring plenty of water, as there is a dearth of refreshment stops en route. Boaters should exit the river, however, *above* the derelict Enfield Dam (preferably at the Thompsonville Town Ramp) and should not attempt to run the falls there.

Miles and Directions

Mile 81.5: Car-top boats and small trailers can access the river at **Perjovski State Ramp** off South Main Street in South Hadley Falls, below the **Holyoke Dam**. On the Holyoke side of the river, you could portage small boats down a steep gravel fisherman's path to Slim Shad Point, where shad anglers congregate in large numbers. The annual Holyoke Gas & Electric Shad Derby is held every spring at various river points in Holyoke, South Hadley, and Chicopee. The world-record eleven-pound, six-ounce American shad was caught by a local resident in this stretch. An innovative "fish elevator" above the Holyoke Dam allows passage of more than 250,000 migrating fish every spring—mostly shad, but also some salmon, lamprey, herring, bass, and trout. Its fish-viewing station is well worth a side trip (on land, of course) to learn

The Holyoke canals carried river water that powered its once vibrant factories. Photo © Al Braden

more about the various fish and their aquatic habitats.

Mile 81.2: Just below the dam you will experience the only turbulence of the trip in the form of quick, shallow water urging you past many canal outlets, brick dikes, and riprap, and then under the Massachusetts Route 116 bridge. Large, overhanging willows grow among the cobbles and bricks, so it is surprisingly green even in the center of this old, industrial city.

Miles 79.5–77.5: After passing at a good clip under the Interstate 391 bridge, the river will bend south, and the **Jones Ferry Landing** appears in another 2 miles on the right bank. Once home to a ferry between Holyoke and Chicopee, this is now a paved public boat launch.

Mile 76.5: Downstream of Jones Ferry, as you near the Interstate 90 (Massachusetts Turnpike) bridge, keep your eyes peeled for a huge bald eagle nest. *Caution:* Give these magnificent birds a wide berth. The U.S. Fish and Wildlife Service owns this

The Enfield rapids are enticing but don't try them in your boat. Photo courtesy of Connecticut River Watershed Council

land, and disembarking from your boat is *prohibited* at this site.

Mile 76: Just beyond the Massachusetts Turnpike bridge, on the left bank, the **Medina Street Ramp** lies north of the confluence with the **Chicopee River**. Just 17 miles long, but with a 721-square-mile watershed, this little river drops more than 250 feet and thus sports no fewer than six hydropower dams along its length. The Chicopee River Watershed Council suggests several lovely hikes and canoe trips on the Chicopee; check the group's Web site (www.chicopeeriver.org) for more information. You could picnic on one of the sandbars at the river mouth, but might be deafened by the large military aircraft taking off from nearby Westover Air Force Base.

Miles 75–73: Passing under the I–91 bridge, you may see some enormous tree trunks wedged high into the abutments, testimony to the height and power of the river in flood. The **North End Bridge** (U.S. Route 20) passes over the river approximately 2 miles downstream.

Mile 72: On the approach to the heart of Springfield, you will pass under the **Memo-**

rial Bridge, Massachusetts Route 147, which links U.S. Route 5 and I–91 across the river. This lovely landmark lights up beautifully at night. First built in 1922 and rebuilt in 1996, it spans more than 1,500 feet from shore to shore with graceful arches.

Mile 71.8: The downtown **Springfield Riverwalk and Bikeway**, on the left bank, are the city's only direct points of access to the river. It's awkward for boaters to access the 3.7-mile-long park from the river—there's no place to tie up safely, and a steep, concrete staircase ascends the bank. Parking is about 400 yards away, making this area useful only for lightweight car-top boats. About 0.1 mile from this "landing" (which once housed the cruise boat *Tinkerbell*) is the Springfield Visitor Center.

Mile 71.5: Bondi's Island Launch Ramp is downstream of the Riverwalk, on the river's right bank. From here to the mouth of the Westfield River, the river becomes very shallow. *Caution:* Larger boats often run aground at low water here.

Mile 71: The river shoals up around its culverted confluence on the left bank with the **Mill River**, one of literally dozens of "Mill Rivers" in Massachusetts that fueled the Industrial Revolution.

Mile 69.7: The **Westfield River** enters the Connecticut on the right bank. **Pynchon Point**, named after Springfield's first settler, is a sandy access point and shady beach at the confluence of the Westfield on its south bank. The City of Agawam is in the process of cleaning up this site and adding picnic tables in the near future. The 78-mile-long Westfield is another cleanup success story. The U.S. Department of Interior has designated 45 miles of its upper reaches as wild and scenic, helping to protect its many trout-fishing and paddling opportunities. The Westfield River Watershed Association is its watchdog.

Mile 69.5: Shortly below the Westfield confluence, you will pass under the **South End Bridge**, then pass the Springfield Yacht Club on the right bank. Founded in 1850, it's one of America's oldest.

Mile 69: About 0.75 mile south of the Westfield River, and south of the Pioneer Valley Yacht Club on the left bank, is **Riverfront Park**, an undeveloped, pleasant fishing access from which you can launch a car-top boat.

Miles 67–65: From **Willy's Island** south to the Connecticut border, the lands to the east of the river revert to agriculture and floodplain forest, making for spectacular birding; you are almost guaranteed to spot an oriole here. At 2,100 feet, this is the widest point on the Connecticut River north of the Tidelands. The **Fannie Stebbins Wildlife Area** in Longmeadow protects part of this complex of fertile lands. *Caution:* Just south of the confluence with **Longmeadow Brook** (mile 66) on the left bank, a sign points to a dangerous gas pipeline crossing under the river.

Mile 65.5: You will know you are about to pass into Connecticut when you hear

America's First Planned City

In 1633, when Captain Elizur Holyoke first worked his way upstream to the place that would become his namesake, he could not have imagined that this site would become America's first planned industrial city. The falls between Holyoke and South Hadley dropped 57 feet over a 2-mile stretch, creating a great anadromous fishery but posing a serious hindrance to river transport. However, the rich agricultural land, fed by the river, drew settlers in droves to the growing town, first named the "Ireland Parish" of West Springfield.

By the early 1800s Boston entrepreneurs, who had developed the towns of Lawrence and Lowell in the Merrimack River Valley, began to eye the falls for similar industrial purposes. Through land purchases, they expanded the town to 1,100 acres and developed a design for a city centered on the river with an ambitious set of canals and factories. Several churches were shortly established for immigrant Irish, Quebecois, and Polish populations. Workers dug the 4-mile canal system by pick and shovel, then set to work constructing the first dam in 1847. The dam was doomed within hours of its dedication. Terse telegraph communiqués tell the story of its fate:

10:00 A.M.:	"Gates just closed; water filling behind dam."
Noon:	"Dam leaking badly."
1:00 P.M.:	"Leaks cannot be stopped."
2:00 P.M.:	"Stones of bulkhead giving way to pressure."
3:20 P.M.:	"Your old dam's gone to hell by way of Williamansett" (the village just downstream).

Undaunted, the industrialists built a new wooden dam within the year, one that lasted until 1900 when it was replaced by a granite behemoth called the Million Dollar Dam. Factories specialized in textiles and paper; a cotton boom was short-lived due to Civil War shortages. As twenty-five paper mills came online, Holyoke became internationally known as the Paper City of the World. Population peaked in 1920 at 60,000 people (the current population is about 40,000). Downtown streets were graced with striking Gothic buildings, paid for by the Holyoke Water Power Company, constructed of the traprock of the nearby Mount Tom Range. The Holyoke Opera House rivaled the Goodspeed Opera House (see the "East Haddam History" sidebar in Reach 25) for its contributions to Broadway.

After the world wars, however, industry in Holyoke had begun to wane slowly as companies moved south and west to get easier access to raw materials. The recession of the 1970s spelled the end of large-scale manufacturing along the canals. But the historic old factories lining the now clean canals like an American Venice are not lost. Plans are currently underway to create a 2-mile-long Canal Walk with open-air restaurants and cafes to enhance the growth of an Artist District as part of Holyoke's revitalization and reconnection to the river.

To learn more about Holyoke's colorful history—and perhaps to catch a ride on the city's beautifully restored carousel—visit Holyoke Heritage State Park, 221 Appleton Street, Holyoke; (413) 534-1723.

screaming voices and see the big roller coasters and Ferris wheel of **Six Flags New England** on the right bank.

Mile 65: Once you cross the Connecticut state line, houses along the river seem to fade into the woods. A long peninsula lines the eastern bank, with pretty wetlands and woods behind it. Gradually, the bridge abutments associated with Connecticut Route 190 appear in the distance, heralding your approach to the **Enfield Dam.**

Mile 63: The **Thompsonville Town Ramp** on the left bank is a well-equipped area to take out upstream of the Enfield Dam, and by far the easiest portage around the dam. *Caution:* Do *not* run this breached dam at high water; skilled paddlers have run it down the left bank, but you must know what you are doing and which water levels are safe. A more cumbersome alternative is to take out on the right bank just above the breached dam, walk up the steep bank, go left through the parking lot at the Windsor Locks Canal Trail, cross a path on an outlet gate, and put in just below the start of the old canal. If you successfully negotiate this portage, you can take out at the **Enfield Public Ramp.**

Connecticut

A cruiseboat gives passengers a good view of the Hartford skyline. Photo © Al Braden

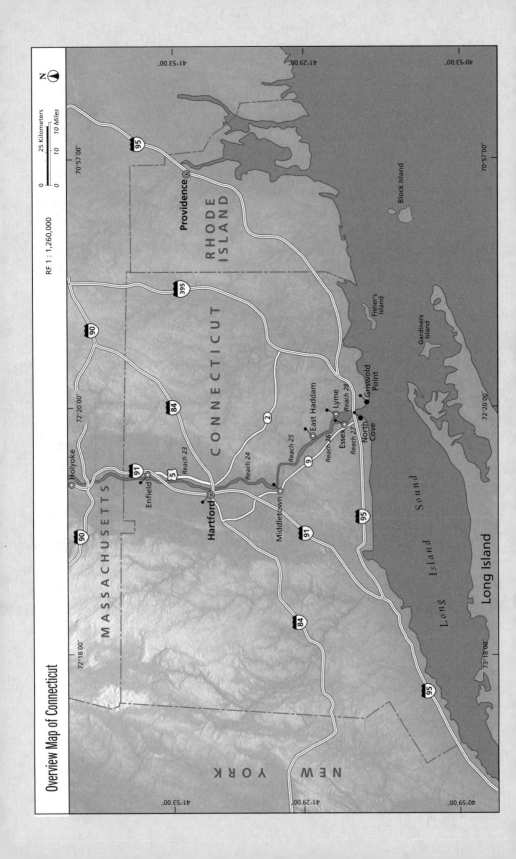

Overview Map of Connecticut

RF 1 : 1,260,000

N

Reach 23 **Enfield to Hartford**

Miles from mouth: 63–49 (14-mile span).
Navigable by: Kayaks, canoes, small powerboats.
Difficulty: Class I through III, flat water.
Portages: None.

Camping: No established sites.
USGS maps: Windsor Locks 7.5, Broad Brook 7.5, Manchester 7.5, Hartford North 7.5.

The Reach

This reach runs from Enfield, Connecticut, to Hartford, Connecticut. It begins with a little excitement, provided by the rush of the Connecticut River over small rapids and falls below the breached Enfield Dam, and ends with the thrill of approaching the stirring skyline of the Connecticut River's only big city, Hartford. Along the route you will pass gorgeous islands, the lush floodplains at the Farmington River confluence, and the historical novelty of the Windsor Locks Canal. You may never quite avoid the noise of the busy commuter roads, but perhaps, if you are enjoying a day off from rush hour, you can gloat a bit about not being caught in the distant hum of traffic.

The river is easy to navigate here, although novice boaters will want to handle currents carefully below the breached Enfield Dam, and sudden shoals can pop up anywhere around the islands.

Miles and Directions

Mile 63: You can access the river at the **Enfield Public Ramp**, downstream of the breached **Enfield Dam** and rapids. Although the falls over the breached dam may look deceptively small, we do not recommend running the dam. *Caution:* The rapids in summer are Class I, but can be Class III in spring high water. Only very experienced paddlers should attempt these rapids. The rapids below the dam will carry you along quite swiftly and pleasantly. During the annual shad run, the banks may be lined by crowds of hopeful anglers. Later in the year you may see (and smell) the remains of the shad that have spawned upstream; having done their duty, their bodies now float back down to the sound, replenishing the river's nutrients along the way.

Mile 62.5: King's Island is a notable landmark just below the access ramp. Its profile is particularly craggy at the southern end, and it is densely forested with large trees. The island and Enfield rapids, home to bald eagles and spawning territory for blueback herring, are considered Special Habitat Areas by the U.S. Fish and Wildlife Service. The passage to the right of the island becomes shallow at the confluence with **Stony Brook**. Several islands, large and small, are springing up in this dynamic portion of the river; take note of sudden shallow spots. Notice how the vegetation differs among newly forming and older islands: Scrappy young willows and cherries

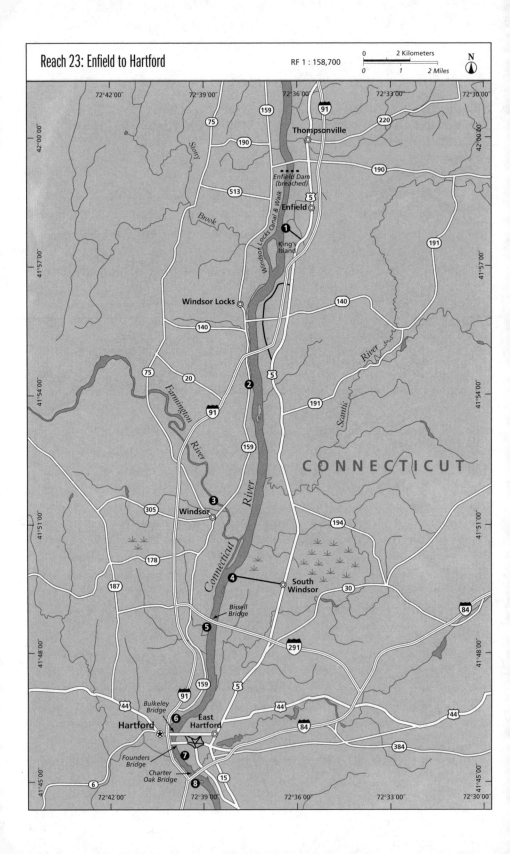

0   2 Kilometers

0   1   2 Miles

N

72°42′00″   72°39′00″   72°36′00″   72°33′00″   72°30′00″

42°00′00″

159

75   91   220

Thompsonville

190

190

Enfield Dam
(breached)

513   5

Enfield

1

Brook

King's
Island

41°57′00″   191   41°57′00″

Windsor Locks   140

140

Stony   Windsor Locks Canal & Walk

75   20   River

Farmington   **2**   5   41°54′00″

91   191   Scantic

159

C O N N E C T I C U T

River

305   **3**

Windsor   194

41°51′00″   41°51′00″

178

Connecticut   84

187

4   South
Windsor   30

Bissell
Bridge   **5**

41°48′00″   291   41°48′00″

159   5

91   44

Bulkeley   44   84
Bridge   **6**

Hartford ★   East
Hartford   84

Founders   **7**   384
Bridge

Charter
Oak Bridge   **8**   15

6   41°45′00″

72°42′00″   72°39′00″   72°36′00″   72°33′00″   72°30′00″

Boating Facilities Table for Reach 23

Access Point, Directions	Boat Type	Fee	Parking	Picnic	Toilets	Camping	Rentals	Supplies
❶ Enfield Public Ramp Parson's Road, Enfield, CT *Just south of junction of Bridge Street and Parson's Road (north of junction with Old King Road), west of railroad tracks in Enfield.*	Improved ramp for all boat types	N	Y	N	N	N	N	N
❷ Windsor Locks Public Ramp 1530 Palisado Avenue (CT 159), Windsor, CT *Turn east toward river off CT 159.*	Improved ramp for all boat types	N	Y	N	N	N	N	Nearby
❸ Windsor Town Ramp (Farmington River Access) Pleasant Street Park, Windsor, CT *Behind Bart's Bait and Sporting Goods Store on CT 159, 1 mile north from junction of CT 75/305/159 in center of Windsor. Put in after noon, when releases from hydro dam upstream provide enough water to launch.*	Improved ramp for all boat types	N	Y	Y	Y	N	N	Nearby
❹ South Windsor Public Ramp Vibert Road, South Windsor, CT *Turn west onto Pleasant Valley Road from US 5; jog right onto Main Street and immediately left onto Vibert Road.*	Improved ramp for all boat types	N	Y	Y	N	N	N	N
❺ Bissell Bridge Boat Launch East Barber Street, Windsor, CT *From CT 159, turn east onto Barber Street; launch is at terminus.*	Improved ramp for all boat types	N	Y	Y	Y	N	N	N
❻ Riverside Park Reserve Road, Hartford, CT *Take I-91 south to exit 33. At end of ramp, turn left onto Jennings Road. Take first right onto Liebert Road. Park entrance is 0.5 mile on left.*	Improved ramp for all boat types	N	Y	Y	Y	N	N	Nearby
❼ Great River Park East River Drive, East Hartford, CT *Take I-84 east to exit 53, East River Drive/ CT 44. Follow ramp signs to East River Drive and turn right onto East River Drive at end of ramp. Park entrance is 0.75 mile on right.*	Improved ramp for all boat types	Y for motor-boats	Y	Y	Y	N	N	Nearby
❽ Charter Oak Landing Reserve Road, Hartford, CT *Take I-91 to exit 27; at end of ramp, turn left onto Airport Road. At end of Airport Road, turn left onto Brainard Road. Take first left onto Reserve Road. Park entrance is 0.5 mile on right under Charter Oak Bridge.*	Improved ramp for all boat types	Y for motor-boats	Y	Y	Y	N	N	N

The Hartford skyline frames these paddlers. Photo by Wendy Sinton

colonize this year's new gravel bars, while larger, more stately maples and sycamores have a firm foothold in the older, more stable sediments.

Miles 62–57.5: From the beginning of the reach, you will be paralleling the historic **Windsor Locks Canal**, which begins north of the Enfield Ramp, just below the Hazardville Avenue (Connecticut Route 190) bridge on the right bank of the river. This 5-mile-long engineering marvel was built out of huge fieldstones in 1829 to accommodate shipping between southern Connecticut and Holyoke, Massachusetts, and beyond (see the "Connecticut River Canals" sidebar in Reach 18). After passing under the Connecticut Route 140 bridge, you will see the center of the historic nineteenth-century industrial town of Windsor Locks. Boats are no longer allowed in the canals, although from the river you can peek into the terminus on the right bank, just north of the Interstate 91 bridge. On land you can enjoy nice views of the river and canal from a scenic, 4.5-mile **Canal Walk**. There is good fishing access from the parking area.

Mile 57.5: Windsor Locks Public Ramp, with a paved access and nearby restaurant, lies on the right bank of the river, below the I–91 bridge. The river buoys you pleasingly along this stretch, so you have time and momentum to take out binoculars and bird-watch. Ducks are frequent visitors to this part of the river, and you may spot a cormorant perched on a log, drying its splayed-out wings.

Mile 54.5: Approaching the **Scantic River** mouth on the left bank, you may be inadvertently "buzzed" by low-flying planes out of the neighboring airstrip. Explore the twisty Scantic if you can navigate around the large downed trees that frequently block access. The rapids on the upper river host the annual Scantic River Spring Splash Canoe and Kayak Race. You might also want to take a terrestrial wander through Scantic River Park, a greenway connecting Somers, Enfield, East Windsor, and South Windsor.

Mile 53.5: The mouth of the **Farmington River** on the right bank is hidden behind a long, forested island, and invites a leisurely exploration. We have seen as many as twelve great blue herons congregating at the confluence, which is overhung with enormous trees. The **Windsor Town Ramp** boat launch at Pleasant Street Park in Windsor is a convenient upstream access point to the Farmington River, and it's just 2 miles from here to the Connecticut River. The Farmington River is the first river in Connecticut to receive national Wild and Scenic designation, and its watershed supplies about a third of Connecticut's population with clean water. Visit the Web site of the Farmington River Watershed Association (www.frwa.org) to learn more.

Mile 53: Opposite the southern tip of the island enclosing the Farmington confluence is the paved **South Windsor Public Ramp.** As you move downriver through this stretch, you will encounter several more small islands, which at low water have sandy beaches that are great for a picnic and a swim.

Mile 52: The **Bissell Bridge Boat Launch** will shortly come into view on the river's right bank, just under the Bissell Bridge (Interstate 291). A 1.8-mile bike path starts here.

Miles 52–50: Below the Bissell Bridge, the river regains some of its former velocity on the stretch into Hartford. You will pass many willow-dominated, sandy banks all the way to the Hartford Landfill. Look for clusters of holes in the upper layers of these sandy cuts; these are the home of bank swallows, which swoop and dive, skimming the water for insects. Your nose may alert you to the presence of the Hartford region's landfill, which is otherwise well hidden from view. Looking at the river bottom here, you may notice multitudes of clams with shells about 1.5 inches across. These are invasive Asiatic clams (*Corbicula fluminea*), which are becoming increasingly common in the calm, warm waters of the southern Connecticut River. *Caution:* The river gets unexpectedly shallow near the banks at the base of the landfill.

Miles 50–49: The river makes one of its few turns along this reach at Hartford's large **Riverside Park,** just north of the Bulkeley Bridge (Interstate 84 and U.S. Route 44). Rounding the bend of the densely forested banks, you will be astonished by the dramatic Hartford skyline suddenly rising before you. You have three options for exiting the river here: Riverside Park on the right bank, **Great River Park** farther down on the left bank in East Hartford, and **Charter Oak Landing** opposite Great River Park on the right. You are in the heart of downtown, so be sure to catch the sights!

The Greenway Concept

The Connecticut River passes through some of the densest population centers in central New England, but for the most part you would hardly know it. Certainly, houses and some condominiums cluster in places along the shore, and past and present heavy industry dominates the river in Bellows Falls, Brattleboro, Holyoke, and other locales. But from a spaceship the Connecticut River would appear to traverse a narrow swath of amazingly green lands—covered in forests or farmland—over most of its course. Partly we can attribute this to the fact that it's hard to set up shop in a floodplain, and despite all its dams, the Connecticut still floods regularly. Partly we can thank strong legislation that protects rivers from unwise development, protecting people from disaster and polluted water in the process. But more and more the open lands that line the Connecticut River stay open for all to enjoy thanks to the many organizations whose activities protect the river as a greenway.

A *greenway* is a corridor that is maintained in a semi-natural (vegetated and so "green") state; it provides linkages between sites that people find valuable and worthy of preservation and appreciation. You can visit multiple, diverse sites without ever leaving the scenic and protected route that links them. Being essentially linear features, rivers lend themselves well to the construction of greenways.

Greenways fall into three general (but not mutually exclusive) categories. Recreational greenways provide safe, car-free places for people to have fun by the river. These include paths such as the Bissell Bridge bike trail, Scantic River Park, Hockanum River Trails, and the Windsor Canal Walk. Cultural greenways connect sites of historic, architectural, or social importance. Hartford-based Riverfront Recapture, for example, has pursued waterfront renewal in metropolitan Hartford, building networks of parks and trails. Its ambitious restoration of river parks is a model for how towns can celebrate the river's presence. Ecological greenways provide natural pathways by which animals (and plant seeds, and other mobile living things) can move from place to place. Large, unfragmented forests along the banks of the Farmington River, for example, allow animals with large home ranges—like black bears—to wander large areas without crossing roads. Migrating flocks of birds home in on the greenways of the Pioneer Valley section of the river, navigating by these large, forested landmarks.

The greenway idea isn't especially new. The term dates back to Frederick Law Olmsted's designs for New York's Central Park and Boston's 10-mile "Emerald Necklace" from the 1850s to the 1870s. City planners and landscape architects adapted Olmsted's ideas in the 1970s to develop urban plans that connect many areas in large cities through greenways.

Greenways promote cultural, recreational, and ecological goals simultaneously: enhancing the quality of life for visitors and residents of rivers, protecting water quality by reducing runoff and bank erosion, and attracting economic returns from tourism. Conservationists, watershed councils, and land planners now take much broader, watershed-level views of greenways, attempting to design large-scale systems of public-use areas across state and even national boundaries. Imagine the view from space if every river on earth had its own greenway!

Reach 24 Hartford to Middletown

Miles from mouth: 49–30 (19-mile span).
Navigable by: Kayaks, canoes, powerboats.
Difficulty: Flat water.
Portages: None.
Camping: No established sites.

USGS maps: Hartford North 7.5, Hartford South 7.5, Glastonbury 7.5, Middletown 7.5, Middle Haddam 7.5.
NOAA charts: Connecticut River: Bodkin Rock to Hartford #12377.

The Reach

This reach passes through the heart of Connecticut, taking boaters from Hartford to Middletown, Connecticut. The reach begins at Hartford, an industrial city, which, like others in New England, is recovering from post-industrial doldrums. Beloved of writer Mark Twain in the nineteenth century and Alexander Calder, the great mid-twentieth-century artist and sculptor, Hartford also boasted one of this country's greatest poets, Wallace Stephens, who would take a lunchtime stroll along the city's riverbank.

Hartford's riverfront has become an anchor for economic and recreational development, thanks to the work of government agencies and, above all, Riverfront Recapture, a nonprofit organization that has succeeded in redeveloping parks, docks, and riverwalk paths and promoting recreational activities and youth programs in three lovely parks on the river. On the river's left bank in the towns of East Hartford and Manchester, local residents and town governments have developed extensive paddling, biking, and hiking trails along the Hockanum River, a Connecticut River tributary.

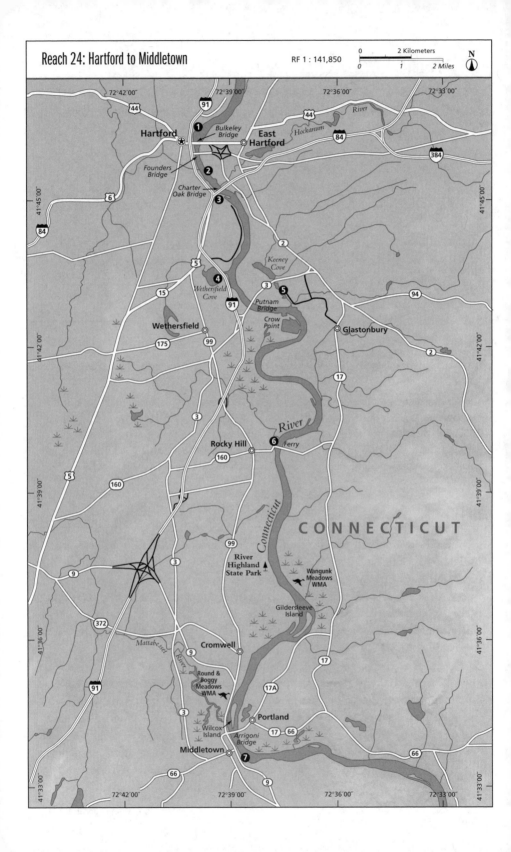

Reach 24: Hartford to Middletown

RF 1 : 141,850

0   2 Kilometers
0   1   2 Miles

N

72°42'00"   72°39'00"   72°36'00"   72°33'00"

44

91

Hartford

Bulkeley
Bridge

East
Hartford

44

River

Hockanum

84

384

41°45'00"

6

Founders
Bridge

Charter
Oak Bridge

84

2

Keeney
Cove

5

Wethersfield
Cove

15

91

3

Putnam
Bridge

Crow
Point

94

Glastonbury

41°42'00"

Wethersfield

175

99

River

17

2

3

Rocky Hill

160

Ferry

41°39'00"

5

160

CONNECTICUT

99

River Highland
State Park

Wangunk
Meadows
WMA

9

Connecticut

Gildersleeve
Island

41°36'00"

372

91

Mattabesset
River

Cromwell

9

Round &
Boggy
Meadows
WMA

17

17A

3

Wilcox
Island

Portland

Arrigoni
Bridge

17   66

66

Middletown

66

9

72°42'00"   72°39'00"   72°36'00"   72°33'00"

Boating Facilities Table for Reach 24

Access Point, Directions	Boat Type	Fee	Parking	Picnic	Toilets	Camping	Rentals	Supplies
❶ Riverside Park Liebert Road, Hartford, CT *Take I-91 south to exit 33. At end of ramp, turn left onto Jennings Road. Take first right onto Liebert Road. Park entrance is 0.5 mile on left.*	Improved ramp for all boat types	N	Y	Y	Y	N	N	Nearby
❷ Great River Park East River Drive, East Hartford, CT *Take I-84 east to exit 53, East River Drive/ US 44. Follow ramp signs to East River Drive and turn right onto East River Drive at end of ramp. Park entrance is 0.75 mile on right.*	Improved ramp for all boat types	Y for large boats	Y	Y	Y	N	N	Nearby
❸ Charter Oak Landing Reserve Road, Hartford, CT *Take I-91 to exit 27; at end of ramp, turn left onto Airport Road. At end of Airport Road, turn left onto Brainard Road. Take first left onto Reserve Road. Park entrance is 0.5 mile on right under Charter Oak Bridge.*	Improved ramp for all boat types	Y for large boats	Y	Y	Y	N	N	N
❹ Wethersfield Cove Public Ramp Main Street, Wethersfield, CT *From CT 15, head south on Hartford Avenue. Turn east onto State Street, then north onto Main Street. Ramp is at end of Main Street.*	Improved ramp for all boat types	Y	Y	Y	Y	N	N	N
❺ Glastonbury Public Ramp (Keeney Cove) Point Road, Glastonbury, CT *Turn west off Main Street onto Glastonbury Boulevard and take to end; jog left, turn right onto Point Road, and enter park.*	Unimproved ramp, car-top boats only	N	Y	Y	Y	N	N	N
❻ Rocky Hill Public Ramp Rocky Hill, CT *From CT 3 in Rocky Hill, turn south onto Elm Street. Bear left onto Second Lane and follow signs to Rocky Hill Ferry.*	Improved ramp for all boat types	Y	Y	Y	Y	N	N	Nearby
❼ Harbor Park Middletown, CT *At 80 Harbor Drive, park is accessible via exit 12 or 14 off CT9.*	Improved ramp for car-top and small trailer boats	N	Y	Y	Y	N	Y	Nearby

In this reach you will also find the historic town of Wethersfield, among the first handful of colonial settlements in the Connecticut River Valley and the largest historic district in Connecticut.

You end at Middletown, Connecticut, an early industrial town founded in 1653 and named for its location equidistant between the mouth of the river and Windsor, Connecticut. Middletown began as a vital industrial and commercial link in eighteenth- and early-nineteenth-century New England, but without a major port or transport facilities, mid-nineteenth-century railroad and industrial capital bypassed the town, shifting to the Hartford–New Haven axis.

The paddling here is easy, with a negligible current except in a few places. Be aware that the water level can change almost 2 feet between high and low tide at Hartford.

Miles and Directions

Mile 49: Car-top boats, sculls, and motorboats can put in at lovely **Riverside Park** on the river's right bank smack in the middle of downtown Hartford. The Victorian-style structure near the docks is the Greater Hartford Jaycees Community Boathouse. If you are coming from the east, **Great River Park** in East Hartford features a public boat launch, an amphitheater, a picnic area, and an extensive riverwalk.

Miles 49–47.2: Shortly after putting in at Riverside Park, you will pass under the **Bulkeley Bridge** (U.S. Route 44/Interstate 84), the **Founders Bridge** (Connecticut Route 2), and the **Charter Oak Bridge** (U.S. Route 5/Connecticut Route 15). About halfway between the Founders and Charter Oak Bridges, you will see a large culvert where the Park River (aka Hog River) used to flow into the Connecticut. Lined with tenements in the nineteenth century, the river was infamous for its pollution levels, although part of it flowed through genteel Bushnell Park. Following the disastrous 1936 flood, however, the Park River was confined to an underground tunnel to prevent future flooding; water quality has improved since. The **Hockanum River** joins the Connecticut River just upstream of the Charter Oak Bridge. If you can manage a portage here and there, it's possible to paddle the Hockanum upstream to two lakes that, despite their proximity to downtown East Hartford, are surrounded by relatively pristine marsh.

Mile 47.2: The large boat moored at the Charter Oak Bridge belongs to Lady Katharine Cruises (named for the actress and Connecticut resident Katharine Hepburn), which offers regular dinner cruises around the river. There is a public boat access to the river at **Charter Oak Landing**, with parking. Below the bridge, the Trinity College boathouse and Hartford Yacht Club are near each other on the left bank.

Mile 47: *Caution:* There is a no-wake zone near the power plant breakwater just below the Charter Oak Bridge at Hartford Jetty. The river briefly becomes quite turbulent here, affording small boaters their only potential adrenaline rush of this reach.

The Turnstile Railroad Bridge is a striking landmark in Middletown, Connecticut.
Photo © Al Braden

The riverbanks are populated by industry, private homes, and occasional remnants of floodplain forests.

Mile 47: South of Hartford, huge log pilings dot the left shore; these once accommodated barges that brought oil to a large oil depot in East Hartford. Changes in that industry mean oil barges no longer come up this far, but in their time, they must have made an impressive wake.

Mile 45: Two miles on, the entrance to **Wethersfield Cove** beckons on the right shore. This cove is the gateway to the quaint town of Wethersfield, which is well worth a ramble to see its historical colonial buildings clustered around the water. Small boats should take care entering through the narrow channel that links the cove with the river; the wake of larger motorboats can create unexpected turbulence. Keep to the left after entering the cove, and the well-equipped **Wethersfield Cove Public Ramp** will come into view. There is a paved ramp and ample parking, with a fee for its use. The private Wethersfield Cove Yacht Club occupies the western shore of the cove.

Miles 44–43: The river takes an easterly turn as it passes beneath the **Putnam Memorial Bridge** (Connecticut Route 3). The inlet to **Keeney Cove** soon appears on the left bank, a state wildlife area surrounded by pretty marsh. The city of Glastonbury has an unimproved ramp at Point Road Park at the northern end of the cove. Anglers visiting the cove to fish need to assiduously clean their propellers; the cove

High school and college crew races are a common sight on the river. Photo by Ruth Bergengren

contains water chestnut, an invasive weed (with nasty, sharp-spined nuts) that has been the focus of removal efforts since 1999.

Mile 42.5: Within 0.5 mile boaters with shallow drafts can duck into **Crow Point** on the right bank. Beware of submerged bars at the entrance. A glance at the shore or a navigational map will puzzle an observant boater: The basin is square. It was created, in fact, as a borrow pit from which sediments were dredged to construct Interstate 91. Despite its artificial flavor and its shallowness, the cove is a popular fishing area. Note the large trees draped in vines of poison ivy, bittersweet, and wild grape; this is a small but lush example of floodplain forest. A bird's-eye view would show a classic series of ridges and swales carved by the river as the river channel gradually meandered east.

Mile 37.5: One more full S-loop of the river will bring you to the **Rocky Hill Public Boat Ramp,** where there is ample parking (for a fee), a picnic area, and the Pilot House restaurant. This is also the berth of the **Rocky Hill–Glastonbury Ferry,** the oldest continuously running ferry in the United States. The ferry has evolved from a small raft steered by poles, to a horse-driven treadmill craft, to a steamboat, to today's gas-powered open flatboat, the *Hollister III*, which can carry three cars across.

Miles 37.5–33.5: The river now straightens out for a few miles. Although the surroundings are pleasantly green and seemingly sparsely populated, boaters will notice a sure sign of "civilization" accompanying them downriver: garbage. This is one of the very few stretches of river in which trash still accumulates. A combination of nearby landfills and roads that closely parallel the eastern shore contributes bottles, cans, and other human debris. The currents here coalesce the garbage into long windrows, sober reminders of what much of the river looked like during much of the nineteenth and twentieth centuries. Boaters can be good citizens and retrieve occasional containers. At about mile 35.5, the river cuts steeply through the bank on the left, and a 150-foot-high bluff is also visible beyond the right bank. These bluffs mark **River Highlands State Park** (accessible only by land), a lovely place for a stroll along the river or a hike along the cliffs. **Wangunk Meadows Wildlife Management Area** lies just downstream on the left bank.

Mile 33.5: After the prolonged straight stretch, the river makes a westerly bend and passes **Gildersleeve Island**; only small boats can pass to its west side. *Caution:* Boaters should watch for gravel bars and a submerged dike, marked by a warning beacon, extending out from the southern end of the island; there are complicated crosscurrents here. Likewise, there is a no-wake zone extending from halfway along the island well past its southern tip. The privately owned island is home to a federally endangered tiger beetle. Farm fields surround this area, even though it is close to a city center. Keep an eye out for fast-moving merlins flying about in search of prey.

Mile 31: On the right shore opposite **Wilcox Island** lies the confluence with the **Mattabesset River**. This little river wends its way over 18 miles and fifteen towns to its meeting with the Connecticut. Once subject to a great deal of pollution (an abating but ever-present concern), the river is recovering here due to the cleanup efforts of the Mattabesset River Watershed Association and other groups. You can take a pleasant detour here for some nice paddling into the **Round and Boggy Meadows Wildlife Management Area** in Cromwell. These wetlands are important habitat for waterfowl such as wood ducks, and provide boaters from the north with their first real glimpse of freshwater tidal marsh.

Mile 30.9: The distinctive arches of the **Arrigoni Bridge** (Connecticut Routes 17/66) loom overhead at the southern tip of Wilcox Island. Only a stone's throw downstream are the equally distinctive ruins of the old railroad bridge linking Portland and Middletown. That bridge was rammed by a steamship in 1876; a memorable photo from the day of the accident shows a crumpled section of bridge unceremoniously draped across the bow of the listing ship. Although steam travel on the river would continue until 1931, this and other accidents presaged the demise of the steamship century.

Mile 30: Exit the river at **Harbor Park**, on the river's right bank in the heart of Middletown. The ramp is paved, and there is limited parking here. Tranquil Harbor Park, a great place to admire the power of spring freshets during a lunch break, is all that's left of what was, for half a century in the 1800s, one of the busiest ports in the United States, shipping out more cargo annually than New York City.

Rocking the Boats

Four hundred and ten miles of river, leading from Long Island Sound to the Canadian border, created the highway that Native Americans in the area used as their main trading route. Early New England colonists joined them in commerce, bringing logs and furs downriver. The first industrialists saw the river's potential for transport, even though it was beset by thirteen major waterfalls. So dams were built and canals were carved to skirt the difficult passages (see the "Connecticut River Canals" sidebar in Reach 18). By the early 1800s the river was open for business, accommodating the traffic of large boats and all they could carry.

The advent of steam power revolutionized shipping on the river. On December 1, 1826, the *Barnet*, the first steamship to ply the river, passed through the South Hadley Canal on its way north. Steamships made convenient alternatives to the rocky, horse-driven roads of the 1800s, too. Thousands of passengers traveled in luxury from New York to Hartford and beyond, with boats such as the *Middletown* carrying upward of 350 people.

By the 1930s, however, the heyday of steamships had passed. A series of unfortunate accidents—boiler explosions, fires, and collisions—destroyed several of the fleet. Trains—and that bane and boom of modern society, the car—made river travel uneconomical. Industrial and urban dumping turned parts of the river into an open sewer for the next fifty years.

The Connecticut River Watershed Council, founded in 1952, was one of the first public voices to warn of the dangers of pollution, joined by more organizations in the chorus of river advocates—the Connecticut River Joint Commissions, the Audubon Society, the Sierra Club, The Nature Conservancy, and many local watershed committees and councils. Cities whose river shores were given over exclusively to industry began to cultivate a new vision for the waterfront.

Today boats are returning to the river in force. Yachts share the channel with kayaks and fishing skiffs. A new generation of passenger boats now fills the role of the old steamships, ferrying delighted passengers around the river and showing people that great things can continue to happen on one of America's most beautiful rivers.

Reach 25 Middletown to East Haddam

Miles from mouth: 30.5–15.5 (20-mile span).
Navigable by: Kayaks, canoes, small and large powerboats.
Difficulty: Flat water.
Portage: None.
Fishing regulations: Boaters should steer clear of the gill nets used by shad anglers from Putnam Bridge (Connecticut Route 3, Glastonbury) to Long Island Sound from April through June.

Camping: *Mile 23:* Hurd State Park, Middle Haddam, Connecticut; river access for nonmotorized boats only.
USGS maps: Middletown 7.5, Middle Haddam 7.5, Haddam 7.5, Deep River 7.5.
NOAA charts: Connecticut River: Bodkin Rock to Hartford #12377, Deep River to Bodkin Rock #12377.

The Reach

This portion of the river flows from Middletown, Connecticut, to East Haddam, Connecticut. This reach is a great outing to enjoy a day of contrasts. You start in the city of Middletown, which has undergone something of an urban renaissance in recent years. Soon, although the highway noises are never far away, greenery closes in. A picnic lunch at Hurd State Park, followed by a walk around the park's many trails, will make you forget there are any cities nearby. But when you approach the East Haddam Bridge and the landmark Goodspeed Opera House (see the sidebar), you have arrived back in civilization.

At Middletown the river takes a sweeping easterly turn, a dogleg that diverts the remainder of its course toward the southeast. The traprock ridges of the Metacomet Range, uplifting 180 million years ago, prevented the river from taking a straight north–south route to the sea; instead, it found its way through a constrained valley of 450-million-year-old bedrock. So instead of heading straight south to New Haven, you will pass through a rugged, steep-sided gorge, reminiscent in places of the French King Gorge in Massachusetts.

The river throughout the reach is calm, though its pace can pick up a bit where it squeezes through deep bedrock fissures near Bodkin Rock. *Caution:* Be aware of tide changes, no-wake zones, and the many navigational markers along this reach that guide deeper-draft boats along the correct channel. Winds and large-boat traffic can pick up substantially as you near East Haddam.

Miles and Directions

Mile 30.5: Car-top boats and small trailers can access the river at **Harbor Park** in downtown Middletown, next to the Harbor Park Restaurant. The parking lot does not accommodate trailer parking, however, so owners of larger boats should consult one of the many marinas in the area for information on alternative access (see Appendix C). It's also possible during the summer to rent kayaks and canoes at Harbor Park

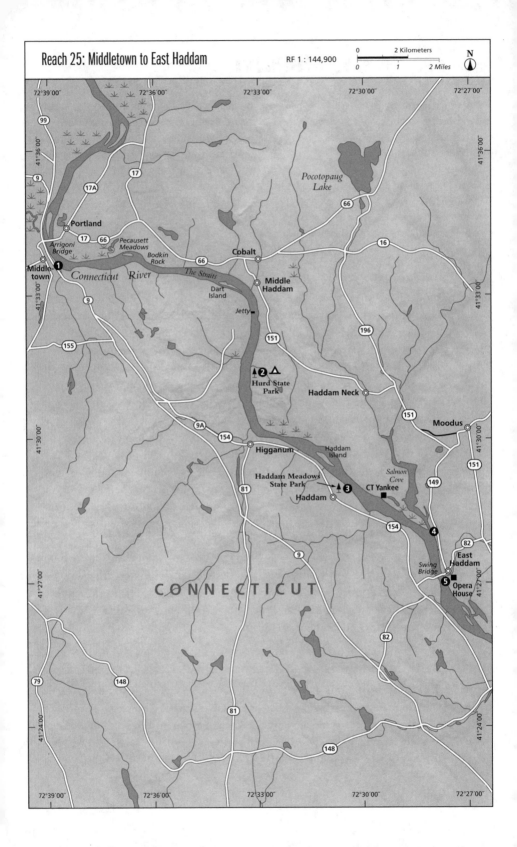

0   2 Kilometers

0   1   2 Miles

N

72°39'00"   72°36'00"   72°33'00"   72°30'00"   72°27'00"

41°36'00"

99

9

17A

17

Portland

Pocotopaug
Lake

66

16

17 66

Pecausett
Meadows

Arrigoni
Bridge

Bodkin
Rock

66   Cobalt

Middle-
town

Connecticut River   The Straits

Middle
Haddam

41°33'00"

9

Dart
Island

Jetty

151

155

Hurd State
Park

Haddam Neck

196

41°30'00"

9A

154

Higganum

151

Moodus

Haddam
Island

151

Haddam Meadows
State Park

81

Salmon
Cove

149

CT Yankee

Haddam

154

CONNECTICUT

9

4

82

East
Haddam

Swing
Bridge

Opera
House

41°27'00"

82

79   148

41°24'00"

81

148

72°39'00"   72°36'00"   72°33'00"   72°30'00"   72°27'00"

Boat Rental. The Macomber Boathouse, which houses Wesleyan University's crew team, is next door to the park; avoid swamping sculls and shells with your wake. Immediately downstream of Harbor Park on the right bank is the Middletown Coast Guard/Police Dock with emergency marine services.

Mile 30: Portland Boat Works and the neighboring **Pecausett Meadows** wetlands are visible on the river's left bank.

Mile 28: Bodkin Rock, a rocky cape on the river's left bank, heralds the new bedrock type, pegmatite, through which the river now threads its course. This complex and hard granite, studded with feldspar, is the product of hundreds of millions of years of violent subterranean pressures and folding spurred by multiple continental collisions. Pegmatite yields many economically important minerals and crystals, including cobalt, which was mined from nearby Middle Haddam and its neighboring village—aptly named Cobalt—from the 1700s on. Steep bedrock now encloses the river through the narrow passage called **The Straits** just beyond Bodkin Rock, and much of the way to East Haddam. Watch for tricky currents around the base of Bodkin Rock, signaled by a warning beacon at its summit.

Boating Facilities Table for Reach 25

Access Point, Directions	Boat Type	Fee	Parking	Picnic	Toilets	Camping	Rentals	Supplies
❶ **Harbor Park** Middletown, CT *At 80 Harbor Drive, park is accessible via exit 12 or 14 off CT 9.*	Improved ramp for car-top and small trailer boats	N	Y	Y	Y	N	Y	Nearby
❷ **Hurd State Park** Middle Haddam, CT *River access only. Reservations required; call (860) 424-3200 or (866) 287-2757.*	Unimproved path, canoes and kayaks only	Y	N	Y	Y	Y	N	N
❸ **Haddam Meadows State Park** Haddam, CT *East side of CT 154.*	Improved ramp for all boat types	N	Y	Y	Y	N	N	N
❹ **Salmon River Ramp** East Haddam-Moodus Road, East Haddam, CT *CT 149 near junction of East Haddam-Moodus Road and Landing Hill Road.*	Unimproved ramp for all boat types	N	Y	N	N	N	N	N
❺ **East Haddam Town Landing** Lumber Yard Road, East Haddam, CT *From CT 82 just east of East Haddam Bridge, turn right onto Lumber Yard Road.*	Unimproved ramp, car-top only	N	Y	N	N	N	N	Nearby

Mile 26: Just before the river turns south, **Dart Island** appears along the right bank, a state park that makes a pretty stop for a picnic (no facilities). *Caution:* There is a no-wake zone around this island. You should approach it from the main channel, not the very shallow lee side.

Mile 24.5: A pier and long **jetty** jut far out into the river here. Deeper-draft boats should give these a wide berth.

Mile 23: Hurd State Park, marked by the towering Split Rock and a long stone breakwater, lies on the left bank. Primitive camping is permitted here for nonmotorized boats only. Access the area by paddling all the way down to the end of the breakwater and making your way into the little embayment it encloses, which can be very shallow at low tide. Walking trails lead from the camping area through the thousand acres of the park. Every July the great Connecticut River Raft Race proceeds from here to Haddam Meadows State Park, attracting a motley array of ingenious human-powered watercraft—just about anything that floats. The race sponsor, Riverside Marina in Portland, donates a portion of the proceeds to various Connecticut children's charities.

Mile 20: Haddam Island appears midriver. It's a state park but does not permit camping. In the ever-changing way of river islands, Haddam Island was "giving birth" to a new island at its northern tip in 2005. *Caution:* Be wary of shoals here. According to the Haddam Historical Society, legend has it that some of Captain Kidd's treasure was buried on the island, although searches to date have not turned up riches. Haddam Island is one of two sites on the river where the magnanimous (or forgetful) pirate is purported to have buried treasure, the other being Northfield, Massachusetts. Once an important fishing spot, the island became a popular recreational destination, complete with refreshment stand, in the early twentieth century. Today its empty, inviting beach is a nice spot for a rest and swim.

Mile 19: Approaching **Haddam Meadows State Park**, just downstream on the right bank, the current may drag smaller craft a bit toward the center of the channel. Once a common pasture for livestock owners in Haddam and a nexus for trains carrying cargo from the steamships plying the river, the open fields of the park are great places for picnics or pickup baseball games. Haddam River Days, celebrating the Connecticut River, occurs here each September. The state park has a boat launch.

Mile 18.5: Looking like extraterrestrials have landed, the domes of the **Connecticut Yankee Power Plant** soon loom on the left bank. The plant opened in 1968 and produced more than 110 billion kilowatt-hours during its twenty-eight-year tenure. Decommissioning began in 1996 and is scheduled to be complete in 2007. Keep an eye out for great egrets, which frequent the area.

Mile 16.5: *Caution:* At the Salmon River confluence on the river's left bank, there is a no-wake zone. The lovely **Salmon Cove** is well worth exploring in smaller boats,

Cormorants are common boating companions, often seen drying themselves in the sun. Photo by Wendy Sinton

which can pass all the way up into the freshwater tidal marshes of the cove; maintain a watchful eye on the tides. The Salmon River is considered one of the state's top trout streams and is the site of a federal Atlantic salmon restoration project. Bald eagles take advantage of the wealth of fish and unfrozen tidal waters here during the winter. A state boat launch with gravel ramp is located at the southern end of the Salmon River mouth.

Mile 15.6: The **East Haddam Swing Bridge** (Connecticut Route 82) signals the homestretch of this reach. One of the oldest turnstile bridges in the country, it was built in 1913 by renowned bridge designer Alfred Boller and spans almost 900 feet. The bridge swings open at scheduled times for tall-masted traffic and on demand for barges. It has been undergoing extensive renovation since February 1999, when it "stuck" open due to stresses resulting from paving.

Mile 15.5: On the river's right bank, in Haddam, Camelot Cruises offers regular cruises down the river on a number of unusual themes such as "Murder on the Connecticut River." You may see several of the firm's large boats in the channel.

The Goodspeed Opera House in East Haddam is world-renowned for its Victorian architecture and musical productions. Photo © Al Braden

Mile 15.5: The unmistakable grande dame of the river, the **Goodspeed Opera House**, sits on the left bank just beyond the bridge. If you call ahead, you can reserve private docking space at the Opera House, just steps away from the theater, should you wish to take in a musical performance; otherwise, public use of the dock is not permitted. Instead, take out at the **East Haddam Town Landing**, a sandy beach just below the Opera House dock. Although you may be tempted to take out immediately downstream at the large dock associated with the Goodspeed Airport, do not do so; it is only for seaplanes and requires permission to use.

East Haddam History

No one should pass through East Haddam, Connecticut (settled 1662), without strolling down its historical streets, which boast shops, a memorable ice-cream and candy parlor, and numerous lovely buildings from the colonial and Victorian eras. Most are only a stone's throw from the river shore. The most visible river landmark is the Goodspeed Opera House, which the merchant and shipbuilder William Goodspeed built in 1876 as an entertainment venue for the many passengers on the river steamships of that era. The Opera House was all but condemned by the mid-1900s, reflecting the decline of steamship travel. Saved from demolition by an eleventh-hour, $1.00 purchase, it was restored and rededicated in 1963. It's now a major seat of musical comedy in the United States, having premiered such famous productions as *Man of La Mancha* and *Annie.*

The nearby Gelston House (8 Main Street) was built in 1736 and now houses an award-winning restaurant with sweeping views of the river. St. Stephen's Episcopal Church (33 Main Street) was founded in 1791 but houses an artifact almost 1,000 years older: its bell. The bell was cast originally for a Spanish monastery in the year 815, but was transported as ship's ballast to Connecticut in 1843. Just behind St. Stephen's, at 29 Main Street, sits the one-room Nathan Hale Schoolhouse, where its namesake presided over thirty-three students for five months in 1773–1774 before being hanged for "espionage" at the age of twenty-one by the British.

A bit farther afield, on Town Street, the Amasa Day House is a Federal-style home built in 1818 and inhabited by generations of descendants of Amasa Day, a wealthy industrialist. It now houses the Antiquarian and Landmarks Society of Connecticut and offers visitors fine examples of interior art and stenciling, plus an extensive photographic collection from the 1920s by Amasa Day Chafee. Also on Town Street, the Congregational church dates from 1794; its grand, arching interior and star-studded ceiling merit a long look. To learn more about the region's colorful history, including its precolonial inhabitants, visit the East Haddam Historical Society Museum at 264 Town Street.

Reach 26 East Haddam-Chester to Essex

Miles from mouth: 15.5–6.0 (9.5-mile span).
Navigable by: Kayaks, canoes, small and large powerboats.
Difficulty: Flat water.
Portages: None.
Fishing regulations: Boaters should steer clear of the gill nets used by shad anglers from Putnam Bridge (Connecticut Route 3, Middletown) to Long Island Sound from April through June.

Camping: *Mile 14:* Gillette Castle State Park, East Haddam, Connecticut; access for nonmotorized boats only. *Mile 12:* Selden Neck State Park, Hadlyme, Connecticut; river access only.
USGS maps: Deep River 7.5, Hamburg 7.5, Essex 7.5, Old Lyme 7.5.
NOAA charts: Connecticut River: Deep River to Bodkin Rock #12377, Long Island Sound to Deep River #12375.

The Reach

This reach can begin in either East Haddam or Chester, Connecticut, and concludes in Essex, Connecticut. This reach has something for everyone: historical architecture, a dramatic ecological transition from fresh to brackish water, secret coves to explore, and accessibility for all types of boats. As such, it's one of the most popular stretches on the entire Connecticut River and can be exceptionally busy on weekends throughout the year. *Caution:* Check tide charts, because shallow coves dot the whole reach. Canoeists and kayakers may need to dodge larger motorcraft, and people piloting deep-draft boats need to watch carefully for paddlers plying the river. For small boaters there are numerous quieter coves and tributaries to duck into should the wakes and chop get too challenging. The Connecticut River Estuary Canoe/Kayak Trail can give paddle boaters lots of alternative trips along the river's estuaries and inlets. We recommend that small boaters stick to either the west or east shores of the river without trying to cross the bustling central channel in heavy traffic or winds. Larger boats can cross the river at will, but will have more choices of access points on the west side of the river.

This stretch lies within the heart of the Tidelands, a globally significant natural area that The Nature Conservancy calls one of the "Last Great Places" on earth. There are no other areas in the Northeast that support such extensive or high-quality fresh and brackish tidal wetland systems as those in the Connecticut River estuary. Since no two marshes here are identical, spend as much time as you can exploring each one. Seabirds and songbirds abound: Look for ospreys hovering overhead and great egrets patiently hunting the shallows. Botanists will enjoy the diversity of interesting plants in the marshes: flamboyant purple spires of pickerelweed, golden daisy-like flowers of beggarticks, and white arum lily spikes peeking out amid the rich green meadows of wild rice. All these species coexist with an increasingly dense population of residents and tourists, who revel in the scenic attractions, campgrounds, and historical sites of the lower river.

Note that since the Connecticut River now becomes a wide estuary, from here on we will refer to the river's east and west shore rather than left or right bank.

Miles and Directions

Mile 15.5: Canoeists and kayakers can find parking and a sandy put-in at the **East Haddam Town Landing**, just downstream of the Goodspeed Opera House and upstream of the small airstrip, on the east shore. Do not miss exploring the charming town of East Haddam (see the "East Haddam History" sidebar in Reach 25).

Miles 14.5: Larger boats can put in at one of the many local marinas on the west shore in this area (see Appendix C). Chester residents with a valid sticker can put in at the **Chester Town Boat Landing**. Both large and small boats can put in downstream at the well-equipped **Deep River Town Landing**. The Essex Steam Train and *Becky Thatcher* Riverboat also leave from here. Deep River (which is named for a tributary and does not reflect bottomless depths of the main stem) served as a major shipping area for 150 years, at one time trafficking in more than 12,000 pounds of African ivory *a month*.

Mile 14.5: You will shortly come to **Rich** and **Lord Islands** on the east shore, which afford some shelter from the wind and current on the main stem. East of Lord Island, a narrow cut leads east to **Chapman Pond**, a Nature Conservancy preserve protecting ecologically unique freshwater tidal wetlands (see the sidebar). The gorgeous wild rice marshes and hiking trails through more than 500 acres of surrounding forests are worth a day to explore in themselves. You may unearth some oyster shells along the shore here; they once formed the raw material for a button factory in the area. Anglers will find good bass fishing here, too. Keep an eye on the tides, however, as you can easily be stranded in the shallow waters of the pond, which are thick with submerged aquatic plants. Although a small creek snakes through marshes and exits the south end of the pond, it's usually best to head back out to the river the way you came in.

Mile 13: Gillette Castle, a startling stone edifice complete with turret, watches over the river's east shore above the landing for the **Chester–Hadlyme Ferry**. Built in 1918 by the actor William Gillette (famed for portraying Sherlock Holmes on the stage), this imposing structure and the 122 acres of woods, trails, and stone bridges surrounding it became a state park in 1943. Primitive, river-access camping is available here; reservations are required, and competition for campsites is keen in the summer. There is a small picnic area on the shore, with signs describing the Impressionist Art Trail of the Connecticut River that highlights the river paintings of Connecticut artist William Chadwick. *Caution:* Car-top boaters putting in at the access point here should avoid getting in the path of the Chester–Hadlyme Ferry. In continuous operation since 1768, it leaves every few minutes for the opposite shore.

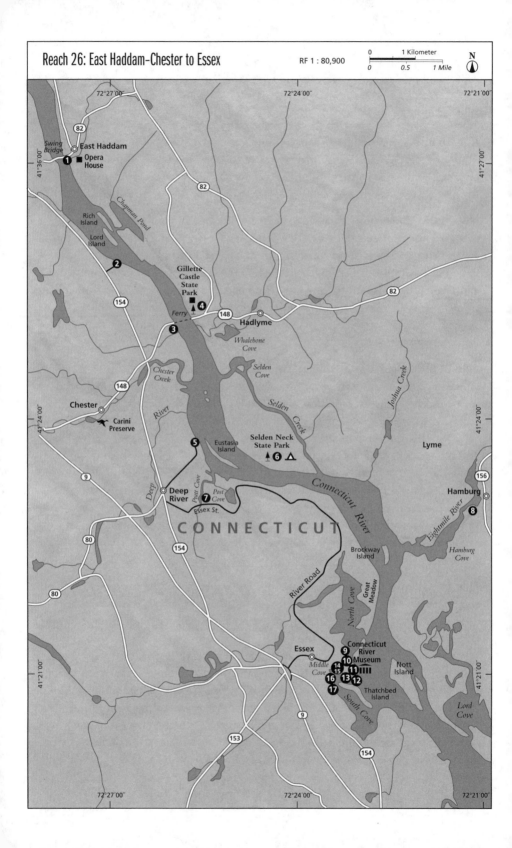

Reach 26: East Haddam-Chester to Essex

RF 1 : 80,900

0   1 Kilometer

0   0.5   1 Mile

N

82

Swing Bridge

East Haddam

1 Opera House

Chapman Pond

Rich Island

Lord Island

2

154

82

Gillette Castle State Park

4

Ferry

3

148

Hadlyme

82

Whalebone Cove

Chester Creek

Selden Cove

148

River

Chester

Carini Preserve

Selden Creek

Joshua Creek

Lyme

5

Eustasia Island

Selden Neck State Park

6 △

9

Deep Cove

Putt Cove

Deep River

Post Cove

7

Essex St.

156

Hamburg

8

Connecticut River

Eightmile River

C O N N E C T I C U T

80

154

Brockway Island

Hamburg Cove

River Road

80

Great Meadow

North Cove

9

Essex

10

Connecticut River Museum

11 ‖‖‖‖

Nott Island

Middle Cove

14
15

16

13 **12**

17

Thatchbed Island

South Cove

Lord Cove

9

153

154

Boating Facilities Table for Reach 26

Access Point, Directions	Boat Type	Fee	Parking	Picnic	Toilets	Camping	Rentals	Supplies
❶ East Haddam Town Landing Lumber Yard Road, East Haddam, CT *From CT 82 just east of East Haddam Bridge, turn right onto Lumber Yard Road. Park in dirt lot at river shore.*	Unimproved ramp, car-top only	N	Y	N	N	N	N	Nearby
❷ Chester Town Boat Landing Parker's Point Road, Chester, CT *Turn east off CT 154 (Middlesex Turnpike) onto Parker's Point Road. Ramp for use by town residents (with sticker) only.*	Improved ramp for all boat types	N	Y	Y	Y	N	N	N
❸ Chester–Hadlyme Ferry Boat Access CT 148, Chester, CT *At terminus of CT 148 on the western shore, adjacent to and just south of the ferry dock.*	Unimproved ramp, car-top only	N	Y Limited	N	N	N	N	N
❹ Gillette Castle State Park Route 148, Hadlyme, CT *Take CT 148 to its terminus at Chester–Hadlyme Ferry; access is north of ferry landing. Call (860) 526-2336 for camping reservations.*	Unimproved ramp, car-top only	Y	Y	Y	Y	Y River access only	N	N
❺ Deep River Town Landing River/Kirtland Street, Deep River, CT *Turn east onto River Street off CT 154 just opposite junction with CT 80.*	Improved ramp for all boat types	N	Y	Y	Y	N	N	Nearby
❻ Selden Neck State Park Lyme, CT *River access only. Call (860) 526-2336 for camping reservations.*	For car-top and shallow-draft boats	Y	N	Y	Y	Y River access only	N	N
❼ Pratt Cove Essex Street, Deep River, CT *South side of Essex Street off CT 154.*	Unimproved path, car-top only	N	Y	N	N	N	N	N
❽ Lyme Town Boat Access Cove Road, Lyme, CT *Just south of junction of CT 156 (Hamburg Road) with Cove Road.*	Unimproved ramp, car-top only	N	Y	N	N	N	N	N
❾ Little Point Street Ramp Little Point Street, Essex, CT *From Middlesex Turnpike/CT 154 in Essex, turn east onto West Avenue. Turn left onto Grove Street. Turn right onto North Main Street. Turn left onto Little Point Street.*	Improved ramp, car-top only	N	Y	N	N	N	N	N

Boating Facilities Table for Reach 26 continued

Access Point, Directions	Boat Type	Fee	Parking	Picnic	Toilets	Camping	Rentals	Supplies
❿ **Bushnell Park** Bushnell Street, Essex, CT *From Middlesex Turnpike/CT 154 in Essex, turn east onto West Avenue. Take slight right onto Champlin Square. Stay straight to go onto West Avenue. Turn slight left onto South Main Street. Turn slight right onto Essex Square. Turn slight left onto North Main Street. Turn right onto Bushnell Street.*	Improved ramp, car-top only	N	Y	N	N	N	N	N
⓫ **Essex Town Dock** Main Street, Essex, CT *From Middlesex Turnpike/CT 154 in Essex, turn east onto West Avenue. Take slight right onto Champlin Square. Stay straight to go onto West Avenue. Turn slight left onto South Main Street. Turn slight right onto Essex Square. Turn right onto Main Street. Follow Main Street to end.*	Improved ramp for all boat types	N	Y	N	N	N	N	Nearby
⓬ **Novelty Lane Water Access Area** Novelty Lane, Essex, CT *From Middlesex Turnpike/CT 154 in Essex, turn east onto West Avenue. Take slight right onto Champlin Square. Stay straight to go onto West Avenue. Turn slight left onto South Main Street. Turn slight right onto Essex Square. Turn right onto Main Street. Turn right onto Novelty Lane.*	Unimproved ramp, car-top only	N	Y	N	N	N	N	N
⓭ **Scholes Lane Water Access Area** Scholes Lane, Essex, CT *From Middlesex Turnpike/CT 154, turn east onto West Avenue. Take slight right onto Champlin Square. Stay straight to go onto West Avenue. Turn slight left onto South Main Street. Turn slight right onto Essex Square. Turn right onto Main Street. Turn right onto Scholes Lane.*	Unimproved access, car-top only	N	Y	N	N	N	N	N
⓮ **Middle Cove, Essex Town Park** Nott Lane, Essex, CT *Turn south off Main Street in Essex onto Nott Lane behind post office; portage boat to small ramp in park.*	Improved ramp, car-top only	N	Y	Y	Y	N	N	Nearby
⓯ **Nott Lane Open Space Access** Nott Lane, Essex, CT *Turn south off Main Street in Essex onto Nott Lane behind post office; portage boat to small ramp in park.*	Unimproved access, car-top only	N	Y	N	N	N	N	Nearby

Boating Facilities Table for Reach 26 continued

Access Point, Directions	Boat Type	Fee	Parking	Picnic	Toilets	Camping	Rentals	Supplies
⑯ Alt Water Access Area Collins Lane, Essex, CT *From Middlesex Turnpike/CT 154, turn northeast onto South Main Street. Turn right onto Collins Lane.*	Unimproved access, car-top only	N	Y	N	N	N	N	N
⑰ Mack Lane Access Area Mack Lane, Essex, CT *From Middlesex Turnpike/CT 154, turn northeast onto South Main Street. Turn right onto Mack Lane. Caution: Access here is steep.*	Unimproved access, car-top only	N	Y	N	N	N	N	N

Chapman Pond and its hundreds of acres of freshwater tidal marsh and wooded hills are well worth a visit. Photo by Chris Joyell

Mile 12: Smaller boats can now explore two lovely east-shore creeks. A few hundred yards below the Chester–Hadlyme Ferry is the entrance to **Whalebone Creek**, an entry point to tranquil, lovely marshes surrounded by forest. *Caution:* Paddlers should stay close in to shore here, as motorboat traffic can kick up large wakes. Downstream is a creek that leads to **Selden Cove** and skirts the length of **Selden Neck**, the largest island in the Connecticut River. Four river-access campgrounds are available at Selden Neck State Park on the island's west shore; reservations are required. Although a few houses overlook Selden Cove, **Selden Creek** itself is very secluded and makes a wonderful swimming, picnicking, and fishing spot. Enclosed by towering pines and stark bedrock outcrops of gneiss studded with pegmatite crystals, this place is easy to mistake for some of the more remote outposts on the northern part of the river. You may come upon rather territorial mute swans here; do not challenge these large birds, especially during nesting season.

Mile 12: Across the river from Selden Cove is the more crowded **Chester Creek**, home to a mixture of freshwater tidal marshes and busy marinas. It was once possible to access Chester Creek from land from the **Carini Preserve**, owned by the Chester Land Trust, with an unimproved access for car-top boats off Connecticut Route 148. However, a beaver dam and several downed trees now obstruct paddling through Chester Creek proper to the Connecticut River; boaters can play in the upper reaches only. Just downstream from Chester Creek lies the **Deep River**, with its own lovely tidal wetlands.

Miles 11–9.5: If you forgo a side trip down Selden Creek, on the west shore you will pass the **Deep River Town Landing** at the northern tip of **Eustasia Island**, an important shad fishery in the eighteenth century. *Caution:* This is a no-wake zone and a rich site for rare mussels. Passing to the right of the island, you will encounter the Deep River Marina, which marks the entrance to **Pratt Cove** and its smaller twin, **Post Cove** (just to the south). These freshwater tidal marshes offer spectacular birding; look for Cooper's hawks, wood ducks, black ducks, marsh wrens, and even the occasional ruby-crowned kinglet here. Land access to Pratt Cove and its associated walking trail is also possible for car-top boats at a small put-in in Deep River. Note that the route from the Deep River all the way to Essex is part of the Connecticut River Estuary Canoe/Kayak Trail. Another 1.5 miles downstream of Pratt Cove is the landing site of the Brockway Ferry, which operated in the 1700s. A flotilla of small sailboats from the local Pettipaug Yacht Club sailing program might greet you as you paddle downriver here.

Mile 10.5: Downstream of the southern outlet of Selden Creek is tiny **Joshua Creek**, followed after another mile by the mouth of **Hamburg Cove**, which lies directly east of **Brockway Island** on the river's east shore. The cove forms the confluence between the Connecticut River and the picturesque **Eightmile River**, which will likely be designated a national Wild and Scenic River in 2007. Anadromous fish are

The Chester-Hadlyme Ferry is one of the oldest continuously operating ferries in the United States. Photo © Al Braden

making their way back upriver due to the construction of clever fishways. Take great care what you catch; except for shad, possession of anadromous fish, including alewives and blueback herring, is strictly prohibited. Lucky boaters may spot one of the resident bald eagles or ospreys here. The numerous dead hemlocks haunting the bluffs above the river were killed by a combination of Hurricane Gloria (1985) and a diminutive but deadly invasive insect, the hemlock woolly adelgid. Car-top boats can be paddled about a mile up the cove to the **Lyme Town Boat Access**. More intrepid explorers can take out at an informal fisherman's access at the top of Hamburg Cove, where Joshuatown Road crosses Hamburg Creek.

Miles 8–6: South of Brockway Island, the river begins a final dramatic widening on its approach to the sea. Traffic on the river picks up considerably as you near the coves of Essex on the west shore. The **Great Meadow** peninsula protects the **North Cove**

Essex has a fine harbor for all kinds of craft. Photo © Al Braden

near Essex. As you head into this quiet cove to explore as far as the mouth of the Falls River, it's easy to forget how close you are to a busy town. Watch the tides so as not to strand yourself while daydreaming. Ospreys and perhaps even a bald eagle will greet you here; in fact, Essex is the site of a very large bald eagle celebration. Connecticut Audubon's Eagle Festival happens every February, attracting thousands of people who welcome the birds home from their winter migration.

Miles 7–6: There are a number of places to take out in Essex, clustered at the mouth of North Cove and around Middle Cove. Moving clockwise around the Essex peninsula, the **Little Point Street Ramp, Bushnell Park, Essex Town Dock, Novelty Lane Water Access Area, Scholes Lane Water Access Area, Essex Town Park, Alt Water Access Area,** and **Mack Lane Access Area** are best suited for car-top boats. The Essex Town Dock, adjacent to the Connecticut River Museum at the end of Main Street, can accommodate all types of boats. You can find restaurants and shops in the colonial town of Essex, for two centuries a major shipbuilding center. Do not leave Essex without a visit to the Connecticut River Museum, housed in a restored steamboat warehouse on the waterfront and replete with all the information you could ever want to know about the river. And consider taking a pleasure ride on the Connecticut Valley Railroad, which begins at the train station, 0.1 mile north of the junction of Connecticut Routes 9 and 154 in Essex.

Wetlands of International Importance

Most people think of tidal wetlands solely as saltwater phenomena, but all great estuaries show a gradation from saltwater to brackish to freshwater tidal wetlands. As the Connecticut River makes its last push to Long Island Sound, tides increasingly shape its course and the natural communities it supports. South of Glastonbury, tides are felt only as rhythmic rises and falls in the level of the fresh water in the river; no salt water penetrates this far upriver. But the subtle daily tides alternately flood the vegetation and leave it high and dry, creating difficult conditions for many wetland plant species adapted for continuous inundation. In these changeable freshwater tidal marshes, a specialized suite of plants takes hold among the more common wetland species. Their hallmark is wild rice (*Zizania palustris*), an exceptionally graceful grass and a critical food source for ducks, rails, blackbirds, and other species, and once a staple grain for Native Americans. You can lose yourself in the tortuous channels that weave through swards of these 10-foot-tall grasses. Another hundred or more plant species grow interspersed with wild rice in these very diverse habitats. Such exuberant growth makes these freshwater marshes among the most productive in the world—producing more biomass during the growing season than most other ecosystems. Plants supply a rich food web, and their annual decay furnishes the river with a bounty of nitrogen and other nutrients that fertilize aquatic vegetation and feed fish and other aquatic animals.

Downstream of Essex, more brackish waters, pushed by tides, mix with the river's fresh water. Here the marshes take on the appearance of other great northeastern estuaries from Merrymeeting Bay, Maine, to the Chesapeake. Plants with spongy roots and high tolerance to salt have adapted specifically to the twice-daily influx of salt water that covers the fine muds and peats of salt marshes, so low in oxygen that they exude the characteristic rotten-egg smell of sulfur. Narrow-leaved cattails, clumps of the tough and wiry salt marsh cordgrasses, and fields filled with chartreuse cowlicks of salt marsh hay ultimately replace all the freshwater plants. Pounded by oceanic storms and rafts of ice, these ecosystems are hardy and resilient. Comparable in productivity to freshwater marshes, salt marshes supply the inshore ocean environments with nutrients while buffering the uplands from waves.

This exceptionally rich complex of wetlands on the lower river is unique in all New England, and almost unheard of on rivers of comparable size and population density. As such, the United Nations has designated them as one of only twenty-two U.S. Wetlands of International Importance.

Reach 27 **Essex to the Sound (Western Shore)**

Miles from mouth: 6.0–0 (6-mile span).
Navigable by: Kayaks, canoes, small and large powerboats.
Difficulty: Flat water; beware of wind, tides, and boat wakes; no-wake zone on river in Essex between North Cove and South Cove.
Portages: None.
Fishing regulations: Boaters should steer clear of the gill nets used by shad anglers from Put-nam Bridge (Connecticut Route 3, Middletown) to Long Island Sound from April through June. No state fishing license is required downstream of the Amtrak Railroad Bridge between Old Saybrook and Old Lyme.
Camping: No established sites.
USGS maps: Essex 7.5, Old Lyme 7.5.
NOAA charts: Connecticut River: Long Island Sound to Deep River #12375.

The Reach

The river is crowded with marinas and public landings in its last 6 miles before Long Island Sound, and small boats are often prevented by currents and large boat traffic from crossing the river near its mouth. Therefore, we are presenting the last reach of the river in two parts: an eastern shore and a western shore. This reach runs from Essex, Connecticut, to Old Saybrook, Connecticut, along the river's west shore. Since the Connecticut River is now an estuary, we will refer to the river's east and west shore rather than left or right bank.

The smell of salt begins to sting your nose; the onshore breezes pick up; the river widens as you begin your final approach to Long Island Sound. Although many private docks, marinas, and stately homes dot the shore, the population density is quite low compared with other coastal areas in the Northeast, and you will still find expansive marshes and creeks to explore. The boater with a taste for nautical history will delight in the old chandleries and moorings of Essex, not to mention the many exhibits at the Connecticut River Museum. After touching base at the very outer reach of land at Lynde Point Lighthouse (but beware of tricky currents and big swells here!), small boats can end their run at the North Cove Town Ramp in Old Saybrook; larger craft should head back upstream to the Baldwin Bridge State Boat Launch.

Powerboats can buck tides and winds, but please be considerate of small craft. Canoes and kayaks, by contrast, must steer clear of the large sportfishing boats traveling to and from the sound. Stick close to the west shore of the river, both to shelter yourself from wind and wakes and to take the opportunity to explore the winding, tranquil creeks.

Miles and Directions

Mile 6.0: Car-top boats and trailers can put in at the public **Essex Town Dock** at the end of Main Street, near the Connecticut River Museum. Note that entering the water (and finding nearby parking) can be a bit challenging here due to the comings and goings of boat traffic at the yacht club next door. Skippers of much larger boats should consult with one of the dozen or more yacht clubs and marinas in the area (see Appendix C). If you'd like someone else to do the tricky navigation, Connecticut River Expeditions runs regular tours of the river mouth. Be sure to take some time to enjoy the historical sites of Essex before your departure or upon your return. **North Cove** and **South Cove**, lobes off the river above and below Essex respectively, are great places to explore, fish, bird-watch, and loll about. The eastern shore of South Cove is protected by The Nature Conservancy's **Turtle Creek Wildlife Sanctuary**, and **Thatchbed Island** guards the mouth. Note that this and many of the fascinating natural areas around the Connecticut coast are well documented at the Long Island Sound Resource Center's Web site (www.lisrc.uconn.edu).

Miles 6–4: As you enter the river's main channel from the town dock, **Nott Island**, a state Wildlife Management Area, will be directly east of you. Another 2 miles downstream on the river's west shore, you will see the mouth of a small unnamed creek, leading to a small marsh that provides some nice fishing. You have now left behind the freshwater tidal marshes: from here on, salt-tolerant cordgrasses form thick stands all the way to the sound, reflecting the ocean's influence. Notice that these marshes have been deeply ditched with channels to control water levels (and, it was originally thought, to control mosquitoes and associated diseases). Much of the ditching happened in the 1930s, with the intent of allowing faster drainage of excess standing water. Unfortunately, ditching profoundly altered the water flow into salt marshes, sometimes lowering groundwater levels and hastening the breakdown of peat and the loss of marsh. When the ditches themselves degraded and eroded, they accumulated stagnant water and supported the very mosquitoes they were supposed to thwart. In recent years managers have reopened tide gates, restoring or augmenting tidal flooding. In many cases the vegetation has quickly recovered and invertebrate populations have rebounded, along with the birds that feed on them.

Mile 3.5: The roar of traffic on Interstate 95 will herald your approach to the **Baldwin Bridge**. Connecticut's largest public boat ramp lies at the foot of this bridge on the west shore. The **Baldwin Bridge State Boat Launch** is an enormous complex with a four-lane boat ramp for trailers and ample parking (for a fee). Smaller boats can take out at an out-of-the-way ramp tucked in a few yards downstream of the big launch.

Mile 3: Rocks and shoals beset the river just downstream of the Baldwin Bridge ramp, so take care at low tide. *Caution:* Watch for turbulence and reduced steerage around the pylons of the bascule-style **Amtrak Railroad Bridge**, which, when closed to accommodate the train, has only a 19-foot clearance (Sailboats: See Appendix B for information on contacting the bridge tender to raise the bridge.) Here the river widens significantly, and the water and fishery take on a decidedly marine quality. About 1.2 miles south of the ramp, the entrance to **Ragged Rock Creek** and its

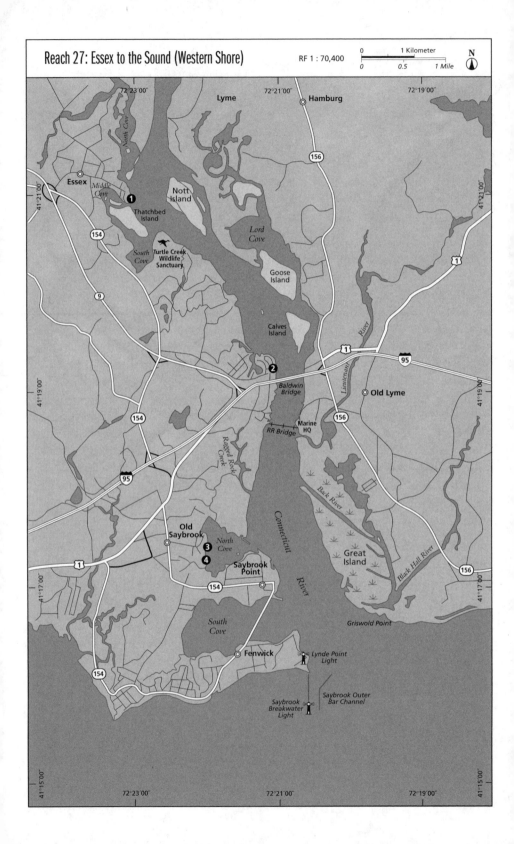

Reach 27: Essex to the Sound (Western Shore)

RF 1 : 70,400

0   1 Kilometer
0   0.5   1 Mile

N

Lyme

72°23'00"

72°21'00"

Hamburg

72°19'00"

156

41°21'00"

North Cove

Essex

Middle Cove

1

Nott Island

Thatchbed Island

Lord Cove

South Cove

Turtle Creek Wildlife Sanctuary

Goose Island

154

9

Calves Island

2

Baldwin Bridge

River

Lieutenant

Old Lyme

72°19'00"

41°19'00"

154

RR Bridge

Marine HQ

156

Ragged Rock Creek

95

Back River

Old Saybrook

3

North Cove

Great Island

4

Saybrook Point

Connecticut

Black Hall River

156

1

154

River

41°17'00"

South Cove

Griswold Point

154

Fenwick

Lynde Point Light

Saybrook Breakwater Light

Saybrook Outer Bar Channel

41°15'00"

72°23'00"

72°21'00"

72°19'00"

41°15'00"

surrounding Wildlife Management Area appears on the west shore. This creek meanders through about 300 acres of marsh, home to migrating black ducks, green-winged
teal, and mallards, and providing wintering habitat for rare species such as the king
rail and the tiny black rail.

Mile 1.4: About 0.4 mile below Ragged Rock Creek, the inlet to Old Saybrook's
North Cove, carved from the remains of an old railroad bed, will come into view.
On your way into the cove, you will pass many fine examples of colonial architecture, including the former Black Horse Tavern, dating to 1665. Most of the cove's
perimeter is very shallow, so stay to the center where a 4-foot rectangular basin is kept
dredged. The town of Old Saybrook maintains the small **North Cove Town Ramp**

Boating Facilities Table for Reach 27

Note: The Essex Town Dock is one of nine points of access to the river in Essex (see the descriptions in Reach 26).
Only one, the Essex Town Dock, is accessible to all types of craft.

Access Point, Directions	Boat Type	Fee	Parking	Picnic	Toilets	Camping	Rentals	Supplies
❶ Essex Town Dock Main Street, Essex, CT From Middlesex Turnpike/CT 154 in Essex, turn east onto West Avenue. Take slight right onto Champlin Square. Stay straight to go onto West Avenue. Turn slight left onto South Main Street. Turn slight right onto Essex Square. Turn right onto Main Street. Follow Main Street until the end.	Improved ramp for all boat types	N	Y	N	N	N	N	Nearby
❷ Baldwin Bridge State Boat Launch Ferry Road, Old Saybrook, CT Take exit 2 off CT 9 or exit 69 off I-95. Turn east onto Essex Road, south onto Ferry Road, and left into parking area.	Improved ramp for all boat types	Y	Y	Y	Y	N	N	Nearby
❸ North Cove Yacht Club Sheffield Street, Old Saybrook, CT Shortly before terminus of Sheffield Street, make easterly turn off CT 154 heading south through Old Saybrook. Drive past public schools to end of road. Open to public with permission; call (860) 388-9087.	Improved ramp for all boat types	Y	Y	N′	Y	N	Y	Y
❹ North Cove Town Ramp Sheffield Street, Old Saybrook, CT Take US 1 to CT 154; turn south, then left onto Sheffield Street. Drive past public schools to end of street. Limited parking.	Improved but narrow ramp for car-top and small boats	N	Y	N	Y	N	N	N

A boat passes Saybrook Breakwater Light for a day on Long Island Sound. Photo © Al Braden

at the western end the cove, at the terminus of Sheffield Street. Next door is the **North Cove Yacht Club,** which is open to guests and boats needing short-term moorings on a first-come, first-served basis (visitors must sign in and pay). *Caution:* These are the last two easily accessible take-out points on the river's west side before Long Island Sound.

Miles 1.4–0: If you want to extend your trip to the very tip of land at the river's mouth, keep heading south, paying close attention to the changeable currents around the jetties that mark the **Saybrook Outer Bar Channel.** Alternatively, consider boarding the Connecticut Riverboat for a tour of the coves and the lights; call (860) 575–9888 for reservations. Rounding the bend of **Saybrook Point,** you see the wide mouth of **South Cove,** marked by a drowned causeway and a roadway that crosses it. The cove is very shallow in most places, with extensive brackish marshes. South

Cove is enclosed by an arm of land that houses the neighborhood of **Fenwick**; that arm is a classic example of a recessional moraine—a place where the end of the receding glacier paused and temporarily dumped its formidable load of sediments (Long Island is the outermost or "terminal" moraine of that glacier). Both North and South Coves are included in the Connecticut River Estuary Regional Planning Agency (CRERPA) Canoe/Kayak Trail. Call (860) 388–3497 for trail maps.

Mile 0: **Lynde Point Light** (Old Saybrook Inner Harbor Lighthouse) marks the effective end of solid land. Initially erected in 1803, Lynde Point Light was refurbished to a 65-foot stone tower in 1838. It is still functional as a navigation aid, but is closed to the public. Its sister beacon, **Saybrook Breakwater Light** (the Outer Light) at the end of a stone breakwater, was built in 1886.

Boatbuilding

The Connecticut River may lack a world-class port at its mouth (see "The Ever-Changing River Mouth" sidebar in Reach 28), but that has never hampered the growth of a vibrant and lucrative shipbuilding trade, one that would last for more than 200 years. Essex Village built its first wharf in 1664, and by the time of the first rumblings of the Revolutionary War, several large ships were being produced here. An impressive early effort was the *Oliver Cromwell,* Connecticut's first real "battleship." With an 80-foot keel, she was built in 1775 for about £1,750 and sailed to New London, Connecticut, to be outfitted in weapons—the largest ship at that time to have successfully breached the Saybrook sandbar. Surviving lightning strikes, a hurricane off the Bahamas, and several outbreaks of smallpox among the crew, the *Oliver Cromwell* captured nine British ships in privateering raids until the British seized her in 1779.

Essex gave rise to other innovative maritime "secret weapons" during this period. The Yale graduate and inventor David Bushnell designed and deployed the nation's first attack "submarine" in Essex in 1776. The *American Turtle,* actually looking more like an outsize 6-foot-wide teapot than a turtle, carried a single mine with a timer delay. It was hand-propelled underwater by one man, who would approach the unsuspecting enemy, affix the incendiary to the ship's hull with a screw, and make his escape before detonating the bomb. When the sub's practiced pilot, Ezra Bushnell (David's brother), became ill, Ezra Lee hastily stepped in to pilot the *Turtle* on its first mission: an attack on the British ship *Eagle,* which was blockading New York Harbor. Lee failed to attach the bomb, however, and had to scurry away when the British ship gave chase. He detonated the mine while fleeing, leaving the enemy ship undamaged but alerting the British that something sneaky was afoot with this peculiar craft. The

British temporarily withdrew their ships from New York Harbor. After this doomed maiden voyage, the *Turtle* would bungle several other combat missions. Almost twenty years later a disillusioned David Bushnell would change his name to Bush and retire to Georgia, keeping his identity and ill-fated invention a secret until his death.

Ship production accelerated following the American Revolution; Essex shipwrights built more than 500 vessels before the Civil War erupted. The industry generated considerable income, which captains and merchants invested in constructing lovely Federal-style homes clustered in downtown Essex, several of which are today on the National Historical Register. By the War of 1812, news that five sleek privateering schooners were under construction at Essex made the British navy quite nervous. In a preemptive strike, more than one hundred British sailors raided Essex Harbor in the predawn hours of April 1814, commandeering the town, burning twenty-eight boats, and capturing two others. Losses were calculated at $200,000, a devastating cost at the time. This skirmish earned Essex the dubious distinction as one of only a handful of towns in the United States attacked directly by a foreign power. To commemorate the disaster, Essex residents still stage a "Burning of the Ships" parade in May every year.

In the ensuing half a century, steamships gradually replaced sailing vessels, and the great shipbuilding era came to a close. Essex remained an important port, however, especially when the 1850s saw a boom in ivory trade with Africa, 90 percent of which passed through the town and its villages, Deep River and Ivoryton. The Connecticut River Museum now houses the last souvenirs of this trade, including two bull elephant tusks.

Today private interests such as the Dauntless Marine Shipyard and the Chandlery at Essex carry on the legacy for recreational rather than military purposes, repairing and housing yachts. And, in 2000, writer Joseph Leary and mechanic Fred Freze teamed up to reconstruct the *American Turtle.* Their whimsical replica proved seaworthy and maneuverable, but hopefully it will not see combat anytime soon.

Reach 28 Lyme to the Sound (Eastern Shore)

Miles from mouth: 5.0-0 (5-mile span).
Navigable by: Kayaks, canoes, small and large powerboats.
Difficulty: Flat water, but watch for wind, tides, and boat wakes.
Portages: None.
Fishing regulations: Boaters should steer clear of the gill nets used by shad anglers from Putnam Bridge (Connecticut Route 3, Middletown)

to Long Island Sound from April through June. No state fishing license is required downstream of the Amtrak Railroad Bridge between Old Saybrook and Old Lyme.
Camping: No established sites.
USGS maps: Essex 7.5, Old Lyme 7.5.
NOAA charts: Connecticut River: Long Island Sound to Deep River #12375.

The Reach

The river is crowded with marinas and public landings in its last 6 miles before Long Island Sound, and small boats are often prevented by currents and large boat traffic from crossing the river near its mouth. Therefore, we are presenting the last reach of the river in two parts: an eastern shore and a western shore. This reach runs from Hamburg village in Lyme, Connecticut, to Old Lyme, Connecticut, along the river's east shore. Since the Connecticut River is now an estuary, we will refer to the river's east and west shore rather than left or right bank.

You are now boating down the last stretch of the Connecticut River where it meets Long Island Sound, spanning more than a mile at its mouth and contributing almost 70 percent of the sound's total fresh water. Hugging the river's eastern shore from Hamburg Cove to the sea, you will see many more marshes than marinas. While not devoid of people and the occasional private dock, the eastern shore is much less crowded than the western. There are many lovely creeks to explore, and the area is a birding paradise; ospreys may outnumber anglers here. You wind through 10-foot-tall marsh reeds around Great Island and Back River. Rounding the southern shore of Great Island, you enter the expanse of Long Island Sound. You can visit the shifting sands of Griswold Point, a mini barrier beach that is home to endangered least terns and piping plovers. On a clear day you can see Long Island and might be tempted to paddle there—but don't; it's farther away and harder to get to than it looks!

Caution: People in large motorized craft must be observant and considerate of small boaters, and small boaters need to steer clear of large boats coming to and from the sound. Stick close to the river shore. Deeper-draft boats have to pay attention to the charts; three-quarters of the mile-wide mouth averages a few feet in depth, forcing motorboats into the west channel. Kayaks and canoes need to pay attention to shallow waters, especially at low tide. The currents around Griswold Point are notoriously tricky, and rip tides and large swells can develop quickly. Standing waves of 7 feet are not uncommon. At ebb tide the combination of river current and tide can be very strong.

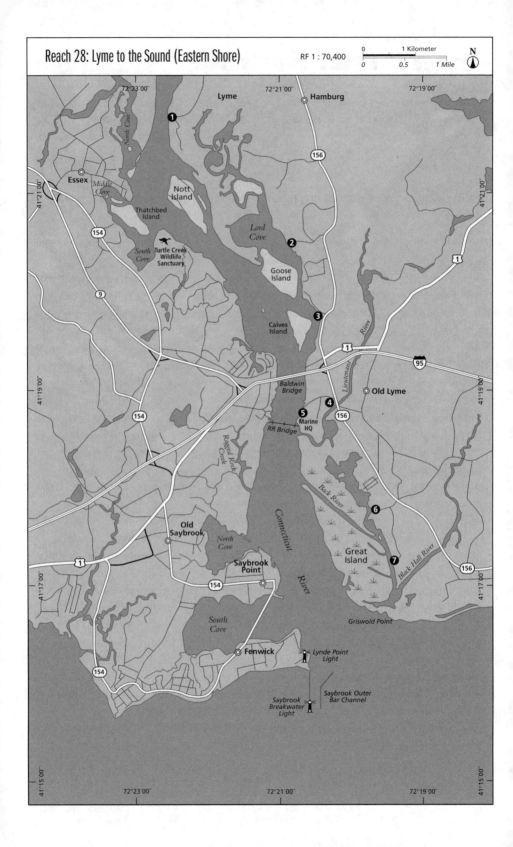

Reach 28: Lyme to the Sound (Eastern Shore)

RF 1 : 70,400

0   1 Kilometer
0   0.5   1 Mile

N

Boating Facilities Table for Reach 28

Access Point, Directions	Boat Type	Fee	Parking	Picnic	Toilets	Camping	Rentals	Supplies
❶ Ely Ferry Road Access Ely Ferry Road, Lyme, CT *From CT 156 in Lyme, turn west onto Ely Ferry Road and follow to end.*	Unimproved access for car-top boats only	N	Limited	N	N	N	N	N
❷ Tantummaheag Town Landing Tantummaheag Road, Old Lyme, CT *From CT 156 (Neck Road) in Old Lyme, turn west onto Tantummaheag Road and follow to town landing on left. Note: Access only at high tide.*	Unimproved access for car-top boats only	N	Y	N	N	N	N	N
❸ Pilgrim Landing Neck Road, Old Lyme, CT *Off CT 156 (Neck Road) in Old Lyme at junction with Pilgrim Landing Road.*	Unimproved access for car-top boats only	N	Limited	N	N	N	N	N
❹ Lieutenant River State Boat Launch Neck Road, Old Lyme, CT *Directly off CT 156 at northwest side of bridge over Lieutenant River.*	Unimproved ramp for car-top boats only	N	Y	N	N	N	N	N
❺ Old Lyme Ferry Road Launch Site Ferry Road, Old Lyme *From CT 156 in Old Lyme, turn west onto Old Ferry Road and follow to end.*	Unimproved access for car-top boats only	N	Y	Y	Y	N	N	N
❻ Smith Neck Town Landing Smith Neck Road, Old Lyme, CT *From CT 156 in Old Lyme, turn west onto Smith Neck Road. At sharp southerly curve in road, turn onto dirt road between two houses, and follow drive to end. Note: Difficult to access at low tide.*	Unimproved access for car-top boats only	N	Limited	Y	N	N	N	N
❼ Great Island State Boat Launch Smith Neck Road, Old Lyme, CT *From CT 156 in Old Lyme, turn west onto Smith Neck Road and follow to end; turn left at brown launch sign into parking area.*	Improved ramp for all boat types	Y	Y	Y	Y	N	N	N

Miles and Directions

Mile 5.0: Small, car-top boats can access the river from unimproved landings at Lyme (Lyme Town Boat Access—see Reach 26—or **Ely Ferry Road Access**) and Old Lyme (**Tantummaheag Town Landing, Pilgrim Landing,** and **Lieutenant River State Boat Launch**). These areas offer limited parking, and can sometimes be difficult to negotiate at low tide. Trailered boats do best either putting in at the Essex Town Dock (on the river's western shore; see Reach 27) or at the well-equipped **Great Island State Boat Launch** on Smith's Neck, Old Lyme.

Mile 5.0: If you head south into the river from the Tantummaheag Town Landing, you will find yourself immediately in the lee of **Goose Island**. Conversely, you can head north from the landing into the wilds of **Lord Cove**. *Caution:* The water between Goose Island and Lord Cove can be very shallow. Several creeks wind their way through the marshes here, with the steep banks of Lord Hill overlooking them. It's possible to spend hours in these twisty passages, watching ospreys fish or putting a line in yourself. There is a vigorous, state-managed effort under way to remove over 200 acres of the tall common reed (*Phragmites australis*) in order to restore native vegetation to the marsh.

Mile 4.0: South of Goose Island is **Calves Island**, and small boats can find protection from wind, currents, and large boats by taking the narrow channel in the lee between it and the mainland. Opposite Calves Island on the eastern shore is **Pilgrim Landing**, a tiny access point for small boats, with limited parking.

Mile 3.5: Baldwin Bridge (Interstate 95) marks the noisiest point of your journey to Long Island Sound. The Baldwin Bridge State Boat Launch lies on the western shore of the river and is often crowded with boat traffic (see Reach 27). *Caution:* Small boats should stay well to the east of this launch.

Mile 3.0: Rocks and shoals beset the river just downstream of the Baldwin Bridge ramp, so take care at low tide. Just above the **Amtrak Railroad Bridge**, there is a very small access point on the eastern shore, the **Old Lyme Ferry Road Launch Site and Dock**. *Caution:* A cable crosses here, so do not use propellers or anchors. The Connecticut Department of Environmental Protection's **Marine Headquarters** (Ferry Landing State Park) is right next door, with a beautiful river overlook and boardwalk where you can learn about marsh ecology from interpretive signs. *Caution:* Watch for turbulence and reduced steerage around the pylons of the railroad bridge, which, when closed to accommodate the train, has only a 19-foot clearance. (Sailboats: See Appendix B for information on contacting the bridge tender to raise the bridge.) Here the river begins to widen substantially and takes on the characteristics of a bay.

Mile 2.8: Shortly after passing under the Amtrak Bridge, you will encounter the mouth of the **Lieutenant River**. Small outboards, canoes, and kayaks can proceed up

The mouth of the river at Griswold Point has tricky shoals and waves that make for an interesting paddle. Photo by Wendy Sinton

the Lieutenant River almost 3 miles to where it widens into a series of old millponds, but be aware of tricky eddies around narrow stone abutments where the railroad crosses the Lieutenant. The **Lieutenant River State Boat Launch** is a large gravel area designed for access by car-top boats, about 0.8 mile upstream where Connecticut Route 156 crosses.

Mile 2.0: The **Back River** divides **Great Island** from the mainland. Great Island is home to the Roger Tory Peterson Wildlife Management Area, a beautiful, wide expanse of marsh named for America's foremost twentieth-century bird expert, who lived in Old Lyme. The island was once ditched to try to eradicate mosquitoes; recently, the State of Connecticut and many conservation groups have worked together to remove the ditches and restore the wetlands here, reviving the natural habitat for all kinds of birds and aquatic life. The flat marshes of Great Island are punctuated by small islands of higher ground, where trees grow on bedrock outcrops. These islands within islands provide habitat for upland plants and animals, increasing the overall diversity of life in the Tidelands. You also will see many osprey nesting platforms on this island, built to encourage the recovery of the once endangered species. These "fish hawks" are returning in large numbers to the river.

Smaller boats can tuck into the Back River at the northern end of Great Island for some great exploring. About a mile after entering the Back River, you can bear

The least tern is an endangered species found on the barrier islands at the river's mouth. Photo courtesy of Connecticut River Watershed Council

left (north) into a large embayment created by the Duck River; this is shallow at low tide. Upstream from this turn is the **Smith Neck Town Landing**, a tiny take-out point that is somewhat muddy at low tide. Watch Rock Park, owned by the Old Lyme Conservation Trust, is a bit farther upstream along the Duck and is a nice spot for a picnic. You can also take the Back River south and take out at the larger Great Island State Boat Launch. This is the southernmost access point on the Connecticut River's eastern shore. Osprey nesting platforms dot Great Island, visible reminders that these raptors are abundant. Please observe these nests from a distance. The **Black Hall River** enters from the east at the southern tip of Great Island.

Mile 0: Griswold Point is a highly changeable barrier beach that guards the confluence of the Back and Black Hall Rivers at the Connecticut River mouth. *Caution:* Beware of unpredictable currents, wind, and tide forces in this area. This sand spit can only be explored completely at low tide. The point provides critical habitat for two federally endangered bird species, the piping plover and the least tern. These shorebirds scoop fragile nests out of the sand and are vulnerable to predators and house pets. *Caution:* Do not disturb the nests of these birds; their nesting areas are marked by signs and fences. Look for an amazing abundance of shorebirds such as oystercatchers, dowitchers, and sandpipers. September and October are great months to observe the migration of hundreds of thousands of birds, including flocks of tree swallows half a million strong that roost nightly near the river.

The Ever-Changing River Mouth

All the other major rivers in Connecticut—including the Housatonic, the Quinnipiac, and the Thames—have large port cities at their deltas. Why have large urban settlements not sprung up on the Connecticut River? The mouth of this river is rife with sandbars and shoals that challenge the passage of large ships with deep drafts. Spring floods and fall and winter storms continually reshape these sediments, making it hard to maintain a deep central channel.

Griswold Point exemplifies the changing nature of these sandbars. The point has existed for at least 400 years, although rising sea levels have caused it to shift northward during that time. Longshore ocean currents in Long Island Sound transport sands to Griswold Point, but the construction of groins to prevent erosion at White Sands Beach to the east has slowed its growth in recent decades, making it more vulnerable to erosion. During the winter of 1992–1993, floodtides from a series of severe storms nearly breached the spit and pushed it farther north and west. Later, in May 2004, the narrow channel separating Griswold Point from Great Island completely closed. It has remained so ever since.

Great Island and Griswold Point form part of the ever-shifting Connecticut River mouth. Photo by Chris Joyell

Many factors contribute to the accumulation of sediments at the mouth of the river. First, the largest river in New England picks up 410 miles worth of sediments on its course to the sea. The river valley itself widens dramatically south of Essex, slowing the current and causing the river to deposit its load quite suddenly. The numerous marshes and islands that line the last few miles of river shoreline are products of millions of tons of fine muds and silts. The northeast tip of Long Island lies almost directly across the sound from the river mouth; tides pushing into this comparatively narrow area tend to push the river sediments east or west rather than allowing them to float farther out to sea. The source of much of this sediment was the last glacier to visit this region, which began to recede about 20,000 years ago. The sands and cobbles that are continuously reworked by the ocean waters of Long Island Sound today may well have been transported by ice and water from far upriver. Today the Connecticut beaches, including Griswold Point, are rimmed with the fine sands of purple garnets that have been eroded and transported from Connecticut's mainland bedrock. It is perhaps fitting that the beaches at the mouth of the Connecticut consists of semiprecious jewels. The forces of sands, winds, and tides conspire to make the river mouth a treacherous place for large shipping interests. At the same time, they foster its appeal for recreation and deep, leisurely appreciation of the river's natural resources.

Appendix A: **Bibliography**

Natural History

Conant, R., and J. T. Collins. *A Field Guide to Reptiles and Amphibians, Eastern and Central North America.* Third Edition. Peterson Field Guide Series. Boston: Houghton Mifflin, 1998.

Dreyer, G. D., and M. Caplis. *Living Resources and Habitats of the Lower Connecticut River.* Bulletin Number 37. New London: Connecticut College Arboretum, 2001.

Fabos, Julius Gy., and Jack Ahern. *Greenways: The Beginning of an International Movement.* Amsterdam: Elsevier, 1995.

Farnsworth, E. "New and Ancient Treasures: The Traprock Mountains of New England [Metacomet Range]." *Conservation Perspectives* (summer 2002). www.nescb.org/epublications/summer2002/farnsworth.html#origins.

Gabriel, M., and P. Huckery. "Freshwater Mussels." *Massachusetts Wildlife* 2: 15–21, 1998.

Gephard, Stephen, and James McMenemy. "An Overview of the Program to Restore Atlantic Salmon and Other Diadromous Fishes to the Connecticut River. . . ." In Jacobson, P., et al., eds., *The Connecticut River Ecological Study (1969–1973) Revisited.* Washington, D.C.: American Fisheries Society, 2004.

Klekowski, E. The Connecticut River Homepage: A World Wide Web Site Containing Information About the Biology, History, and Geology of New England's Largest River. www.bio.umass.edu/biology/conn.river. Amherst: University of Massachusetts, 2005.

Little, R. D. *Dinosaurs, Dunes, and Drifting Continents: The Geology of the Connecticut River Valley.* Easthampton, Mass.: Earth View, 2003.

Maloney, T. *Tidewaters of the Connecticut River: An Explorer's Guide to Hidden Coves and Marshes.* Essex, Conn.: River's End Press, 2001.

Motzkin, G. Uncommon Plant Communities of the Connecticut Valley, Massachusetts. Report for the Massachusetts Natural Heritage and Endangered Species Program, Westborough, Mass., 1993.

The Nature Conservancy. *Submerged Aquatic Vegetation: A Guide to SAV in the Lower Connecticut River and Its Tributaries.* Middletown, Conn.: The Nature Conservancy, 1999.

Preston, J. *Tools for Intelligent Tinkering: A Natural Resource Guide for Lower Connecticut River Land Use Commissioners.* Old Saybrook, Conn., 2005.

Rook, E. J. S. Flora, Fauna, Earth, and Sky . . . The Natural History of the Northwoods. www.rook.org/earl/bwca/nature. Michigan, 2004.

Sikes, D. S. Tiger Beetles of Connecticut (Coleoptera: Carabidae: *Cicindela*): Conservation Status, Taxonomy, and Natural History. http://collections2.eeb.uconn.edu/collections/insects/CTBnew/ctb.htm. Storrs: University of Connecticut, 1999.

Tripp, Nathaniel. *Confluence: A River, the Environment, Politics, and the Fate of All Humanity.* Hanover, N.H.: Steerforth, 2005.

History

Albers, Jan. *Hands on the Land: A History of the Vermont Landscape.* Cambridge, Mass.: MIT Press, 2000.

Bacon, Edwin. *The Connecticut River.* New York: G. P. Putnam, 1907.

Bruchac, Margaret. "Wôbanaki Lifeways" and other essays. http://1704.deerfield.history.museum. Deerfield, Mass.: Pocumtuck Valley Historical Association, 2005.

Calloway, Colin. *Dawnland Encounters: Indians and Europeans in New England.* Hanover, N.H.: University Press of New England, 1991.

————— *The Western Abenakis of Vermont, 1600–1800.* Norman: University of Oklahoma Press, 1990.

Cumbler, John. *Reasonable Use: The People, the Environment, and the State, New England 1790–1930.* New York: Oxford University Press, 2001.

Delaney, Edmund. *The Connecticut River, New England's Historic Waterway.* Guilford, Conn.: Globe Pequot, 1983.

Dincauze, D. "A Capsule Prehistory of Southern New England." In Hauptman, L., and J. Wherry, *The Pequots in Southern New England: The Fall and Rise of an American Indian Nation.* Norman: University of Oklahoma Press, 1990.

Doezema, Marianne, ed. *Changing Prospects: The View from Mount Holyoke.* Ithaca, N.Y.: Cornell University Press, 2002.

Ewald, Richard, and Adair Mulligan. *Proud to Live Here: In the Connecticut River Valley of Vermont and New Hampshire.* Charlestown, N.H.: Connecticut River Joint Commissions, 2003.

Foster, David R., and John Aber. *Forests in Time: The Environmental Consequences of 1,000 Years of Change in New England*. New Haven, Conn.: Yale University Press, 2004.

Gilmore, William J. *Reading Becomes a Necessity of Life: Material and Cultural Life in Rural New England, 1780–1835*. Knoxville: University of Tennessee, 1989.

Grant, Ellsworth. "The Mainstream of New England." *American Heritage* (April 1967).

Hill, E., and W. F. Stekl. *The Connecticut River*. Middletown, Conn.: Wesleyan University Press, 1972.

Hard, Walter. *The Connecticut*. New York: Rinehart & Company, 1947.

Klekowski, Ed. *The Great Flood of 1936*. 2003 film for WGBY-TV. Springfield, Mass. http://wgby.org/localprograms/flood.

Klekowski, Ed, and Libby Klekowski. "Dynamite, Whiskey, and Wood." 2005 film for WGBY-TV. Springfield, Mass. http://wgby.org/localprograms/logdrives.

Marsden, George M. *Jonathan Edwards: A Life*. New Haven, Conn.: Yale University Press, 2003.

Mulholland, Mitchell. "The Connecticut River: 12,000 Years of Exploitation." Unpublished talk at University of Massachusetts. UMASS Archaeological Services, October 2004.

Pike, Robert. *Tall Trees, Tough Men*. New York: Norton, 1967 (reissue 1999).

Sweeney, Kevin. "River Gods and Related Minor Deities: The Williams Family and the Connecticut River Valley, 1637–1790." Ph.D. Dissertation, History Department, Yale University, 1986.

U.S Department of the Interior, National Park Service, Northeast Region. *Connecticut River Valley: Special Resource Reconnaissance Study*. Boston, 1998.

Wetherell, W. D. *This American River: Five Centuries of Writing About the Connecticut*. Hanover, N.H.: University Press of New England, 2002.

Wilentz, Sean. *The Rise of American Democracy: Jefferson to Lincoln*. New York: Norton, 2005.

Appendix B: Useful Web Sites and Contact Information

Flow and Tide Information

All available flow information at: www.h2oline.com or (800) 452–1742 plus six-digit code:

Second Connecticut Lake	335121
First Connecticut Lake	335122
Murphy Dam	335123
Moore Dam	335124
Comerford Dam	335125
McIndoe Dam	335126
Wilder Dam	505121
Bellows Falls Dam	505122
Vernon Dam	505123

U.S. Geological Survey gauging stations: http://waterdata.usgs.gov

For Holyoke and Turners Falls Dams: http://stream-flow.allaboutrivers.com

Tide information: www.tidesonline.com; http://tidesonline.nos.noaa.gov; http://tidesandcurrents.noaa.gov

Local papers also have tide information.

General Information Related to Connecticut River and Boating

American Heritage Rivers: www.epa.gov/rivers

Appalachian Mountain Club: www.outdoors.org

Connecticut River Joint Commissions: www.crjc.org

Connecticut River Watershed Council: www.crwc.org

Connecticut River Byway: http://ctrivertravel.net

First Nations: www.tolatsga.org/aben.html (Native American history)

Flood History in New England: www.serve.com/NESEC/hazards/Floods.cfm #history

Connecticut River Homepage: Biology, History, and Geology of New England's Largest River: www.bio.umass.edu/biology/conn.river

Land Trust Alliance: www.ltanet.org

Silvio O. Conte National Fish and Wildlife Refuge: www.fws.gov/r5soc

The Nature Conservancy: http://nature.org/wherewework/northamerica/states

Trust for Public Land, Connecticut River Program: www.tpl.org

Great North Woods

Connecticut Lakes Headwaters Forest: http://nature.org/success/headwaters.html

Mount Washington: www.mountwashington.org

New Hampshire parks: (603) 271–3628; www.nhparks.state.nh.us

Northern Forest Canoe Trail: www.northernforestcanoetrail.org

Nulhegan region: www.nulhegan.com

Vermont Department of Forests, Parks and Recreation: www.vtfpr.org

White Mountains: www.visitwhitemountains.com

Upper Valley

American Precision Museum: www.americanprecision.org

Crazy Horse Campground, Littleton, New Hampshire: www.ucampnh.com/
crazyhorse/

Ethan Allen: www.virtualvermont.com/history/eallen.html;
www.uvm.edu/~vhnet/hertour/eallen/eahistory.html

Fairbanks Museum: www.fairbanksmuseum.org

Green Mountain Head rowing regatta: http://trust.dosolutions.com/gmh

Lancaster Fair: www.lancasterfair.com

Montshire Museum, Norwich, Vermont: www.montshire.org

New Hampshire Fish and Game Department, public-access boating and fishing sites
in New Hampshire:
www.wildlife.state.nh.us/Outdoor_Recreation/access_sites_table.htm

New Hampshire Outdoors, Enjoying the Waters: www.nhoutdoors.com/nh
_boating.htm

New Hampshire parks: (603) 271–3628; www.nhparks.state.nh.us

New Hampshire Public Access and Put-ins: www.visitnh.gov/publicaccessputins
.html

Saint-Gaudens National Historic Site: www.nps.gov/saga

TransCanada Power Company: www.transcanada.com/power/usne.html

Upper Valley History Education Network: www.flowofhistory.org

Upper Valley Land Trust, Primitive Campsites in Upper River: www.uvlt.org

Vermont Department of Forests, Parks and Recreation: www.vtfpr.org

Vermont Paddlers Club: www.vtpaddlers.net

Vermont River Conservancy: www.vermontriverconservancy.org/index.html

Massachusetts

Cabot Camp: www.umass.edu/greenway/Seniors/MA/CabotCampHist.html

Chicopee River Watershed Council: www.chicopeeriver.org

Connecticut River Greenway State Park: www.mass.gov/dcr/parks/central/
crgw.htm

Deerfield Raid, 1704: http://1704.deerfield.history.museum

Deerfield River Watershed Association: www.deerfieldriver.org

Dinosaurs in Holyoke: www.thetrustees.org/pages/298_dinosaur_footprints.cfm

Eagle Web cam: www.nu.com/eagles/default.asp

Fossils and armored mudballs: www.earthview.pair.com/mudballs.html

French King Bridge: www.mhd.state.ma.us

Great Falls Discovery Center: www.greatfallsma.org

Holyoke Gas and Electric: www.hged.com

Holyoke Heritage State Park: www.mass.gov/dcr/parks/central/hhsp.htm

Holyoke's history: www.holyoke.org/history.htm

Massacre of 1676: www.bio.umass.edu/biology/conn.river

Millers River Watershed Council: www.millersriver.net/mrwc

Northfield Mountain Riverview Picnic and Recreation Area, Northfield Mountain
pumped storage: www.nu.com/northfield

Riverboat cruises, round-trip Barton Cove to Northfield Mountain, Wednesday
through Sunday from Memorial Day to Columbus Day. Northeast Utilities.
Reservations: (800) 859–2960.

Springfield Science Museum: www.springfieldmuseums.org/museums/science

South Hadley Canal: www.bio.umass.edu/biology/conn.river/canal.html

Stacy Mountain: http://nature.org/wherewework/northamerica/states/massachusetts/
preserves/art5332.html

The Trustees of Reservations: www.thetrustees.org

TransCanada Power Company: www.transcanada.com

Westfield River Watershed Association: www.westfieldriver.org

Connecticut

Amtrak Railroad Bridge, Old Lyme/Old Saybrook, VHF 13

Camelot Cruises: www.camelotcruises.com

Chester Land Trust: www.ltanet.org

Connecticut Coastal Access Guide: www.lisrc.uconn.edu/coastalaccess/index.asp

Connecticut Department of Environmental Protection Boating Regulations: http://dep.state.ct.us/rec/boating/boatingregs.htm

Connecticut River Estuary Regional Planning Agency, Old Saybrook: (860) 388–3497; www.crerpa.org

Connecticut River Expeditions, Essex: www.ctriverexpeditions.org or (860) 662–0577

Connecticut River Museum, Essex: (860) 767–8269; www.ctrivermuseum.org

Dinosaurs at Rocky Hill: www.dinosaurstatepark.org

East Haddam Historical Society Museum: (860) 873–3944

Farmington River Watershed Association: www.frwa.org

Goodspeed Opera House: (860) 873–8664; www.goodspeed.org

Hockanum River: www.ci.manchester.ct.us/leisure/canoe.htm

Hurd State Park, Gillette Castle State Park, Selden Neck State Park: http://dep.state.ct.us/stateparks/camping.rvrcmp.htm; camping information (860) 526–2336

Lady Katharine Cruises, Charter Oak Landing, Hartford: (866) 867–4837

Mattabesset River Watershed Association: www.mrwa-ct.org

Old Lyme Conservation Trust: www.oldlymeconservtrust.org/lib_grswld_pt _history.htm

Riverfront Recapture, Hartford: www.riverfront.org

Yacht Clubs and Marina Directory for the lower Connecticut River Valley: www.ctrivervalley.com/4-Connecticut-CT-in-of/Marinas-in-Connecticut-Boats

Birding

Audubon Vermont: http://vt.audubon.org

Connecticut Audubon: www.ctaudubon.org

Connecticut River Birding Trail: www.birdtrail.org

Eagle Web Cam, Barton Cove, Massachusetts: www.nu.com/eagles/default.asp

Massachusetts Audubon: www.massaudubon.org/index.php

New Hampshire Audubon: www.nhaudubon.org

Fish and Fishing

Connecticut Department of Environmental Protection Angler's Guide:
http://dep.state.ct.us/burnatr/fishing/fishinfo/angler.htm

Massachusetts Fish and Wildlife: www.mass.gov/dfwele/dfw/dfwrec.htm#FISH

New Hampshire fishing: www.wildlife.state.nh.us

The Anadromous Fish of the Connecticut River: www.nu.com/environmental/
steward/fish.asp

U.S. Fish and Wildlife Service, Connecticut River Coordinator's Office:
www.fws.gov/r5crc/Who/links.html

New Hampshire: www.wildlife.state.nh.us/Fishing/fishing.htm

Vermont: www.vtfishandwildlife.com

Appendix C: Marinas, Outfitters, and Guides

Reaches 1–18

Hanover Outdoors, 17½ Lebanon Street, Hanover, NH; (603) 643–1263; info@hanoveroutdoors.com; www.lymeangler.com. Fishing guides.

Strictly Trout, David Deen, RFD 3, Box 800, Putney, VT 05346; (802) 869–3116; deenhome@sover.net; www.sovernet/~deenhome. Fishing guide.

Reaches 1–5

Armand Buteau, 177 Round Pond Road, Pittsburg, NH 03592; (603) 538–7001; pathtour@joi.mail. Guided kayak and canoe trips.

Ken Hastings, Osprey Fishing Adventures, P.O. Box 121, Colebrook, NH 03576; (603) 922–3800; www.ospreyfishingadventures.com. Guided fly fishing.

Lopstick Lodge, Route 3, First Lake, NH 03592; (800) 538–6659; Lisa and Tim Savard; www.lopstick.com. Boat rentals, fishing guides.

Metallak Shores Resort, First Connecticut Lake, Pittsburg, NH 03592; (800) 545–6613, (603) 538–6613; www.timberlandlodge.com.

Tall Timber Lodge, 609 Beach Road, Pittsburg, NH 03592; (800) 835–6343; www.talltimber.com. Boat rentals, fishing guides.

Reaches 8–10

Hemlock Pete's Canoe Livery, North Haverhill, NH 03774; (603) 667–5112; www.hpcanoes.bizland.com/index.html.

Reaches 10–15

John Marshall, River Excitement, P.O. Box 65, Hartland Four Corners, VT 05049; (802) 457–4021; rvrxcitmnt@aol.com; www.riverexcitement.com. Float trips and fishing guide.

Reaches 10–11

Fairlee Marine, VT Route 5, Fairlee, VT; (802) 333–9745; www.boatingvermont.com.

Reaches 12–15

North Star Canoes and Rentals, 1356A Route 12A, Cornish, NH/White River Junction, VT; (603) 542–6929; www.kayak-canoe.com. Rentals, guided float trips.

Reach 13

Ledyard Boat Club, Hanover, NH; (603) 643–6709; www.dartmouth.edu/~lcc. Rentals, instruction.

Reaches 14–15

Green Mountain Marina, VT Route 5, Rockingham, VT; (802) 463–4973; www.greenmtnmarina.com.

Reaches 16–17

Norm's Marina, NH Route 119, Hinsdale, NH; (603) 256–6266.

Vermont Canoe Touring Center, 421 Putney Road, Brattleboro, VT; (802) 257–5008. Tours, rentals.

West River Marina, VT Route 5, Putney Rd., Brattleboro, VT; (802) 257–7563; www.vermontmarina.com.

Reach 18

Barton Cove Canoe and Kayak Rentals, MA Route 2, Gill, MA; (413) 863–9300, www.nu.com. Canoe and kayak rentals and shuttle to river access points north to Vernon Dam.

Reach 20

Sportsman's Marina, MA Route 9, Hadley, MA; (413) 586–2426.

Reach 21

Mitch's Marina, MA Route 47, Hadley, MA; (413) 584–7960.

Oxbow Marina, Island Road, Northampton, MA; (413) 584–2775; www.oxbow-marina.com.

Brunelle's Marina, Alvord Street, South Hadley, MA; (413) 586–3132; www.brunelles.com. HGED shuttle pickup for Holyoke Dam.

Reaches 23–24

Long River Adventures, 326 Poquonock Avenue, Windsor, CT; (866) 529–2528; www.longriverllc.com. Kayak and canoe rental, trips.

Petzold's Marine Center, off CT Route 17A, Portland, CT; (860) 342–1196.

Portland Boat Works, Portland, CT; (860) 342–1085.

Seaboard Marina, 684 Tryon Street, South Glastonbury, CT; (860) 657–3232.

Yankee Boatyard and Marina, 54 Riverview Street, Portland, CT; (860) 342–4735.

Portland Riverside Marina, 37 Riverview Street, Portland, CT; (860) 342–1911.

Reach 25

Andrews Marina, Bridge Road, Haddam, CT; (860) 345–2286.

Midway Marina, Haddam Dock Road, Haddam, CT; (860) 345–4330.

Reach 26

Brewers Deep River Marina, 50 River Lane, Deep River, CT; (860) 526–5560.

Chester Marina, 72 Railroad Avenue, Chester, CT. (860) 526–2227.

Castle Marina, 61 Railroad Avenue, Chester, CT; (860) 526–2735.

Chrisholm Marina, 226 CT Route 154, Chester, CT; (860) 526–5147.

Hays Haven Marina, 59 Railroad Avenue, Chester, CT; (860) 526–9366.

Reach 27

Brewer's Dauntless Shipyard, 37 Pratt Street, Essex, CT; (860) 767–2483.

Essex Island Marina, Ferry Street, Essex, CT; (860) 767–1267; www.essexislandmarina.com.

Essex Boat Works Ferry, Street, Essex, CT; (860) 767–8272.

Middle Cove Marina, 19 Nott Lane, Essex, CT; (860) 767–3938.

The Chandlery at Essex, 19 Novelty Lane, Essex, CT; (860) 767–8267.

Between the Bridges Marina, 142 Ferry Road, Old Saybrook, CT; (860) 388–1431.

Ferry Point Marina, 29 Essex Road, Old Saybrook, CT; (860) 388–3260.

Harbor One Marina, 22 Bridge Street, Old Saybrook, CT; (860) 388–9208.

Island Cove Marina, 47 Sunrise Avenue, Old Saybrook, CT; (860) 388–0029.

Oak Leaf Marina, 218 Ferry Road, Old Saybrook CT; (860) 388–9817.

Offshore East Marina, 26 Fourth Avenue, Old Saybrook, CT; (860) 388–4532.

Ragged Rock Marina, 54 Ferry Road, Old Saybrook CT; (860) 388–1049.

Saybrook Marine Services, 2 Clark Street, Old Saybrook, CT; (860) 388–3614.

Saybrook Point Marina, 2 Bridge Street, Old Saybrook, CT; (860) 395–3080.

Van Epps, 15 King Street, Old Saybrook, CT; (860) 388–1211.

Reach 28

Black Hall Marina, 132 Shore Road, Old Lyme, CT; (860) 434–9680.

Cove Landing Marine, 250 Hamburg Road, Old Lyme, CT; (860) 434–5240.

Old Lyme Dock Co., 323 Ferry Road, #2, Old Lyme, CT; (860) 434–2267.

Old Lyme Marina, 34 Neck Road, Old Lyme, CT; (860) 434–1272.

In winter the upper river becomes a snowmobiler's roadway. Photo by David Deen

Appendix D: The Connecticut River Watershed Council

CRWC MISSION STATEMENT: The River Connects Us

The Connecticut River Watershed Council works to protect the watershed from source to sea. From alpine forests to tidal estuaries, rural farmlands to urban riverfronts, spotted salamanders to bald eagles, and mussels to salmon, the Connecticut River watershed unites a diversity of habitats, communities and resources. As stewards of this heritage, we celebrate our four-state treasure and collaborate, educate, organize, restore, and intervene to preserve the health of the whole for generations to come.

CRWC: More Than Fifty Years of Success—Now We Need You!

The Connecticut River sustains us . . . it defines us . . . it connects us to one another. And, when decades of pollution and neglect turned the Connecticut into a 410-mile sewer, the single most important force behind the river's recovery was not government or industry, but ordinary citizens speaking collectively.

For more than fifty years, the Connecticut River Watershed Council (CRWC) has been informing and engaging people in the protection, restoration, and sustainable use of the Connecticut River watershed. CRWC is the Connecticut River's primary watchdog and steward "from source to sea." Our achievements include:

- Helping to restore access to spawning areas for migratory fish, such as Atlantic salmon, that have been blocked by dams for hundreds of years;
- Protecting over 8,000 acres through our Land Conservancy Program, preserving valuable wetlands, forests, farmlands, natural buffers and river access points;
- Supporting three full-time River Stewards who bring CRWC's on-river presence to every region of the watershed, taking action and assisting community groups.

You can read about Connecticut River Watershed Council's many other accomplishments and historic victories at www.ctriver.org. I encourage you to join us today so you can think of our success stories as *your* achievements, too.

The Connecticut River was sustaining life in this beautiful region long before state lines were drawn. As the river flows from mountains to farmland to hamlets to cities, it doesn't know New Hampshire from Vermont or Massachusetts from Connecticut. There is one watershed affecting us all. By working together for a thriving, sustainable river, we enrich our world today, and we leave a positive legacy for future generations— a beautiful, safe, robust watershed instead of an 11,000-square-mile dumping ground.

The River connects us. Let's take care of it together. Please join CRWC today by sending in the membership reply on the following page, by using the reply card at the end of this book, or visiting us online at www.ctriver.org. Thank you.

—Chelsea Reiff Gwyther, executive director
Connecticut River Watershed Council

The River connects us.
Let's take care of it together.
Join the Connecticut River Watershed Council today.

YES! I'll help promote improved water quality, restoration, conservation and sustainable use of the entire Connecticut River watershed. I'm pledging to join CRWC with a gift of:

☐ $25 ☐ $35 ☐ $50 ☐ $75 ☐ $100 ☐ $_____

Members receive CRWC's quarterly newsletter, discounts on publications, and other benefits.

Mr/Ms:_____

Address:_____

City:_____ State:_____ Zip Code: _____

Telephone:_____ E-mail: _____

☐ Take Action!

I want to join the hundreds of other CRWC members who are getting their feet wet and their hands dirty to make the Connecticut River watershed cleaner by volunteering for the Source to Sea Cleanup. Please contact me about volunteer opportunities.

Please copy and mail to Connecticut River Watershed Council
15 Bank Row Greenfield MA 01301 (413) 772-2020
Save time and postage by joining online at
WWW.CTRIVER.ORG
or by sending an email to: membership@ctriver.org

Index

Upper Island, 136
Upper Valley, 13

V

Vaughan Meadow campsite, 85
Vermont borders, 48
Vermont Yankee Nuclear Power
    Plant, 128
Vernon, VT, 136
Vernon Dam, 123, 128, 133, 136

W

Waits River, 85
Walpole, NH, 119
Wangunk Meadows Wildlife
    Management Area, 183
Wantastiquet Campsite, 128
Wantastiquet Mountain, 127
Watch Rock Park, 214
water-milfoil, Eurasian, 122–23
Wells River, 78
Wells River–Woodsville Bridge, 78
Westfield River, 165
West Lebanon, NH, 98, 102

Westminster Station, VT, 119
West River, 123, 126, 127
Wethersfield, CT, 180
Wethersfield Cove, 181
wetlands, 187, 193, 201
White Mountains, 67
White River, 102–3
White River Junction, VT, 98, 102
Wilcox Island, 183
Wild Ammonoosuc River, 74
Wilder Dam, 80, 89, 94, 95, 98, 102
Wilder Picnic Area, 95
Wilder Waterfowl Management
    Area, 92
Wilgus State Park, 106
Williams River, 114
Willy's Island, 165
Windsor, CT, 175
Windsor, VT, 102, 104, 106
Windsor Locks, CT, 174
Windsor Locks Canal, 139, 171, 174
Windyhurst campsite, 121
Woodsville, NH, 74, 75, 78, 80
Wyoming Dam, 61–62, 63

About the Authors

Authors John Sinton, Wendy Sinton, and Elizabeth Farnsworth.
Photo courtesy of the authors

The Connecticut River Watershed Council

This book is authored by, and published in cooperation with, the Connecticut River Watershed Council, the leading organization devoted to management of the river and its watershed. Founded in 1952, the Council, with headquarters in Greenfield, Massachusetts, is the river's primary watchdog and steward "from source to sea."

John Sinton

John Sinton grew up as a river rat on the Truckee River in California, helping make log rafts and learning to cast flies with his grandfather's bamboo rods. Much of his work as a professor of geography and regional planning focused on river systems. Now retired, he hikes, fishes, and kayaks the Connecticut River watershed with his wife, Wendy.

Wendy Sinton

Wendy Sinton became an avid boater when, at age 14, she fell in love with sailing. Between sailing, canoeing, and kayaking, she has spent many wonderful hours on the water. Growing up in South Hadley, Massachusetts, on the Connecticut River when it was polluted, she returned later in life to find a renewed and vibrant waterway. She has spent the last two years with her husband, John, exploring and appreciating the varied landscapes of the river.

Elizabeth Farnsworth

Elizabeth Farnsworth, biologist, illustrator, and musician, lived for several years overlooking the Connecticut River in Holyoke, enjoying the river's many moods. After building her own wooden kayak in 1999, she took her maiden solo voyage downriver from Turners Falls to Long Island Sound. She continues to do research on the ecology of the river and to work for its conservation.

FALCONTRAILS on the WEB

To learn more about Falcon or to get detailed information about our more than 10,000 published trails and routes, go to **www.falcontrails.com.** While there, purchase custom topo maps, view real-time weather, post and review trail reports, and much more.

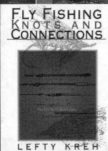

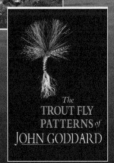

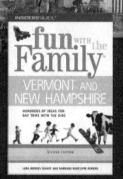
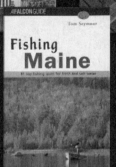
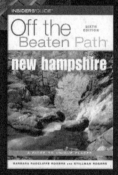